A
HANDBOOK
OF
CHURCH
MUSIC

A
HANDBOOK
OF
CHURCH
MUSIC

edited by
Carl Halter and Carl Schalk

Publishing House
St. Louis

Concordia Publishing House, St. Louis, Missouri
Copyright © 1978 Concordia Publishing House
Manufactured in the United States of America

Library of Congress Cataloging in Publication Data

Main entry under title:

A handbook of church music.

    1. Church music—Lutheran Church. I. Halter,
Carl, 1916-   II. Schalk, Carl.
ML3168.H33   783'.026'41   77-16272
ISBN 0-570-01316-X

Contents

Abbreviations

CB	*Church Book* (1868)
CS	*Common Service* (1888)
CSB	*Common Service Book* (1917)
CW	*Contemporary Worship* (1969f)
DM	*Deutsche Messe* (1526)
EpH	*The Hymnal 1940* (Episcopal)
FM	*Formula missae* (1523)
ILCW	Inter-Lutheran Commission on Worship
KO	Kirchenordnung (church order)
KOO	Kirchenordnungen (church orders)
LBW	*Lutheran Book of Worship* (1978)
SBH	*Service Book and Hymnal* (1958)
TEH	*The English Hymnal* (1906)
TLH	*The Lutheran Hymnal* (1941)
WS	*Worship Supplement* (1969)

Preface

Of all the activities in which the church is involved, worship stands at the heart and center of its life and mission. At its best, Lutheran worship has always held music in high regard and given it a place of great importance and distinction. Church music—in the Lutheran tradition—has always been next to theology. It has always been the "living voice of the Gospel." This book is an attempt to follow in that tradition and is for organists and choir directors, pastors and church music committees, members of congregations with a particular interest in worship and church music, all who are interested in growing in their understanding of what church music is about, and who are interested in helping to lead congregations into a parish practice of worship and church music that is rich and varied, historical yet truly contemporary.

It should be emphasized that this book is for parishes small and large, where musical resources are modest and plentiful. Perhaps it is particularly in smaller parishes with more modest musical resources that the suggestions in this book may be most necessary and most helpful.

In varying degrees, music in Lutheran worship has always reflected two seemingly different tendencies. The one looks back to the roots of its tradition and practice; the other looks forward to the future. At any given moment parish practice usually represents a mixture of these elements, a mixture determined largely by how a parish and its leaders in worship and church music see the relative importance of these elements in the realities of their own situation. At times, some church musicians have indulged themselves in an exclusive preoccupation with the past; at other times some have seemed to float along in a rootless present, imprisoned in a cult of the current. The underlying thesis of the various contributions to this volume is that a truly contemporary church music practice can exist only as it is solidly rooted in the best of the church's tradition. To be truly Lutheran today means to affirm both past and present at the same time, never one at the expense of the other.

This *Handbook of Church Music* and its companion *Key Words in Church Music* are intended as tools for practicing church musicians and for all who care about the musical life of the church at worship. To help the reader see these two books as a single tool, references are given at the end of each chapter to related readings in the companion book. The section on "Resources for the Church Musician" details additional helps.

It is our hope that this book together with its companion volume may be a useful tool for parishes large and small as they seek to develop a rich, varied, and exciting parish practice of worship and church music that will glorify God and edify the Christian community. To attempt anything less would not only fail to meet the challenges of our time. It would effectively deny the very heritage of worship and church music that these volumes seek to affirm and advance as a continuingly viable and effective vehicle for an exciting church music practice for our day.

Carl Halter
Carl Schalk

A
HANDBOOK
OF
CHURCH
MUSIC

Music in Lutheran Worship: An Affirmation

The public worship of God's people is only rarely what we know it can or should be. A lack of understanding on the part of pastors, church musicians, and laity alike as to what Lutheran worship really is or might be is all too common. Inadequate experience and education in living the liturgy in colleges, seminaries, and in the local congregation has resulted in confusion and misunderstanding about worship, worship forms, and worship practices on the part of clergy, laity, and church musicians alike. In large part, this confusion is the result of being cut off from the basic understandings that enabled Lutheran worship and church music to achieve such a glorious history.

As more people in our congregations reflect backgrounds, traditions, and practices other than Lutheran, it is increasingly important that basic guidelines be set out that reflect Lutheranism's understanding of its worship, and particularly the role of music in that worship tradition.

Lutheranism has a distinct point of view in matters of worship and church music. It is hoped that this affirmation will help focus attention on that point of view for pastors, church musicians, and laity alike. In this way may it help in fostering a parish practice that is both faithful to Lutheran traditions and, in returning to Lutheranism's roots, help to realize a more vital worship practice in our parishes.

Worship and Music

What place does music have in a Lutheran understanding and traditon of worship?

The answer to that question is rooted in how Lutherans have seen themselves throughout their history. While the 16th century ultimately saw a separation of Lutherans from the catholic church of its day, Martin Luther and those who followed him did not see themselves primarily as a new church, but rather as a distinctive confessional movement within a larger Christianity. That understanding is a key one as Lutherans approach the matter of worship—how they see themselves in relation to the larger Christian tradition, and how they view music and its role in their corporate praise and prayer.

The Lutheran church is a worshiping church. Lutherans concern themselves seriously with all aspects of the church's worship life. Particular emphasis, however, is given to corporate, congregational worship, where Christians gather to hear the Word and to share the Sacrament. For Lutherans, corporate worship is not simply a pleasant option; it is the indispenable and central work of the gathered Christian community from which all other facets of the church's life and mission, including one's individual worship life, derive their strength, purpose and direction.

The Lutheran church is a liturgical church. With much of Christianity it shares a concern for ordered worship. Its worship is characterized neither by eccentricity nor faddishness. Lutheran worship underscores the elements of stability and continuity with worship forms and practices that place them in the long line of worshipers from the New Testament to the Parousia. Lutherans worship not in subjective isolation, but " . . . with angels and archangels and with all the company of heaven," in concert with Christian believers of all times and places.

Lutheran worship offers a richness and variety of forms and practices that give fullness to the celebration of corporate worship. As Lutherans worship with the recurring cycles of the church year, as they hear the Word proclaimed through ordered readings and preaching that recount the full council of God, and as they celebrate the sacraments, Lutherans are united with Christians of other times and places and receive strength for their task in the world.

Lutherans receive their heritage of worship forms and practices with thanksgiving and appreciation. Lutherans understand that their heritage is a meaningful source of continuity with their own past as well as with that of the whole church catholic. Yet Lutherans do not deify, ossify, or accept their heritage uncritically. Lutherans also see their heritage as a basis for moving toward the future. Thus Lutheran worship is simultaneously conservative and open to the future.

As music in Lutheran worship builds on these understandings, as it helps to nourish the faith, as it works to the glory of God and the edification of the neighbor, it has always had a welcome and important role among Lutheran Christians. Where it has fallen short of these understandings, where it has substituted other goals, where it has become man-centered rather than God-centered, to that extent it has ceased to be Lutheran in motivation, realization, and result.

Music in Lutheran worship—whether the music of congregation, choir, pastor, organ, solo voice, or instruments—finds its most *natural and comfortable place in the context of the liturgy.* It is in the liturgy, in all its fullness and completeness, that music in Lutheran worship finds its highest goal and achieves its greatest fulfillment. At its best, Lutheranism upholds this priority. When Lutheran worship forsakes its roots in the liturgy, as it substitutes other priorities, or as it seeks to imitate sectarian practices, it loses its orientation and perverts the role of both music and worship.

For Luther, music was next in importance to theology, a living voice of the Gospel (*viva vox evangelii*), a gift of God to be used in all its fullness in Christian praise and prayer. As the implications of these concepts begin to permeate our understanding and our practice, music in Lutheran worship will move ever closer to a fuller realization of its potential in the hearts and lives of worshipers everywhere.

Luther's View of Music in Worship

Martin Luther, alone among the reformers of the 16th century, welcomed music into the worship and praise of God with open arms. For Luther, music was a "noble, wholesome, and joyful creation," a gift of God. For Luther, music was a part of God's creation with the power to praise its Creator, and it found its greatest fulfillment in the proclamation of the Word.

> "Therefore accustom yourself to see in this creation your Creator and to praise Him through it."
> "If any would not sing and talk of what Christ has wrought for us, he shows thereby that he does not really believe . . . ."[1]

For Luther to "say and sing" was a single concept resulting from the inevitable eruption of joyful song in the heart of the redeemed. In contrast to some other reformers who saw music as always potentially troublesome and in need of careful control and direction, Luther, in the freedom of the Gospel, could exult in the power of music to proclaim the Word and to touch the heart and mind of man.

In emphasizing music as God's—not man's—creation and as God's gift to man to be used in His praise and proclamation, and in stressing particularly the royal priesthood of all believers, Luther laid the foundation for the involvement of every Christian—congregation, choir, composer, instrumentalist—in corporate praise at the highest level of ability. In seeing all of music as under God's redemptive hand, Luther underscored the freedom of the Christian to use all of music in the proclamation of the Gospel. The music that developed in this tradition is eloquent testimony to the fact that the church's musicians and its people found that Luther's views provided a healthy and wholesome context in which to work, to sing, and to make music in praise of God.

Luther encouraged the most sophisticated forms of the music of his day—Gregorian chant and classical polyphony—to be taught to the young and sung in church together with the simpler congregational chorales. In contrast to both the Latin tradition and that of the Calvinist reformation, it was the Lutheran reformers' understanding of music as a gift of God that successfully encouraged the reciprocal interaction of simple con- gregational song and art music of the most sophisticated kind. A flourishing tradition of church music was the happy result.

A Lutheran View of Tradition

Because it views itself as part of the one, holy, catholic and apostolic church, Lutheranism looks to the experience of the church at worship throughout its history as an important source of its way of worship. Its use of forms and practices with which the church has prayed and praised for centuries—forms that have been tested, tried, and found nourishing through the experience of countless Christians—affirms Lutheranism's continuity with the whole church. In its life of worship Lutheranism gives such forms and practices a central place. Luther's view, which sought to retain from the past all that was useful, rejecting only what could not be retained in good conscience, was no flight into a wistful nostalgia; it was rather a pastorally responsible attempt to demonstrate the continuity and unity of Lutheranism with all of Christendom.

Lutheranism, on the other hand, does not hesitate to critically examine its heritage from the past, subjecting it to sound theological, psychological, and sociological examination for its meaning and usefulness for our own time. In doing so, Lutheranism is reminded that a sentimental return to any earlier age, ignoring later history, is no more adequate an answer than to suggest that each age must start anew to fashion structures of worship and prayer.

For Lutherans, the word tradition—in the sense of the gathered experience of the church at worship throughout its history—is an important working concept. For Lutherans, their worship tradition is always a living tradition, continuously developing and living in a vital parish practice. Building on the experience of the past, the church moves confidently into the future.

In some places the word tradition is misunderstood to mean merely conventional practices that may have developed in some place and have no relation to the experience of the whole church. Often it means no more than "what we in this parish are used to" or "how we did it last year." More often than not such "traditions" merely reflect sectarian fads that have become conventional through repetition.

It is a Lutheran conviction that the needs of people at worship are most effectively met by forms and structures of prayer which draw on the collective experience of the whole church at worship. For some, such structures and practices—when used for the first time—will be new and, perhaps, disconcerting. Once they become a normal part of the life of worship, however, their richness, strength, diversity, power to nourish faith and life, and their ability to help Christians praise God and enjoy Him forever soon become apparent.

The Music of the Congregation

The chief musical reform of the Lutheran church in the 16th century was the establishment of congregational singing as a vital ingredient in corporate worship. It was not enough for Luther that people merely be present at worship—their faith should erupt in song.

> God has made our hearts and spirits happy through His dear Son . . . . He
> who believes this sincerely and earnestly cannot help but be happy; he
> must cheerfully sing . . . .

Thus what was only tolerated in the medieval church—and then only on infrequent occasion—became a central feature of worship in the church of the Lutheran Reformation.

Congregational singing, then as now, centers in the hymnody of the people, particularly in the Lutheran chorale. This unique body of words and melodies, which took shape in the early years of the Reformation— drawn from the chants of the medieval church, from the many popular pre-Reformation "Kyrie songs," from nonliturgical Latin and Latin-German songs of pre-Reformation times, from secular melodies to which sacred words were adapted, and from newly written texts and melodies—became known as the Lutheran chorale. Its texts spoke clearly of sin and salvation, of death and resurrection; they recounted the story of man's fall into sin and his redemption won through Christ's victory over death and the devil. Its melodies—sung by the congregation in unison and without accompaniment—were vigorous, rhythmic, and truly popular.

The chorale spread rapidly and achieved a remarkable popularity wherever Lutheranism took root. The words and tunes of the chorale have continued to provide strength and comfort to worshipers wherever they have been used, and they have served as the basis for an ever-growing body of church music by composers since that time. There is hardly a Christian hymnbook that has not been enriched through the inclusion of Lutheran chorales, just as Lutheran hymnals have been enriched by the hymnody of others.

This unique wedding of words and melody which is the Lutheran chorale gave rise to the uniquely Lutheran custom of singing hymns in alternation between congregation, choir, and organ. Alternating stanza for stanza throughout the entire hymn, this manner of singing offered not only variety in the musical presentation of the hymn, but also provided opportunity for meditation on the words of the stanzas presented by the alternating groups. Each musical entity had a place in the singing of the chorale; at the heart and center, however, was the congregation.

The uniqueness of Lutheran hymnody lies in the fact that from the very beginning it has been an important part of the liturgy, not—as in most other traditions—a general Christian song loosely attached to worship. It was and continued to be *the* vehicle for congregational song.

Luther himself led the way in encouraging the creation of new texts and melodies through which the congregation could give voice to its faith in corporate song. The result has been the incorporation into Lutheran worship of a large body of hymnody reflecting a wide diversity of origins and musical styles.

For worshiping Lutherans, congregational song centers in the singing of hymns of proclamation and praise, prayer and adoration. And wherever a Lutheran understanding of worship and congregational song prevails, the chorale—among all the many jewels in the treasury of the church's song—continues to hold a place of special prominence.

In more recent history, Lutherans have also encouraged congregational singing of such other portions of the liturgy as the great prose songs of the mass (Kyrie, Gloria, Sanctus, Agnus Dei), various canticles (Venite, Magnificat, Nunc dimittis), together with a variety of shorter responses in the liturgy. Most of the early ventures in this development consisted of not too successful adaptions for congregations of music originally intended for choral performance. Only in very recent years has the attempt been made to fashion music for the liturgy that is truly congregational in its conception and realization.

Whatever its characteristics may be, true congregational song operates within the musical limitations of largely amateur singers, yet has a musical integrity and character distinctly its own. True congregational song is neither simplistic, undistinguished melody whose only purpose is functional; neither is it essentially choir music simplified for the purposes of group singing. True congregational song is a genre all its own, and its prototype and model—in terms of an accessible unison melody with rhythmic life and variety—is the Lutheran chorale.

The Music of the Choir

In the Lutheran tradition of worship the choir functions liturgically as a helper and servant to the congregation, enlivening and enriching the worship of the entire assembly. It does this in three ways. In order of importance they are:

1. The choir supports and enriches the congregational singing of hymns and of the liturgy.
2. The choir brings richness and variety to congregational worship by singing the portions of the liturgy entrusted to it.
3. The choir enriches congregational worship by presenting attendant music as appropriate and possible.

1. *The choir supports and enriches the congregational singing of hymns:* by regularly devoting time in rehearsals to practicing the hymns to be sung in the various services, thus establishing a nucleus of singers who can confidently lead the singing; by helping to enlarge the congregation's repertoire through learning new hymns of worth and introducing them appropriately to the congregation; and by participating with the

congregation in the regular festive presentation of the Hymn of the Day (Hymn of the Week, Gradual Hymn, de tempore hymn).

The choir supports and enriches the congregational singing of the liturgy: by devoting time, on a regular basis, to rehearsing the liturgy, so that the choir can lead the congregation most effectively; by teaching and introducing to the congregation the portions of the liturgy that have not yet been learned, or learned only incompletely; by helping the congregation enlarge the dimensions of its participation through learning new musical settings of the liturgy or portions of the liturgy as appropriate. By helping the congregation, of which the choir is a part, sing the services it already knows more effectively, and by introducing—over a period of time—several different musical settings of the service that the congregation can use with the changing moods of the church year, the choir will be assuming more fully its role of leader in the liturgical worship of the congregation.

The uniquely Lutheran tradition of the "hymn mass,"[2] while not suggested as a norm, might well be used as occasionally appropriate to substitute for the prose texts of the major songs of the service.

2. *The choir also adds variety to congregational worship by singing the portions of the liturgy that have been entrusted to it by the congregation.* In the singing of the liturgy, certain texts, because of their unique appropriateness to the Sunday, festival, or season of the church year, change from week to week. Thus these texts are more suitable for singing by a group that meets regularly for rehearsal. At different times in the church's history these texts have been assigned to various groups; their use, however, is crucially important since they provide part of the variety that is important to liturgical worship.

In the services at which Holy Communion is celebrated, the "proper" texts traditionally assigned to the choir are:

> The Introit (Entrance Psalmody)
> The Gradual (Gradual Psalmody)
> The Alleluia
> The Tract
> The Sequence
> The Offertory
> The Communion

In the services at which Holy Communion is not celebrated, chiefly Matins or Morning Prayer, Vespers or Evening Prayer, or other services centered on the Word, the chief variable texts are:

> The Antiphons
> The Psalms
> The Responsory or Response
> The Canticles

This rich selection of texts provides the basis for the participation of the choir in the varying portions of the liturgy, a participation for which the choir is uniquely suited and through which it can make a contribution of major significance. In certain newer liturgies some of these texts occur in slightly different contexts. They remain, however, the basic texts to which the choir must address itself as it prepares for its participation in the varying portions of the liturgy.

3. *The choir also enriches congregational worship by presenting attendant music as appropriate and as possible.* The term attendant music refers to that entire spectrum of motets, anthems, Passions, cantatas, and other music not covered in the preceding discussion. As attendant music is planned for use in worship, three considerations are crucial:

a. Attendant music should be liturgically appropriate to the Sunday, festival, or season of the church year.
b. Attendant music should be appropriately placed in the liturgy. (Here special emphasis should be given the traditional Lutheran practice of music *sub communione*—during the distribution of Holy Communion.)
c. Attendant music should always be within the musical limitations of the choir.

In preparing attendant music, care must always be taken that the time and effort involved does not displace preparation for those other functions of the choir in worship that have prior claim in liturgical worship.

The choir has a unique and significant place in Lutheran worship. It can fill that role with music ranging from the simplest to the most complex; but complexity is never a criterion of liturgical suitability. What is important and crucial is that choirmaster and singers together—as well as the pastor and congregation—understand what the real function of the choir in liturgical worship is, and that, understanding their priorities, they work toward carrying them out in interesting, effective, and meaningful ways that will contribute to the worship of the whole congregation.

A Note on the Soloist

The use of the solo voice in Christian worship finds its roots in the Jewish cantorial tradition and the continuation of elements of that practice in the use of solo voices in the Christian chant of the medieval church. In Lutheran worship that practice was continued, and the music of Lutheranism from Luther to Bach in particular reflects the continued development of that traditon.

The soloist in Lutheran worship always functions liturgically. Where a solo voice is used in the service, for example at times when a choir is not available, a Lutheran understanding of corporate worship assumes that the soloist—in reality a "one-person" choir—will provide the liturgical music necessary for the particular service. Then, when possible and desirable, the soloist may present additional attendant music according to his or her ability. The liturgy offers many opportunities for participation by the solo voice in ways—characterized by a spirit of modesty and restraint—that give richness, variety, and greater meaning to liturgical worship.

As a particular matter, soloists drawn from the ranks of choirs where the singing of appropriate liturgical music is the norm will usually see their function as soloists in a liturgical context more readily than will soloists who see their role to be exclusively that of presenting "special" music.

The Music of the Pastor

The corporate worship of Lutheran Christians has traditionally been sung. This is true also of the parts of the liturgy that are the unique province of those leading the service. The singing of the liturgy by pastor and people together adds a beauty and solemnity not possible in any other way. It elevates the doing of the liturgy to a place that moves beyond the personalistic and idiosyncratic to that of truly corporate song.

Certain portions of the liturgy are essentially *liturgical conversation* between pastor and people. Such familiar exchanges as "The Lord be with you—And with thy spirit," "Lift up your hearts—We lift them up unto the Lord," "Let us give thanks unto the Lord our God—It is meet and right so to do" naturally call for singing by both participants in the dialog. In many other places in the various orders of worship this kind of liturgical conversation is important. When such liturgical conversation occurs, it is the most natural and desirable practice that both portions of the dialog be sung.

Other parts of the liturgy given to those leading in worship are essentially a kind of *monolog.* Examples include the Scripture lessons, the Collect, and the Words of Institution. These portions of the liturgy are usually sung on one tone with simple inflections. Luther himself took care to provide such simple recitation formulas for use in these instances. Most musical settings of the liturgy provide such simple recitation formulas, and congregations should encourage their pastors to use them when the rest of the service is sung by the congregation.

Many pastors already sing certain parts of the liturgy. This is a most commendable practice. Pastors and other worship leaders should be encouraged by their congregations—wherever they may be hesitant—to assume their fuller role in the singing of the complete liturgical service whenever the rest of the service is sung by congregation and choir.

The Music of the Organ

The organ has played a significant role in Lutheran worship since Reformation times, even though various aspects of its role have changed since that time. In its unique way the organ, too, can be the "living voice of the Gospel" and its use in Lutheran worship has demonstrated that possibility.

The Lutheran organist is a liturgical organist. This means that the way the organist functions in the service is determined by the movement and requirements of the liturgical action. It is not the function of the organist to entertain, to provide meaningless meanderings at the keyboard, or to fill every quiet moment with music. It is the function of the liturgical organist to lead the congregation in the singing of the hymns and chorales, to accompany, as appropriate, other portions of the liturgy sung by the congregation or choir, and to present other liturgical and attendant music alone or in ensemble.

The most important role of the organist is that of introducing and leading the congregational singing of the hymns and the liturgy. The practice of using the organ to accompany congregational singing was unknown at Luther's time, when the chorales were sung unaccompanied and in unison. But today the common practice is for the organist to accompany most, if not all, the stanzas of the hymns. Effective leadership here can do much to make worship the exciting adventure it is at its best. Through the use of effective introductions, careful choice of tempos, rhythmic playing, appropriate registration, judicious use of varied accompaniments, the occasional singing of a hymn stanza without the organ, and especially through the use of alternation between the congregation, organ, and choir, the organist sets the spirit and carries the momentum of hymn singing from the introduction through to the final stanza. When the organ accompanies other portions of the liturgy sung by the congregation it should do so with a forthrightness and vigor appropriate to the circumstances. In all situations the organ *leads* the congregational singing; it does not merely provide a bland and lifeless accompaniment.

It is customary in many places that the organ play at the beginning of worship, during the gathering of the gifts, and as the congregation disperses at the close of worship. It is most helpful and meaningful if the organ music at these times is based on the hymns or chorales sung in the service. At the least such music should clearly reflect the spirit of the particular celebration.

In general, the Lutheran organist plays less rather than more. When the organist does play it should be liturgically, functionally, and practically to the point. When it has no particular liturgical function it should remain silent. While the liturgical organist seeks to avoid a self-centered flamboyance and pretension in his playing, at the same time he uses all his skills in highlighting the inherent drama of the liturgical celebration. Only in this way will the organ's role as a liturgical instrument be more readily apparent.

The Music of Instruments

At its best the Lutheran church has always welcomed the use of a variety of instruments as a particularly festive way of expressing the celebrative aspects of joyful worship. Luther encouraged all Christian musicians to "let their singing and playing to the praise of the Father of all grace sound forth with joy from their organs and whatever other beloved musical instruments there are."[3]

The organ has always had a place of special prominence in Lutheran worship. Lutherans have also used a great variety of instruments of all kinds in praise of God. Brass instruments, stringed instruments, woodwinds, bells, percussion—all these and more have been used in Lutheran worship, some of these even being preferred over the organ in the early Reformation era.

A rich treasury of music, intended for use in Lutheran worship using instruments, developed in the centuries after the Reformation. This music includes instrumental pieces intended as preludes, postludes, and interludes, both chorale-based and free compositions for organ and one or more solo instruments, and countless large- and small-scale concerted works for voices and instruments together. Special attention has been given in more recent times to providing a variety of solo and concerted music for small numbers of instruments with organ, or in concert with voices, that can be performed by instrumentalists of modest ability.

Instruments can play an important part in corporate worship, helping us to sing and dance our faith, helping us to express more fully and clearly the changing moods of Christian worship, from the leanness and spareness of such seasons as Advent and Lent to the more exuberant character of the Easter and Christmas seasons. Instruments can help foster communion with God and with our fellow worshipers and can serve as an extension of the human voice in sounding the special joy in the heart of the Christian as— through faith in his Lord—he affirms the totality of God's creation.

The Pastor and the Church Musician

It is only when pastor, church musician, and people work together toward the accomplishment of these goals that a truly living and vital parish worship practice in the Lutheran tradition can result. Each participant plays his own distinctive role, yet each role complements and reinforces the others.

Regular planning sessions are an important part of this mutual preparation for worship. Pastors and church musicians, especially, need to meet often to exchange ideas and to discuss plans for future services and the role each will play. But whatever the vehicle for planning, pastor and church musician need to work carefully together. Only in that way will worship be the best we can offer and God's people be truly inspired and edified.

CHAPTER I

The Liturgical Life of the Church

Eugene L. Brand

The Churchly Ordering of Time

The Calendar

The evolution of the calendar of the Christian church covers many centuries and is a good example of Christianity's accommodation to general religious practice. That the church evolved a calendar evidences the human need for a framework in time according to which faith and natural experience can be harmonized. Primitive religious calendars, for example, coordinate myths about the gods with the cycles of nature.

How the church understands and uses its calendar, however, evidences its transformation of general religious practice—a transformation rooted in the religion of Israel. Most of Israel's major feasts were determined by seasonal changes—Pentecost at the corn harvest (first fruits), the Feast of Booths as "harvest home," the Day of Atonement at the beginning of a new year. But the Jews did not celebrate some dying-god-fertility myth; they celebrated the mighty acts of God *in history,* events which had given irreversible direction to history. Pentecost, for example, became associated with the giving of the Law. By the middle of the second century B.C. it was regarded as the feast of covenant renewal—a covenant that had universal implications.

The Christian church followed in this historical understanding and, though it borrowed dates for its feasts both from the Jewish tradition and from other religions with which it came in contact, it observed its feasts as celebrations of the mighty acts of God in Christ. The church could borrow an ancient celebration of the winter solstice dedicated to the birth of the god Aeon from Kore the Virgin —a feast connected with the waters of the Nile—and transform it into Epiphany, the celebration of the birth and baptism of Jesus. Or it could build on the covenant renewal traditions of Israel's Pentecost, transforming it into the celebration of the outpouring of the Holy Spirit and the establishment of the people of the new covenant.

Throughout the period during which the system of feasts (and fasts) was evolving, Christians continued to celebrate Sunday as the weekly remembrance of the resurrection. Sunday had a strong eschatological thrust—that to which the sabbath had pointed is fulfilled in Jesus; Sunday is the eighth day, the symbol of fulfillment of the new creation. For many years this weekly celebration of the resurrection was sufficient. But in course of time the church saw its role cast increasingly in the transformation of history. One of the dimensions of that new role was accommodation to the forms of religion.

The church's calendar, then, rests primarily on the weekly cycle of Sundays and partly on a system of major feasts. The method of determining these major feasts is itself a testimony to historic evolution. Easter, the most ancient and most central of the feasts, is determined, as is the Passover to which it is related, by the lunar calendar. It, therefore, moves through a span of weeks from year to year. Christmas, on the other hand, is a fixed calendar date because it is determined by the solar cycle, reflecting the Graeco-Roman heritage of Christian history.

The variance between these two systems creates the need for flexible seasons of Epiphany and post-Pentecost to accommodate the varying time span between Christmas and Easter from year to year. Many would like to fix the date of Easter to tidy up this variance.

The system of Sundays and major feasts is related to the history of salvation in Jesus Christ. It is truly a Christian year. Movements to insert a variety of special days overlook this fundamental point. From the First Sunday in Advent to the last Sunday after Pentecost, the life and mission of Jesus are rehearsed and the implications for the mission of the church are celebrated. This system is rooted in a sacramental understanding that recapitulates salvation history not as a timeless myth but as a unique event that influences ongoing time. Though the system itself is obviously cyclical, it does not impose that quality on the Christian understanding of time. The days and weeks march on from the Resurrection to the Final Coming. As they do, the church celebrates repeatedly those great events that relate it at any given moment both to the beginning and the end of that linear progression of history. A cyclical religious device with all its formative value for human consciousness has been appropriately transformed for faith in a God who is ever at work in history to accomplish His purposes.

It is not surprising that the calendar of Sundays and major feasts has been related primarily to the celebration of the Eucharist. The liturgy of Holy Communion embodies the same polarity as the calendar itself. Through its appointed Propers—especially its lessons from the Scriptures—it focuses on specific aspects of salvation history. This specific focus is brought into the present moment by the preacher whose task is an exposition of the lesson(s) in the current milieu. But through the hymns of the ordinary and through the thanksgiving over the bread and wine, the wholeness of the gospel is recalled. The fullness of the eucharistic rite makes it the only adequate liturgical vehicle to reflect the fullness of the church's year.

The so-called lesser festivals or saints days are also part of our calendar heritage. Originally the veneration of the saints was centered in their burial places. Only later did it enter the eucharistic halls, where it eventually was merged with the system of corporate worship. The churches of the Reformation have taken differing attitudes toward the sanctoral cycle. They have reacted strongly against superstitious practices associated with veneration of the saints and against the subtle shift of emphasis away from Christ in the popular mind. Sometimes, however, they have overreacted by simply banishing these days, if not from the calendar, then from actual church life.

Heirs of the Reformation are again beginning to appreciate the observance of the sanctoral cycle as a means of affirming God's continued work throughout history. It is possible for an exclusive emphasis on the ministry of Jesus, especially if His humanity is not really affirmed, to lead to an a-historical viewpoint. Remembering God's actions through a variety of figures throughout the centuries can help keep Christians anchored in history. To do that, of course, the sanctoral cycle must venture beyond the perimeters of the New Testament church and risk including Christians from all periods.

A final ingredient in this mixture of observances is the day itself. Each day marks a basic unit of life. It is natural, therefore, for Christians to mark at least the beginning and ending of each day with worship. A rich heritage of very ancient hymns and prayers shows how parallels were drawn between sunrise, new birth, resurrection, the day's tasks, and opportunity; between lighting the lamps and Christ, the light of the world. The liturgical observance of morning and evening prayer originally centered in psalms, hymns, lessons, and prayers and was determined more by daily personal need than by the seasons of the church year.

The function of all these aspects of the church's ordering of time—Sundays and major feasts, lesser festivals, daily prayer—is not to sanctify time, at least not in the cyclical, religious sense. It is, rather, to make real in time what God has done in Christ through anamnesis.[1] Such vital remembrance through reading, proclamation, Baptism, and the Lord's Supper, is access to God's gracious accomplishing of man's salvation.

The Propers

It has been the special genius of the Western church to flesh out its calendar with a system of propers—liturgical elements specifically related to the specific occasion. These propers bring the point of the particular observance into the holistic sweep of the eucharistic celebration. The propers for Christmas provide a strong accent on the Incarnation while the Great Thanksgiving recalls the whole sweep of salvation history, keeping the service from undue domination by one theme.

The propers, then, are the insurance that worship will dwell on each point of the Gospel, keeping them in balance and insuring full coverage. They keep the prayers, praise, and preaching of the church from the subjective whim of the preacher or musician by keeping both under a discipline imposed by common agreement of the whole church. Thereby, an individual Christian fellowship retains its sense of communion with the whole church by forming its liturgical life according to common patterns.

The Lutheran churches preserved the calendar and propers of the Western tradition because the Reformers appreciated their value. They prized especially the calendar of Sundays and major feasts with its lectionary.

The lectionary has been prominent in the Lutheran tradition because of its great emphasis upon Biblical preaching. In his first liturgical pamphlet, "Concerning the Order of Public Worship" (1523), Luther laid down the thesis that all the church's ills would be corrected if the proclamation of the Gospel were again given free rein. From that day to yesterday, the so-called historic pericopes have been part of the Lutheran liturgical books.

Lutherans have not limited the impact of the lectionary to preaching, however. Many Reformation hymns were written with specific lessons in view. These hymns developed into "propers" of their own; the appointment of de tempore hymns became common in Lutheran circles.

These hymns, in turn, stimulated composers to write a wealth of derivative music for choir and organ that was also related, through them, to the lectionary. The church cantatas of J. S. Bach are perhaps the best known example of such de tempore music.

In addition, there is a body of choral literature that set the Bible passages themselves to music. These pieces were originally intended for use in conjunction with the readings. Heinrich Schuetz, among many who wrote such settings, is the unparalleled master of this sort of de tempore music.

Other parts of the Western system of propers have not fared so well in Lutheran circles. The introit, gradual, and other proper psalmody gradually disappeared after the 16th century, partly due to the tradition of the *Deutsche Messe* (*DM*; "German Mass"; 1526) and its substitution of hymns for most liturgical song. In North America, it was not until the *Common Service Book* (*CSB*) that Lutheran liturgies had restored the complete series of historic introits, collects, and graduals. Since then their use has again become common among Lutherans in North America.

Since the mid-1960s the calendar and propers have undergone revision in all major branches of Western Christianity. Often the changes have been made jointly by various confessional groups. The publication in 1969 of the Roman *Ordo lectionum missae* marked a formal break by the largest church in the West with the "historic" calendar and lectionary. Rather than a one-year system of Epistles and Gospels, a three-year system of three readings was introduced. This three-year system has become the basis of lectionary reform in the Presbyterian, Episcopal, and Lutheran churches as well as the bodies of the Consultation on Church Union. At least provisionally, a new lectionary consensus has emerged replacing the older one-year system.

A new lectionary requires a revision of the other propers as well. The Inter-Lutheran Commission on Worship (ILCW) has offered a new system of psalmody and a new series of collects related to its provisional lectionary.[2] It will also provide de tempore hymns appropriate to the new system. All this will, of course, require the rearrangement of the vast musical literature designed for the historic pericope series. Little of it need be lost; often it will merely fall on different days. See Table A for a calendar comparison.

The church's ordering of time is fundamental to its system of corporate worship. Through its calendar and propers it provides breadth of coverage of Biblical material and a dramatic sequence within seasons and among the seasons themselves. It further provides tangible contact with the religion of Israel and even the pagan traditions of the Graeco-Roman world. In North America the church's calendar does not always mesh with the civil calendar. That, at least, reintroduces a vestige of pre-Constantinian days before the church had transformed culture. For though the church lives in time, it does so as the community that has been placed to be the eschatological sign of God's purpose for the world beyond time.

Eucharistic Worship

Eucharistic Liturgies

We have no description of how the New Testament church celebrated the Eucharist. Whether such celebrations regularly included readings from the Old Testament and the letters of the apostles or whether there was a separate preaching service continues to be debated among scholars. For a while, synagog services probably continued to be services of the Word. The Lord's Supper itself was called "the breaking of the bread" and was celebrated with the joy of eschatological expectation—a foretaste of the anticipated heavenly feast. The Pauline correspondence shows the struggle to regard Christian worship as both separate and exclusive (especially 1 Corinthians).

Even before the end of the apostolic age the Lord's Supper was being separated from its context of a meal (the agape) and was losing the character of eschatological expectation. How quickly it assumed the basic form common to most historic liturgies is shown in the *Didache* ("Teaching of the Apostles"), c. 100, probably from Syria; the *First Apology* of Justin Martyr, c. 155, written in Rome; and the *Apostolic Tradition* of Hippolytus, c. 200, also from Rome. The latter contains a liturgy with this shape: Kiss of Peace, Offering of bread and wine, Prefatory Sentences, Great Thanksgiving (thanksgivings, *verba Christi* [i.e., Words of Institution], anamnesis, epiclesis, doxology), Offerings of the people, Communion prayers, Communion, Blessing, dismissal. Missing are the Sanctus and the Our Father. The prayers show their dependence on Jewish thanksgivings both in form and content. The text is only a model, however, indicating the structure according to which the bishop would form his own prayer. Though it would be a mistake to assume that the liturgy outlined above was used everywhere, the *Apostolic Tradition* does exhibit the basic shape of the later Latin or Roman rite.

When the service of readings and proclamation is added, the liturgy assumes an even more recognizable shape. The tradition of the synagog was preserved in Christian worship—readings separated by the singing of psalms. A series of three readings developed: an Old Testament pericope, part of an apostolic letter, a Gospel pericope.

The major metropolitan centers developed their own liturgical traditions and tended to impose them within their spheres of influence: Antioch, Alexandria, Constantinople, Jerusalem, Milan, Rome. The first four determined the traditions of the Eastern churches, the latter two determined the Western tradition. Space limits us to a consideration of the Western tradition. As Christianity spread northward and westward, other types of liturgical usage developed about whose origins little is known. The Roman Rite is distinguishable fro the Ambrosian liturgy of Milan, the Mozarabic liturgy in Spain, the Celtic liturgies in Scotland and Ireland, and the Gallican liturgy of the Frankish kingdom.

The Roman, or Latin, rite underwent a significant transformation under Gregory the Great (pope 590-604). Gregorian revisions were undertaken to standardize and abridge the inherited rite, and make it more practical. The result formed the basis of the *Gregorian Sacramentary;* it and the *Gelasian Sacramentary* are the chief transmitters of the Roman liturgy. The *Gelasian Sacramentary* known to us is an eighth-century document, but it contains elements of pre-Gregorian Roman practice.

In the interest of liturgical uniformity, Charlemagne introduced an evolved form of the *Gregorian Sacramentary,* the *Hadrianum* (received from Hadrian I) throughout his kingdom. He entrusted work on the books to Alcuin. Even so, the *Gelasian Sacramentary* continued to be copied and used. Finally, in the ninth century an unknown scholar made a more practical edition of Alcuin's sacramentary, which fused the Gregorian and Gelasian books and laid the foundation for medieval sacramentaries. It contained rather few Gallican elements.

The Middle Ages continued to be marked by a variety of practices, and it was not until the *Missale Romanum* (1570) that the Tridentine Roman Church had liturgical uniformity. The *Missale Romanum* was substantially the same as the first printed service book, the 1474 *Ordo missalis secundum consuetudinem Romanae curiae,* which, in turn, resembled the widely used Franciscan missal of the 13th century.

The uniform Roman Rite, then was a mixture of the traditions of the Gregorian and Gelasian sacramentaries with a few Gallican characteristics. The 1570 missal remained the norm for four centuries, until the reforms of the Second Vatican Council culminated in the *Missale Romanum* of 1970.[3] See Table B.

Eucharistic Piety

Sketching the structural development of the eucharistic rite is only a beginning. We must also sketch the evolution of eucharistic piety.

For some time the church remained small enough for the eucharistic celebration to have the domestic character of a meal shared in common. This remained true even where the Eucharist was separated from the agape. Third-century frescoes still show people seated at table for Eucharist. Two forces conspired against this domesticity, both related to the success of the Gospel. First, as numbers of converts grew, services outgrew a patron's home and then even the houses that congregations adapted to their cultic use (house churches). Congregations began to build buildings for worship that, by their scale, militated against the family feeling of those gathered. Second, with the conversion of Constantine and the emergence of Christianity as a public cult, domesticity was destroyed by the absorption of imperial patterns of ritual behavior. A fourth-century basilica in Rome, with its vast spaces and rich embellishments, was hardly the setting for a simple meal! Even so, the congregation continued to participate through singing, offering gifts, and sharing bread and wine.

Popular participation, however, steadily decreased in proportion to the increase of clericalism. To preserve orthodox faith against the inroads of heresy, most of the participatory functions were put in the safe (ie., educated and disciplined) hands of clerics. The church had simply not been able to keep up instructionally with the vast number of converts. Furthermore, there was a conscious effort to consolidate authority and orthodoxy by defining *the catholic faith* over against the rich variety of teaching and life of the first two centuries. In defense of the truth, therefore, the laity was increasingly relegated to second-class status.

The transformation of the role of the clergy was furthered by an emergent concept of priesthood that owed more to the Old Testament— and perhaps to the mystery religions—than it did to the New. When the Roman Empire collapsed, the episcopacy was thrust into a civil role to preserve a modicum of order, since it was in control of the only disciplined network available. The Roman bishop became Pontifex Maximus; the pomp of empire was transferred to the church.

In the light of all this, the celebration of the Eucharist became more and more a sacerdotal act in behalf of the people, influenced in part by the ethos of the Roman state cult.

By about the ninth century, the growing theological and devotional focus on the transformation of elements of bread and wine suggested that special bread was required for such a holy destiny; it could not be taken from the ordinary loaves offered by the people. The link between the elements and the offering was lost; it was required in the Latin Church that the bread be unleavened and specially prepared.

The presence of Christ in the transsubstantiated bread and wine was painted so palpably that people responded in awe and dread. Sacramental materialism led to liturgical acts of veneration in the presence of the consecrated host and raised the question of withholding the cup from the laity because of the profanation that spilling consecrated wine could constitute.

The development of the concept of the sacrifice of the mass spotlighted the sacerdotal role of the clergy and minimalized the concept of communion. The Eucharist was transformed from the shared thanksgiving meal of the early centuries to the awesome sacrifice of Christ himself. It was the witnessing of this sacrifice and the adoration of the host that brought one to church. Most lay persons received the bread and wine only a few times a year.

Churches developed from eucharistic halls to shrines. The marvelous structures of the Middle Ages are eloquent witnesses to peoples' awe in God's presence and their desire to build a temple worthy of the eucharistic presence and the relics of the saints, but they militate aggressively against corporate worship. They are awe-inspiring clerical theaters. Even the music—often quite splendid—had long since ceased to have popular participation as its goal.

The devotion of the people in the Middle Ages, then, was not oriented to what was taking place about the altar except at the moment of consecration. Otherwise, the mass became *the* occasion for one's personal prayers and devotion.

It is easy from a later point in history to judge these developments too harshly. While there clearly were instances of lust for power and prestige among the bishops and clergy which led them to exploit their people through the sacramental system as it had evolved, the questionable eucharistic piety of the Middle Ages was the product of many disparate ingredients and needed reforming. Many realized that even before Luther.

Eucharistic Fullness

Why should Christian worship be centered in the Eucharist? Purely for historic reasons? Only because the Lutheran Confessions said Lutherans did not abolish the mass? Hardly. Only the Eucharist can function as the center of worship because only it is full and rich enough liturgically to be a focus for truly catholic church life. Catholic means whole. It brooks no false separation of mind and body, spirit and flesh, black and white, ruler and subject, clergy and laity, male and female. Such a vision can be shared only by those to whom God has revealed the mystery of His will and purpose. Such a life requires for its ritualization a liturgy with more than words.

There are two primary streams in the devotional life of the church. One is congregational, centered in the Eucharist; the other is, originally, domestic, centered in daily prayer and praise. All congregational services are spin-offs of the eucharistic rite (even Matins and Vespers function as spin-offs in Lutheran practice) and thereby lack its fullness. A service that is largely verbal risks promoting a bourgeois intellectualizing of the Christian life and scarcely allows for sensate experience. Both conceptual and transconceptual communication and experience are part of the full eucharistic celebration. The promise verbalized in the lessons and sermon has its initial tangible fulfillment in the bread and wine.[4] The Supper keeps preaching anchored in the salvation event; the sermon, on the other hand, keeps the Supper from sub-Christian religious observance.

The offerings and the subsequent sharing of bread and wine as Christ's body and blood, where properly accompanied by Gospel proclamation, give ritual expression to the sacrificial shape of the Christian's vocational life—the arena of diaconal service. The ritual expression is devastated by the preaching service offering that leads nowhere symbolically.

The poles of sermon and Supper allow both for a pointed, thematic emphasis and the full expression of the essential Gospel. Without the Supper, the service easily gets too monochrome, too deadly thematic. A service dominated by one theme cannot be a satisfactory liturgical vehicle for the assembled congregation with its complex needs. Too much thematizing leads to manipulation and harangue, the enemies of corporate action.

Understood as foretaste of the heavenly feast (note Mark 14:25 and parallels), the Lord's Supper keeps the worship of the congregation properly eschatological in tone. Without a keen sense of worship's thrust into God's future, the ground for joy and celebration is lost. Christian worship is not merely a celebration of life; it celebrates the death and resurrection victory of the Lord Christ and the congregation's anticipation of the life of His kingdom. When that is grasped, joyous worship is the natural result.

Other Liturgical Orders

Liturgy of the Hours

Services of prayer and praise, especially morning and evening, were originally domestic, as we have noted. We have also noted the observance of the day as a unit of time. Stated times for daily prayer were part of Jewish piety; they corresponded to the hours of sacrifice in the temple. Prayers in the morning and evening are a natural expression of devotion, marking the beginning and ending of the day's work—anciently marking the rising of the sun and the lighting of the lamps.

Initially, Jewish Christians may have observed the prayer hours in the accustomed way. Finally, their observance was transferred to the churches where it began to undergo a process of elaboration. Impulses for this change are still being sorted out by scholars. It is now thought likely that the developed form of hours for prayer reflects the Roman division of the day into *prima, tertia, sexta and nona,* and the night into four watches: evening, midnight, cockcrow, dawn. But the prayers at dawn and dusk should be common to either system and trace their origins back to temple sacrifice. These services were attended by the laity. The additional hours tended to be observed by the ascetics and later by monks.

The cycle of observances now called canonical hours or divine office developed in the monasteries. Perhaps echoing Psalm 119:164, the cycle consists of seven hours: Matins-Lauds (3:00 a.m.), Prime (6:00 a.m.), Terce (9:00 a.m.), Sext (12:00 noon), None (3:00 p.m.), Vespers (6:00 p.m.), and Compline (9:00 p.m.). St. Benedict of Nursia, from whose order for Monte Cassino the list springs, prescribed eight hours; Matins is derived from the Nocturns observed prior to Lauds. The cycle can be divided into the *Officium nocturnum* (Vespers, Compline, Nocturns/Matins, Lauds) and the *Officium diurnum* (Prime, Terce, Sext, None; called "little hours" because they never were as important as Lauds and Vespers).

Monastic communities have been the major locus for the observance of the hours corporately, though they have often adjusted the schedule to fit practical circumstances. The hours have also been sung in cathedral chapters and collegiate churches. Priests have traditionally been obligated to say the office privately.

During the Middle Ages the office became unwieldly because of complexities introduced into its structure by multiplying psalms and lessons and by the burgeoning calendar of saints. In the 12th century the office as used in the papal chapel spread its influence, abbreviating the lectionary, modifying the calendar, and standardizing the hymnal. The process was furthered in 1241 by the approval of a revision undertaken by the Franciscans that ended the celebration of double offices. The festival offices suppressed that of the day. As a result of this reform the old daily office gave way in practice to a procession of saints' day festivals with their readings from often spurious lives of the saints. The office had become the formalistic business of the clergy, with little attendance by the laity except on Sundays and festivals, at morning prayer sung before mass and at Vespers. C. W. Dugmore has noted how, even here, the ancient tradition of morning and evening is observable. After several unsuccessful attempts, a new reformed office, promulgated in 1568 by Pius V, greatly simplified the medieval mass and tried to restore the daily office concept.[5]

The Second Vatican Council, while not wishing to repudiate the model of the monastic choir office, did wish to involve the laity again in daily services of prayer and praise. Lauds and vespers have, therefore, been designated as major hours and are designed for celebration with a congregation in a parish church. The new *Liturgia horarum* was authorized by Paul VI in 1970; the four volumes of the *editio typica* (1971-72) will appear also in vernacular translations.

Christians continued the practice of using the psalms for daily prayer, eventually adding the Gloria Patri as a Trinitarian ascription of praise. The psalter was supplemented by Greek hymns and odes, some of which have survived as office hymns. Latin hymns of the Ambrosian tradition have also been connected with the office.

The components of the hours services were: psalmody, hymnody, lessons, responsories, prayers, canticles. Numbers of psalms and lessons have varied considerably, reaching ludicrous proportions in the Middle Ages. The use of the psalms has usually been based on the principle of covering the psalter within a given time. The lessons have generally followed the *lectio continua* pattern. A canon of hymns developed, prescribed for each hour and day—the origin of the office hymn concept. The *Benedictus* was associated with Lauds, the *Magnificat* with Vespers, the *Nunc dimittis* with Compline. The *Te Deum* and other canticles structured from Old Testament materials and the Apocrypha were also used.

Due to the clericalization of the office and the fact that it was rarely sung outside monastaries, great musical treasures were virtually lost to the laity and, for all practical purposes, to most of the clergy. The classical hymnody of Greek and Latin writers, the psalter, the canticles, and the responsories were virtually embalmed in the breviary. The post-Vatican II attempt to further corporate use of the breviary among the clergy and return Lauds and Vespers to congregational services should release this material for renewed attention by musicians.

Ideally, the hours provide participants with a disciplined form of prayer, use of the psalter, and reading of the Bible. These orders can be adapted to both simple and festal corporate use, but they can also be used in personal devotions. They can be an antidote to individualism in one's devotional life, keeping personal prayers in tune with the liturgical rhythm of the whole church. These values would seem to outweigh the demonstrable hazard of mechanical and perfunctory use.

Preaching Services

While it is true that preaching was not often part of the medieval mass, it is not true that there was little preaching in the medieval Church. But the preaching was seldom done by the parochial clergy, many of whom were trained only to say mass. It was done by monks, some of whom gained sizable reputations as itinerant preachers; an obvious example is St. Bernard of Clairvaux. These men would deliver series of sermons in a local church much in the style of a present-day preaching mission.

Preaching services were part of the Gallican tradition from the sixth century; their roots are uncertain. They were focused on the pulpit, which, in pre-Reformation churches, was in the nave, where people could gather around. Their form was freer than the eucharistic liturgy, and usually they were vernacular services. Latin sermons were preached, of course, where schools or universities offered a learned congregation.

Part of the liturgical reform under Charlemagne was an emphasis on preaching. He ordered sermons to be preached within the eucharistic liturgy, where they were to exert a strong educational influence. For pedagogical reasons the sermon was followed by the Creed, the Our Father, and the Decalog.

Out of these elements a paraliturgy called the Prone (*Pronaus*) developed within the mass itself. Into its orbit came also the public confession (as preparation for Communion), the Ave Maria, and hymns that were at first Leisen attached to the Kyries of the Intercessions. A highly evolved form of the Prone is reflected in this outline from Basel: (1) Latin "In nomine . . . ," (2) Sermon text in Latin, (3) German Votum with congregational "Amen," (4) Text in German, (5) Invocation of the Holy Spirit, (6) Sermon, (7) Parish notices, (8) Prayer of the Church, (9) Our Father and Ave Maria, (10) Apostles' Creed, (11) Decalog, (12) Public Confession, (13) Closing Votum. A simpler structure is this form from Biberach: (1) Bells rung, (2) Ave Maria, (3) Reading of the Holy Gospel, (4) Sermon on the Gospel, (5) Parish notices, (6) Public Confession, (7) Giving Holy Water, (8) Hymn, if feast day.[6]

It is not surprising that such a developed service separated itself from the mass. The Prone was often done before the mass; sometimes it was altogether independent. By the 15th century the importance of the preaching service is reflected in the establishment in large churches and foundations of the office of preacher (*Praedikaturen*). Preachers had only minor liturgical responsibilities and were comparatively well trained theologically. In the 16th century, it was through these preachers that the Reformation often made its first appearance.

Impact of the Reformation on Liturgical Life and Forms
The Eucharist

Lutheran polemic against the mass was directed more at eucharistic theology and piety than the liturgical structure itself. The mass as sacrifice struck at the heart of Luther's doctrine of justification by grace through faith—the synoptic doctrine of the Reformation. Luther taught that the Eucharist is God's gracious gift to us; our offering to God can only be a grateful sacrifice of praise. *Beneficium*, not *sacrificum*, is the core of worship.

Luther undertook liturgical reform himself somewhat reluctantly and tried to prevent his efforts from becoming normative outside Wittenberg. But because of his enormous prestige, the *Formula missae et communionis* (1523) and the *Deutsche Messe und Ordnung Gottes Diensts* (1526) did dominate liturgical reform.[7] Doeber's *Evangelische Messe* for Nuernberg (1525), however, was also of great influence.

The call in Luther's first liturgical tract, *Von Ordnung Gottesdiensts in der Gemeine* (1523), for setting the Gospel in motion through preaching set the tone for the pastoral and theological nature of the Lutheran reform. Fundamental to a proper concept of worship is the grasp of the Gospel itself. That required a strong accent on preaching, teaching, and vernacular worship. At first, the latter need was met by vernacular hymns. Luther himself wrote, and encouraged others to write, such hymns, thereby forging a major weapon for Reformation theology. He touched off a flood of hymn writing the likes of which had not been seen since the day of St. Ambrose.

When compared with the work of the Swiss reformers, Luther's eucharistic rites are seen to be conservative. He had no illusions about restoring the forms of the primitive church. He wished to purge the tradition only of that which was objectionable theologically, and he exhibited a pastoral concern for moving slowly in reform of ceremonies to prevent unnecessary shaking of popular piety. His conservative approach was not rooted in a romantic awe of the liturgical tradition itself.

As a comparison of Tables C and D indicates, the *Formula missae (FM)* is structurally more conservative than the *Deutsche Messe (DM)*. Lessons, sermon, and hymns are the only vernacular portions of the *FM*. The *synaxis* retains its synagog-inspired shape. The major changes of the medieval mass are the restoration of the sermon as a necessary part of the service (either before the introit or after the creed), and the excision of the offertory and most of the Roman canon. The cup is restored so that all receive both kinds in the sacrament. In calling Luther a conservative reformer, one must be aware that he removed most of what had for at least 15 centuries been the heart of the eucharistic liturgy—the Great Thanksgiving. Only the Preface Dialog/*Vere dignum* and the Words of Institution remained, being connected by the *Qui pridie*. The Sanctus was sung (accompanied by the elevation of the bread and wine) after the *Verba*.

The *DM* shows a greater simplification of structure. Such parts of the ordinary as the Sanctus were replaced with metrical paraphrases in German. This was done partly because of Luther's aversion to setting vernacular texts to plainsong melodies—a German liturgy must have German music—and partly because simple folk in village churches could scarcely be expected to master the complexities and subtleties of chant. The tradition of the *Liedmesse* was launched. On the one hand it established vigorous popular participation in liturgical song; on the other hand it estranged folk piety from the prose texts of the traditional ordinary.

As the Reformation spread, each province or city developed its own church order (Kirchenordnung [KO; plural: KOO]), which contained either its reformed rites or its basic ritual legislation. Liturgically, the KOO in northern Europe followed either the *FM* or the *DM*, sometimes being more conservative than Luther. Elements of the medieval Prone are often observable in connection with the sermon. It became common to transform the *Confiteor* into a confessional service for the congregation. Public confession thus became part of the Lutheran eucharistic liturgy before the traditional entrance rite.

The KOO are sometimes classified according to two types: the Bugenhagen type, which followed the *DM* tradition, and the Brandenburg-Nuernberg type, which adhered to the *FM*. Lutheran liturgical reform in America in the 20th century has been strongly influenced by the latter type. See Table F.

What resulted from the Lutheran reform of the eucharistic liturgy? A high degree of congregational participation in the singing of hymns and other liturgical music; greater understanding of the Gospel and thus of sacramental worship because of preaching; restoration of fellowship as a major accent in the Eucharist (highlighted by the restoration of the cup); retention of the architectural and artistic heritage of the church. Not having suffered a breech in musical practice, the evangelical emphasis on proclamation and hymns gave new impulses to church music and led to a rich musical practice which was largely de tempore.

What did not result? In spite of efforts to the contrary, frequency of reception of the Sacrament did not increase much. Overtones of dread-presence piety remained, perhaps reinforced by Lutheran liturgical conservatism intensified by polemics against the Swiss Reformation. Since the Eucharist could be celebrated only when there were communicants, the weekly celebration stressed by the Reformers gradually either disappeared or was reduced to an appendix to the Sunday service. Lutherans retained a sacramental theology without a sacramental piety to support it.

Reticence in disrupting traditional architectural arrangements allowed them to militate against teaching about corporateness in worship and gathering about the Lord's table. The building still said "clerical theater," and the architecture won, as it always does. Their artistic conservatism spared Lutherans the horrendous excesses of Puritanism, but it also worked against breaking the clericalist orientation to worship.

Until the recent past virtually all liturgical leadership was in the hands of the pastor. In addition to their rightful roles as celebrant/preachers, the clergy assumed the roles of liturgical deacon, lector, cantor, and sometimes even choirmaster. Except for singing, the Lutheran congregation has been largely passive. The floor plans of churches more than 25 years old usually reinforce the pastoral monopoly. People come to hear, not to do. Until that basic posture is changed, Lutherans will never be able to inherit their Reformation birthright of sacramental worship. They will be content with a sermon-dominated service.

The Preaching Service

As a result of the importance of preaching and the relative infrequency of the Lord's Supper, the service most familiar to Lutherans is a preaching service. By the same accidents of history, however, that service has generally been in the form of the first half of the Eucharist. In this Lutherans differed from Anglicans, for example, who adapted Matins to become their preaching service. Corporate Lutheran piety has thus remained wedded to the eucharistic liturgy (half of it) despite the infrequency of Holy Communion.

This is the tradition that has influenced most of Lutheranism in North America; it has its roots in northern Europe. The Continental situation was not so uniform, however. In some places the preaching service developed out of the medieval Prone. Such a service is reflected in the KO for Wuerttemberg (1553): (1) Latin Introit sung by school boys, (2) Hymn, (3) Votum, Prayer, silent Our Father, (4) Text, (5) Sermon, (6) Parish notices, (7) Decalog, Creed, Our Father, (8) General Prayer, (9) Our Father, (10) Hymn, (11) Benediction. The entire service was led from the pulpit. When the Eucharist was celebrated, public confession followed the hymn version of the Creed, and a simple eucharistic liturgy followed. The Prone-type preaching service paralled liturgical developments in Strasbourg and Geneva.[8] It did come to influence a portion of American Lutheranism in the early 19th century.

Liturgy of the Hours

Luther's complaints about the burden of the medieval office are well known. It is no surprise that the KOO prescribe no such regulation for the clergy. In principle, whatever was retained from the office would have to be congregational. In 1523 Luther prescribed Matins and Vespers as the congregational services for weekdays, augmenting them with the Eucharist on Sunday. Though no one expected the entire congregation to attend daily, the services were seen as good pedagogical opportunities for schoolboys, clergy, and students, all of whom lived in community anyway. Matins should consist of continuous reading of the Old Testament with exposition, psalms (3 at most), responsories, antiphons (2 at most), and the Te Deum or Benedictus. Vespers should contain readings from the Prophets or the New Testament and use the Magnificat as canticle. Prayers at noon and night prayers are left to free choice.

On Sundays the congregation was expected to be present for Matins and Vespers. These were to contain sermons on the Gospel and Epistle respectively.

Treatment of liturgical form was directed toward simplicity. The emphasis was clearly on Bible reading and instruction, a different purpose from the original intention behind the hours.

No real system for the office evolved in Lutheran areas, however. In some places it lasted longer than others. The few surviving remnants after the Reformation were destroyed during the era of the Enlightenment. As liturgical system, the liturgy of the hours disappeared from Continental Lutheranism.

The concept of morning and evening prayer remained, however, returning to its domestic and personal roots. In the *Small Catechism* Luther offered a brief personal "prayer office." Other materials followed. One of the most influential was the "house breviary" of Johann Habermann, *Christliche Gebett fuer allerlei Noth und Staende.* Pietists, of course, placed strong emphasis on such personal and family devotions. One of their widely used books was Johann Friedrich Stark's *Taegliches Handbuch in guten und boesen Tagen* (1728), later to become available in English for use in North America.

Through family-oriented devotions, therefore, the observance of the day often remained alive in Lutheran circles, albeit not in traditional liturgical form. The restoration of the liturgy of the hours has been part of the liturgical renewal since the end of the 19th century.

Our treatment of the Reformation has been focused primarily on Germany. Developments in Denmark were closely related because of the influence there of Bugenhagen. Developments in Norway, subsequently, were influenced by close political ties with Denmark. The Swedish Reformation was influenced liturgically both by the *FM* and Doeber's *Evangelische Messe.* The liturgy prepared by Olavus Petri in 1531 became, through the 1614 prayerbook, the standard for the Swedish Church. Developments in Finland were tied to those in Sweden.

Decline and Recovery

By the beginning of the period of Enlightenment, Lutheran worship was centered in some form of preaching service with occasional celebrations of the Eucharist. The spirit of the Enlightenment was destructive of liturgy in the traditional sense. Liturgy tended to be identified with medieval baggage that the Reformation had not jettisoned. It was, therefore, thought to be time to complete what the Reformation had begun, and to rid the church of everything that did not contribute directly to instruction and the furthering of morality. That meant the destruction or at least disuse of whatever had survived from the 16th century KOO.

Churches were built or remodeled to resemble concert or lecture halls. Except for the high festivals and a few days regarded as important for moral teaching, e.g., St. Sylvester's Day (Dec. 31; New Year's Eve), the last Sunday after Trinity (*Totenfest,* observed especially in the Evangelical Church of Prussia to commemorate the departed), and Good Friday, observance of the calendar declined.

Lectures on religion replaced sermons; hymns were willfully revised; prayers became highly verbose homiletical outpourings; the creeds were recited in free paraphrases; the Lord's Supper became an appendage to the Sunday Service.

In the nineteenth century things began to change.Under the influence of romanticism, which desired a return to earlier and richer liturgical practice and Gregorian music, of psychological awareness that desired to restore beauty and solemnity, and of renewed allegiance to the classic confessions the so-called liturgical movement was born.

Since that time, Continental Lutheran churches have reordered their worship on a pattern related to the *FM,* restored the liturgy of the hours, witnessed a resurgence of Biblical preaching, purified their hymnals, and cultivated the great treasury of church music, especially that of J. S. Bach, Heinrich Schuetz, and their predecessors. The Eucharist has become more central, though preaching still far outweighs it in importance. Matins and Vespers have gained a foothold.

Liturgical Development in Lutheranism in America

As Lutherans came to North America from the various countries of northern and central Europe, they brought with them the liturgical books and traditions with which they were familiar. Since then, the history of Lutheranism in America has been marked by the merging of more than 100 groups and by acculturation. Merger proceeded first along linguistic lines, later across them. Acculturation meant learning to pray and sing in English and, to a varying degree, to borrow the habits of Anglo-American ecclesial tradition.

Because Lutheran groups arrived in different periods, the picture is complicated further by the varying degrees to which merger and acculturation have progressed. Liturgical development, then, should not be expected to be uniform across the land or among the various Lutheran churches. Congregations on the Eastern seaboard, for example, tend to show greater Anglo-American influence than those in the Midwest.

Eucharist

The liturgical tradition that has become dominant because of the wide acceptance of the *Common Service (CS)* began with the liturgy drafted by Henry Melchior Muehlenberg, Peter Brunnholtz, and Johann Friedrich Handschuh. It was adopted by the first meeting of the Ministerium of Pennsylvania in 1748. Though never printed, it was circulated in handwritten copies. With it Muehlenberg wished to unify the German congregations in America—a first step toward his dream of "one church and one book."

Muehlenberg's *Kirchen-Agende* contained five parts: (1) Of Public Worship, (2) Of Baptism, (3) Of Proclamation and Marriage, (4) Of Confession and the Lord's Supper, (5) Of Burial. It was significant for future developments in at least two respects: in establishing the *FM* fullness (though with metrical paraphrases of the ordinary and other traces of the *DM*), and its use of the synaxis (the first part of the service centering on the Word) as the preaching service.

The Muehlenberg *Agende* was said to be based upon that of the German Lutheran Congregation at Savoy in London—the only service book at hand. That liturgy was, in turn, based upon the so-called Antwerp Agenda (1567). But, as B. M. Schmucker has pointed out, except for the invitation to Communion, the Muehlenberg *Agende* does not resemble Savoy at all. Rather, it is based on the KOO of Lueneburg (1643), Calenberg (1569), Brandenburg-Magdeburg (1739), and Augustine Saxony (1580, 1712).[9]

A revision of the 1748 *Agende* was printed in 1786, and it showed signs of the inroads of Enlightenment thinking. See Table H. It signaled the beginning of a steady trend away from the Reformation liturgical tradition. As congregations began to worship in English, the traditional Lutheran pattern often suffered further erosion from influences adopted along with the language. The first English liturgy was published in 1795 by the Ministerium of New York.

The English liturgy of 1817, prepared by Frederick H. Quitman and Augustus Wackerhagen for the Synod of the State of New York can stand as an example of the farthest departure from the *FM* tradition. No form for the synaxis is given; only materials are offered: (a) two forms of Confession of Sin and two other introductory prayers, (b) eight General Prayers, with the suggestion that they be halved before and after the Sermon, (c) four prayers after the sermon, (d) Scriptural Benedictions, (e) a table of Epistles and Gospels, though the congregation is not to confine itself to these year after year.

In six small printed pages, the service for the Lord's Supper has no responses for the congregation. Their only role was to sing a hymn at the end. Even the Sanctus and Lord's Prayer are said by the pastor alone. The lengthy prayer that precedes the *Verba Christi* has echoes of the Prayer of Humble Access from the *Book of Common Prayer*. The form itself is more related to the South German and Reformed preaching service tradition derived from the Prone.

By the middle of the 19th century, efforts at recovering the Reformation Lutheran traditions had begun. These were evident in the *Liturgie und Agende* (1855), jointly prepared by the Ministerium of Pennsylvania and the New York Synod. An English version published in 1860 printed the Order of Morning Service and The Holy Communion sequentially. But the General Council's *Church Book (CB)* of 1868 was the major step on the path to recovery. It is in the *FM* tradition once more; it has introits for Sundays and Festivals (though not complete); it frees the Kyrie from the Confession; it permits a reading from the Old Testament; it has seasonal graduals; Prone elements have disappeared from the sermon; the Nicene Creed is mandatory at Communion; it has a set of Proper Prefaces; no alternates to the Agnus Dei are offered. The complete ordinary is restored in prose texts! In the German version of the *CB* (1877) further progress is evident: its collects were so excellent that they were incorporated into two subsequent liturgies in Germany. The General Prayer is more intercessional than homiletical. It introduced full orders for Matins and Vespers.

In 1884 work on the *Common Service (CS)* was begun jointly by representatives of the General Synod, the General Council (formed in 1866 because of confessional disputes in the General Synod), and the General Synod South (formed in 1863 because of the Civil War). A letter from B. M. Schmucker to Edward Traill Horn (Oct. 23, 1885) indicates the mood of the workers:

> If the coming generations of Lutherans have put into their mouths and hearts the pure, strong, moving words of our church's Service from week to week and year to year, they will be brought up in the pure teaching of the church, and the church of the future will be a genuine Lutheran Church. [10]

Common was not understood in the sense of public (as in the Book of *Common* Prayer), but in the sense of consensus. The committee's working principle:

> . . .the rule which shall decide all questions in its preparation shall be: The common consent of the pure Lutheran liturgies of the sixteenth century, and, where there is not an entire agreement among them, the consent of the largest number of those of greatest weight. [11]

The Reformation liturgies considered to have greatest weight were *FM* and *DM,* Brandenburg-Nuernberg (1533), Wittenberg (1533), Saxony (1539) and Mecklenburg (1552). That the principle was not applied woodenly is clear from Edward Traill Horn:

> While it [*CS*] exhibits the *consensus* of the pure Lutheran liturgies of that age [16th cent.], in strict accordance with the spirit of Christianity embodied in our Confessions, it freely rejects what was temporary and adapts the whole to this new age. [12]

Tables K and L indicate the structural debt the *CS* owed both versions of the *CB*. Its advance lay in its official adoption by three bodies (a factor in their subsequent merger into The United Lutheran Church in America, 1918), its full calendar, complete set of historic introits (choir preferred) and collects, orders for Matins and Vespers, historic pericopes, and selected psalter. The framers continued the use of the diction of the Book of Common Prayer, thus placing Lutheran worship firmly in the classical stream of English devotion. They defended their choice by pointing to the similarities between the 1549 Prayer Book and the KOO.

The *CS* tradition climaxed in 1917 with the publication of the *Common Service Book (CSB)*. Only minor modifications were made in the structure of the *CS* (see Tables K and L), but the liturgy was given a musical setting, largely Anglican in origin, to fit its prose texts of the ordinary. A full system of historic propers was included, an advance over progress on the Continent. Finally, it provided a wide-ranging collection of hymns that gave prominent place to the Anglo-American tradition.

The *CS*, therefore, marks not only the return to the *FM* tradition of Lutheran worship in its fullness but also the absorption of the classical Anglican diction and chant forms (these were understood to make it American). The former made possible its adoption by other Lutheran bodies; the latter made such adoption desirable.

It is impossible to deal adequately with other Lutheran traditions in one chapter. Because their founders left Europe later and for different reasons, the German churches of the Midwest did not live through the same kind of decline and recovery that marked the *CS* tradition. Until they faced the crisis of English worship, they perpetuated the traditions of the homeland at the time of their departure. Threats to the Lutheran tradition for them were union with German Reformed groups and frontier revivalism. Because of their pietistic bent, the influence of revivalism was great, often influencing their hymn preferences.

In 1904 the Joint Synod of Ohio published an English hymnal whose liturgy was remarkable for continuing a type of eucharistic prayer derived from the KO of Pfalz-Neuberg (1543) that had been part of the 1855/1860 liturgy cited above. The Missouri Synod published a *Kirchen-Agende* in 1856 with both halves of the Eucharist printed sequentially. The ordinary used metrical paraphrases of the Kyrie, Gloria, Creed, and Agnus Dei, but the prose Sanctus/Benedictus. It had a highly developed pulpit office that included the Confession and the General Prayer. An English service published by the English Lutheran Conference appeared in 1889 and was remarkable for its dissimilarity to the 1856 liturgy. Another English service book appeared in 1892 that incorporated the *CS*.

In 1930 the *American Lutheran Hymnal* appeared, with a liturgical section virtually identical with the *CSB*. Though part of the American Lutheran

Church, many congregations of the antecedent Iowa Synod continued to use the *CSB,* which English-speaking congregations had adopted before the merger. In 1941 the Synodical Conference (Missouri Synod, Wisconsin Synod, Slovak Synod, Norwegian Evangelical Lutheran Synod) published *The Lutheran Hymnal (TLH),* whose eucharistic rite and preaching service are borrowed from the *CSB,* though given a different musical setting. The Confession in the Eucharist replaces the *CS*'s declaration of grace with a personal confession and an absolution; a different General Prayer is also used.

Immigrants from Sweden were among the first settlers on the eastern seaboard and witnessed the first Lutheran ordination in America, that of Justus Falckner (1703). When the Church of Sweden found it virtually impossible to send help to this New Sweden, many congregations affiliated with the then established Episcopal Church. The great Swedish immigration that led to the founding of the Augustana Church (1860) began early in the 19th century.

So long as they spoke Swedish, Augustana congregations continued to use liturgies derived from Church of Sweden sources. In 1901 work was completed on a revised edition of the Swedish liturgy and an English translation—*Hymnal and Order of Service.* In 1925 a new English liturgy was published. It reflected, in part, the Church of Sweden's 17th revision (1917) of Olavus Petri's first vernacular liturgy. This *Hymnal and Order of Service* contained (a) The Service [synaxis only], (b) The Holy Communion with Full Service, (c) The Holy Communion Without Full Service [omitting almost the entire synaxis], (d) The Common Service.

The full service is *FM* in shape. Use of Decius' Agnus Dei paraphrase as the hymn before the Preface creates an interesting doublet with the Agnus in its more traditional location. The Sanctus, following Swedish tradition, follows the Words of Institution and the Our Father. Another Swedish tradition is preserved in adding the Trinitarian blessing to the Aaronic benediction (also done in the Muehlenberg *Agende* and the *Service Book and Hymnal).*

Among Norwegian-speaking Lutherans, the *Lutheran Hymnary* set the official liturgical tone. Its 1913 edition contained two eucharistic liturgies: (a) a translation of the Danish-Norwegian service of 1887—89, and (b) the *Common Service.* The former influenced a 1915 revision of an English translation of the Norwegian *Alterbog* made in 1902. Unique are the opening and closing prayers said by "An Assistant," i.e., a layman. Prayers and other texts are often taken both from the *CB* and the *CS*. The distribution formulas are also unique: "This is the true Body/Blood of Christ." Six hymns are prescribed during the liturgy with a possible seven if the Preface Dialog is omitted. Hymns have always been of great importance in the Danish-Norwegian tradition.

In 1927 the American Evangelical Lutheran Church and the United Evangelical Lutheran Church published the *Hymnal for Church and Home*. It contained a liturgy based on the authorized liturgy of the Church of Denmark (1910). The Preface shows the attitude toward the liturgy:

> An order of divine service...and a selection of scripture readings have been added *for the convenience* of those congregations that may wish to use them (p. 3, italics added).

Informality was the keynote of Danish worship, which depended heavily on the use of hymns.

Though a biligual edition of the 1694 *Handbook of the Church of Finland* (based on the Swedish liturgy of 1693) was published in 1935, its English version was not felicitous. English-speaking congregations of Finnish origins tended to use either the liturgy of the Augustana Synod or the *CSB*.

By the middle of the 20th century, almost all Lutherans had made the painful break with their mother tongues and had begun—or were beginning—to think of themselves primarily as American. Virtually all of them were using the *CS* every Sunday either as a preaching service or to celebrate the Eucharist. The *CS* had helped create the United Lutheran Church. Its wide use formed the base for even greater merging.

In 1946 work was undertaken jointly by The Danish Evangelical Lutheran Church of America, the American Lutheran Church, the Augustana Evangelical Lutheran Church, The Evangelical Lutheran Church, The Finnish Evangelical Lutheran Church of America, the Lutheran Free Church, The United Evangelical Lutheran Church, and The United Lutheran Church in America on a new hymnal. Three years after the publication in 1958 of the *Service Book and Hymnal of the Lutheran Church in America (SBH),* the participants had merged into The American Lutheran Church and the Lutheran Church in America.

The liturgical portion of the *SBH* is virtually identical in content with the *CSB*. A pericope from the Old Testament is added to the Epistle and Gospel, allowing for a Psalm to be sung after it. A hymn is inserted before the Preface Dialog. The Words of Institution are set in the context of a

Great Thanksgiving. In other ways the structure followed that of the *CS*. See Table O. Within the structure, a new Prayer of the Church with congregational responses replaced the General Prayer of the *CS*, and a Proper Preface for Advent was added. The three-fold Kyrie of the *CS* was expanded to a litany based on the Deacon's Litany of Eastern liturgies. This change was motivated by a desire to remove from the Kyrie its penitential accretions and restore its original character as an acclamation.

The expanded Kyrie and the Great Thanksgiving point beyond the consensus of the KOO and evidence an openness to the broader tradition of the church. But reintroduction of the Great Thanksgiving can be affirmed on more than traditionalist grounds. It permits a broader expression of the various facets of the Sacrament—thanksgiving, communion, commemoration, sacrifice, presence—than is possible with the isolated *Verba*. More important still, the Great Thanksgiving again puts the church in touch with the Jewish roots of the Eucharist and the tradition of *berakah*.

The *SBH* contains two musical settings for the Eucharist. The first perpetuates the Anglican style of the *CSB*. The second restores to American Lutherans an authentically Lutheran type of chant—plainsong modified by the influence of the *Kirchenlied*. A third, plainsong, setting was published separately.

The *SBH* marks a high point of the effort to restore to Lutherans in America the fulness of their Reformation heritage. At the same time, through its adherence to Prayer Book language and its inclusion of a large number of English and American hymns, it keeps Lutherans in the midst of the Anglo-American tradition of worship. Above all, the *SBH* opens the door to an ecumenical spirit, indicating the readiness of Lutherans, having now found themselves liturgically, to move out beyond the confines of their own tradition. This time they moved *as* indigenized, not in order to become indigenized.

The *SBH* is a tribute to the indefatigable efforts of Luther D. Reed (1873-1972). He had been the secretary of the joint committee that produced the *CSB* and, as such, had served on each of its subcommittees. He was professor of liturgics and church art in the Lutheran Theological Seminary, Philadelphia. And when the Joint Commission on the Liturgy for the *SBH* got under way in 1946, Dr. Reed was named chairman. His textbook, *The Lutheran Liturgy* (1947, rev. 1959), influenced generations of seminarians and pastors.[13]

The Calendar and Propers

The *CSB* included a complete calendar for the church year, a set of introits (from *CS*) and graduals, and a set of Epistles and Gospels—all derived from the northern European tradition of the medieval church and retained in the Reformation. Its calendar retained the traditional system of Sundays and major feasts. The lesser festivals were limited to Presentation, Annunciation, Visitation, Apostles and Evangelists, Nativity of St. John the Baptist, St. Michael and All Angels, All Saints' and the Reformation, Harvest Festival, and Day of Humiliation and Prayer.

TLH added St. Mary Magdalene to the lesser festivals; otherwise its calendar is identical. It also presents historic introits, collects, and graduals.

The lectionary of the *SBH* added an Old Testament series and contains a slight revision of the Epistles and Gospels.[14] Calendar and propers were continued from the *CSB*.

The Liturgy of the Hours

The fate of Matins and Vespers in the post-Reformation period has been discussed above. The German version of the *CB* (1877) introduced Matins and Vespers to North American Lutherans. By means of the *CS* and the *CSB*, these services have been restored to mainstream Lutheran worship, even though scant use is made of them in many parishes. In some places, Matins has been used as a Sunday preaching service.

A discussion of the content and use of these services would be repetitious. Matins contains elements of historic Matins and Lauds. Vespers contains elements of historic Vespers and Compline. The form familiar to Lutherans is virtually the same both in *TLH* and the *SBH*. See Table N.

In addition to these complete services, the Lutheran books present other orders derived from the historic Liturgy of the Hours: General Suffrages (from Lauds and Vespers), Morning Suffrages (Prime), Evening Suffrages (Vespers).

The Inter-Lutheran Commission on Worship

At the invitation of The Lutheran Church—Missouri Synod, the Lutheran Church in America, the Synod of Evangelical Lutheran Churches, and The American Lutheran Church joined in 1966 to form the Inter-Lutheran Commission on Worship (ILCW). The Synod of Evangelical Lutheran Churches has begun a merger process with the Missouri Synod and is a District of it. The Evangelical Lutheran Church of Canada was formed from the Canada District of The American Lutheran Church. The ILCW remains a cooperative agency of four bodies in North America.

At the time of its invitation, the Missouri Synod was engaged in preparing a new hymnal of its own. A selection of hymns and liturgical materials in preparation by the Missouri Synod was published in 1969 as the *Worship Supplement.*

Toward its primary goal of a new hymnal and service book for virtually all Lutherans in North America, the ILCW has issued a series of provisional materials. In addition to the new calendar and lectionary, two collections of hymns, a set of services of the Word, and orders for Holy Communion, Baptism and Affirmation of the baptismal covenant, marriage, and burial have been published in a series entitled *Contemporary Worship.* On the basis of experience with this series, decisions were made about more permanent materials included in the *Lutheran Book of Worship.*

The Liturgical Movement

To conclude this chapter, it is appropriate to take a brief look at the so-called liturgical movement. That is the label given to efforts across the breadth of the Western church to restore full and vital *corporate* worship that centers in a eucharistic celebration where Sermon and Supper coexist in complementary fashion. Its 19th-century roots were reactions to the pietistic stress on individual experience and the arid rationalistic stress on intellectualism.

Key figures in Roman Catholic circles were Ildefons Herwegen of Maria Laach, Prosper Gueranger in Solesmes, Odo Casel, Romano Guardini, Pius Parsch, and the great historian J. A. Jungmann. The liturgical movement was molded by encyclicals of Pius X and the *Mediator Dei* of Pius XII. The Centre de Pastorale Liturgique exemplifies the uniquely French development. In America the movement was influenced by such men as Virgil Michael and Godfrey Diekmann. Its American voice was *Orate Fratres,* which became *Worship* in 1951. The climax of the liturgical movement in the Roman Church came in the Constitution on the Sacred Liturgy of the Second Vatican Council and its subsequent implementation.

In its Anglican form the liturgical movement harks back to the Oxford Movement and people such as John Keble and John Henry Newman. Later, A.G. Hebert and the historian Dom Gregory Dix exerted great influence.

Still more recently the scholarly side of the movement had an influential voice in the Cambridge liturgiologist Edward C. Ratcliff and continuing attention from members of the Alcuin Club. In the Episcopal Church, Massey H. Shepherd Jr. has been a distinguished leader.

European Lutherans were similarly engaged in recovery and renewal, abetted by the neoconfessional movement of the latter half of the 19th century. Theologians such as Theodor Kliefoth and A. F. C. Vilmar had their impact, but the greatest contribution was made by Wilhelm Loehe, a man far ahead of his time. His *Agende fuer christliche Gemeinden des lutherischen Bekenntnisses* (1844), dedicated to Friedrich Wyneken, caused his work to influence American Lutheranism, perhaps more so than his own German milieu. Erlangen professors Adolf Harless, Johann W. F. Hoefling, and Theodosius Harnack stimulated the German liturgical awakening. After the turn of the century such scholars as Friedrich Heiler, Rudolf Otto, Hans Lietzmann, Friedrich Spitta, Yngve Brilioth, and Julius Smend gave the liturgical movement impetus and direction. More recently, leaders have included Karl Bernard Ritter, Frederick Buchholz, Wilhelm Staehlin, Christhard Mahrenholz, Karl Ferdinand Mueller, Peter Brunner, Bo Giertz, and Olaf Herrlin.

The liturgical movement among American Lutherans was, of course, influenced directly by the Lutheran movement in Europe. Indeed, given the state of communications, a scholar like B. M. Schmucker was surprisingly in touch with European developments. The movement was also influenced by both the Roman and Anglican movements. But, in many ways, the American Lutheran form of the movement was not a transplant; it was truly indigenous, responding to typically American problems.[15]

Developments in the late 19th century were behind the restoration that has been traced already from the *CB* to the *CS*. The Lutheran Liturgical Association, Luther D. Reed, president, flourished from 1898 to 1905. Its seven volumes of Memoirs, containing papers read at the monthly meetings, is a valuable resource still. The association also sponsored a series of instructional meetings for laymen.

This stream of the movement, largely eastern in orientation and tied to the *CS*, placed its accents differently from another stream. Here the problem was recovery from a church life dominated by the pulpit and a grossly unliturgical form of worship. The strategy was to persuade people that in their true heritage was a worship of great beauty and dignity, properly balanced, and truly Lutheran. The goal was to win the congregations back to a way of worship that was, historically, genuinely Lutheran. Their chief instrument was the *CS*. Proximity to strongholds of the Episcopal Church made it natural for this part of the movement to borrow models of ceremony, vestments, etc. In addition to those already mentioned, Paul Z. Strodach was an influential figure.[16]

The other stream of the movement flowed out of The Lutheran Church—Missouri Synod. The Society of St. James was founded in Hoboken, N. J., in 1925, with Berthold von Schenk as its president. For a time its voice was *Pro Ecclesia Lutherana,* which began publication in 1933. Early articles show the group to have been especially sensitive to charges of Anglo-Catholicism and Romanizing tendencies.

While the St. James Society also faced a church life dominated by preaching, it had not been shaped by the same sort of decline typical of the first group mentioned. The liturgical roots had remained demonstrably Lutheran and no one was arguing about the propriety of a service largely centered about the altar. The strategy, accordingly, was different. Members of the St. James Society did not place the emphasis on beauty, dignity, and perfection of form—they had no *CS* to rally around—but rather on the catholicity of the true Lutheran tradition. An article in the first volume of *Pro Ecclesia Lutherana* stated:

> We have always gloried in the fact that our Lutheran Church, because of her catholic confessions, and because we have continued in the apostolic doctrine is not a sect, but a branch of that Holy Church founded upon the noble confession of Peter . . . .Therefore, the heritage of the Church from the time of the apostles is our heritage (I, 1, p. 5).

Though the goals of the two parts of the Lutheran liturgical movement were similar, the strategies, with their divergent aspects, gave to each a different character. The first tended to appear more Anglican in orientation (cassock and surplice, economy of gesture, divided choirs), and the second more catholic (albs, historic Western gestures, priestly concept of clergy). This latter thrust was characteristic of *Una Sancta,* a liturgical journal and the bearer of the St. James Society variety of emphases.

As Luther D. Reed was the embodiment of one stream of the Lutheran liturgical movement, so Arthur Carl Piepkorn was the embodiment of the other. Through personal example, many articles, encyclopedic knowledge of the Lutheran Confessions and the history of the church in general, an important monograph on Lutheran vestments, and many years of seminary teaching (not liturgics!), Piepkorn helped several generations of Lutheran pastors to catch the vision of a Lutheran style of life fully catholic in shape and ethos, yet solidly confessional in allegiance.

Both of these streams belong to the recovery phase of the liturgical movement. They helped the Lutheran churches to find again their rightful heritage in worship. And while they followed different strategies, in their best manifestations they were not at odds one with another.

In the 1960s, however, liturgical renewal received new impulses. A new awareness of worship within the total mission of the church began to dawn. This diverted the liturgical movement from its preoccupation with history (what is proper?) to a more pastoral concern (what is relevant?). While the relevance binge has already been declared bankrupt, the pastoral character of liturgical renewal continues.

The challenge before Lutherans in America today, seen in the light of this discussion, is threefold: (1) to achieve a creative synthesis of the two streams in the recovery phase of the liturgical movement, (2) to take further steps beyond the consensus marked by the CS into the broader tradition and life of the Western church, (3) to apply the pastoral concern for renewal in such a way that the results are authentically Christian worship.

See also the related articles in Key Words in Church Music: canonical hours; canticle; Catholic pronouncements and decrees on church music; church music history, Renaissance—the Latin tradition; church music history, Renaissance—the Reformation tradition; church music history, American Lutheran; de tempore hymn; all articles on hymnody; Leisen; mass; office hymn; organ, use in the mass and offices; sequence; all articles on theology of church music

CHAPTER II

Sketches of Lutheran Worship

Carl F. Schalk

How have Lutherans worshiped throughout their history?

Portraying Lutheran worship from the Reformation to the present is fraught with considerable difficulty. Perhaps the chief danger lies in the temptation to oversimplify an activity that by its very nature is complex and given to considerable variety. Various source materials are at hand, but they are often not as complete as one would wish, especially in the details that would best reveal exactly what went on as Lutherans gathered for worship. Moreover, the general tendency in Lutheran practice, from Luther's time to the present, to avoid a dogmatic prescriptiveness in matters of worship forms and practices makes generalization from limited material precarious. Where basic forms and orders were indeed followed, there were large areas of latitude that were determined by local considerations and circumstances. Luther himself, who suggested somewhat different patterns for larger cities and towns, where greater musical resources might be at hand and where somewhat more educated congregations might be supposed to be in existence, than for the simpler situations and resources of smaller towns and rural parishes, reflects the kind of diversity recognized and, in many ways, encouraged and sought by Lutheran congregations. Likewise in America, the conditions of early Lutheran church life often necessitated adaptations and adjustments not always evident in the orders that were at least nominally followed. That problem is no different in our time.

In spite of such problems and difficulties, however, the broad outlines of the worship practices of Lutherans throughout the centuries are quite clear. It is in that context that the following sketches of Lutherans at worship in various places and at various times in its history are presented, illumined by as much detail as historical accuracy and the documents themselves allow.

These descriptions of Lutheran worship are based on the orders themselves and on other material that sheds light on the subject. Rather than saying more than can with good reason be said, I have chosen to say less.[1]

What follows, then, is the beginning of an answer to the question "How have Lutherans worshiped through the centuries?" It is the beginning of an answer, not the last word.

Germany

The 16th Century

The worship and piety of the Western church of the late Middle Ages and the early Renaissance serves as the appropriate background against which Martin Luther's ideas about worship need to be seen and understood if his contribution to the liturgical and musical life of the church of the Reformation are to be placed in proper perspective. While some details remain problematic, the principal thrust of his thinking and the ways it worked itself out in the worship and musical practice of 16th century Lutheranism are quite clear.

The worship and music of the medieval church reflected a wide variety of situations and practices. At papal chapels, courts, cathedrals, and other places where artistic and financial resources were great there was the pomp and ceremony of brilliantly sung polyphonic masses. In the more secluded monastic communities, where worship and musical traditions were carefully nurtured and maintained and where musical innovation—as much as might be allowed—flourished, there was the daily round of chanted services. In the more modest circumstances of most parish churches the spoken mass (*missa lecta*) was the rule.

In addition, popular piety—nurtured by various extra- or para-liturgical practices, pilgrimages, and devotions—was marked by increasing isolation of the people from the action of the mass. Over the centuries a situation had developed in which the sacrifice of the mass was reenacted by the priest at the altar, the people meanwhile attending to their own private devotions. Such sporadic attempts by the people to involve themselves more directly in worship, as in popular vernacular singing—a movement with its own history in pre-Reformation centuries in connection with popular devotions—were usually opposed or, at best, grudgingly allowed only on special occasions and then within strict limits, often only outside the church doors.

Educated as a priest, Luther had been trained in the liturgical and musical tradition of the Western church. As a priest, his daily association with the liturgy and chant served to develop an appreciation for these forms, especially as unique textual and musical vehicles for the worship of the entire church.

Moreover, Luther was a musician whose capabilities extended beyond those of the amateur. He had a knowledge of music and music theory, he sang (in his "small, stupid voice," according to his own words), and he played the lute. According to his own account he not only improvised lute accompaniments for singing, but transcribed polyphonic compositions for that instrument as well. A brief four-voiced motet on Ps. 118:17 (*Non moriar sed vivam*) is most likely from Luther's own pen, attesting to some modest ability in composing.

The particular contribution of Luther to the worship of the people of God—especially his recovery of the sermon, the introduction of vernacular hymns to a place of prominence, and the restoration of the cup to the people—must be seen against this background. Luther was steeped in Augustinianism (he was an Augustinian monk), motivated by a fresh understanding of the doctrine of the universal priesthood of all believers, and prompted by a high view of music as a gift of God in the service of the church. This gave his thinking direction and force for a determinative effect on the worship practices of the Reformation.

Luther's Formula missae (1523) and Deutsche Messe (1526)

By the early 1500s some kind of worship reform was in the air. On Christmas Day 1521, with Luther secluded at the Wartburg, Andreas Carlstadt appeared at the Castle Church in Wittenberg without vestments and conducted a "purified Mass" with various innovations radical for the time—innovations that elicited an even bolder iconoclasm from certain sectors of the populace. In 1522 Kaspar Kantz, another of the more impatient pastors, who was prior of the Carmelite brothers at Noerdlingen, published an "Evangelical Mass" in the vernacular. Thomas Muentzer, whose various activities included publication of two German Mass orders in 1524, added to the controversy and to Luther's concern. Luther referred to "the widespread demand for German masses and services and the general dissatisfaction and offense that has been caused by the great variety of new masses."[2]

Luther's immediate response to the developing ferment included a series of eight sermons preached in 1522. In them he urged moderation and inquired as to the love of innovators who pursue their own courses of action without regard for the consciences of their weaker brethren. The following year Luther published the first of two worship orders, the second following three years later; these two served as the poles between which German Lutheran congregational worship worked out its way in the 16th century. These orders were: the *Formula missae et communionis* of 1523 and the *Deutsche Messe* of 1526. (See Tables C and D.) The first provided an entirely Latin mass for use particularly in "monasteries and cathedrals"; the second provided a vernacular German mass for use particularly in smaller towns and country parishes. Neither of these orders was simply taken over and used as it was. Rather, local parishes or geographical areas used Luther's orders as models or patterns, incorporating changes and adaptions particularly suited to their own requirements or stemming from local customs and traditions. It is both interesting and instructive to examine these two models, between which Lutheran worship in the 16th century was to make its way.

The *FM* of 1523 followed the Catholic Latin mass very closely. The Latin language, the vestments, candles, the sign of the cross, the elevation of the host—all these and more were retained. The order itself can be briefly outlined: the Introit (or Psalm), during which the priest approached the altar and prepared for the service by silently confessing his sins; a ninefold Kyrie; Gloria in excelsis; Salutation; Collect; Epistle; Gradual and Alleluia; Gospel; Creed; Sermon (Luther also suggested the possibility of placing the sermon at the very beginning); Preface; Sanctus (with Hosanna and Benedictus) during which the elevation of the host took place, a practice Luther wished to retain "because of the weak"; the Lord's Prayer; the proclamation of peace and forgiveness; the distribution of the elements in both kinds (bread and wine); the singing of the Agnus Dei and other Communion chants; the post-communion prayers; Salutation; and the Benediction.

The music that Luther envisioned for the Latin mass was the traditional music he knew; it was customarily used in the Catholic service: Gregorian chant and, where possible, polyphonic settings of appropriate texts. Thus, the Introit, Kyrie, Gloria in excelsis, Gradual and Alleluia, Creed, Sanctus, and Agnus Dei might well have been sung in polyphonic settings by a choir. The Scripture lessons were chanted to simple recitation tones, along with other appropriate dialog portions of the service. In theory there was no place in this service for vernacular German hymns, though it is clear that Luther wanted the congregation to sing them after such portions of the liturgy as the Gradual, Sanctus, and Agnus Dei, and after Communion. For Luther, the celebration of the mass seemed to be a more festive form when sung completely, or at least in part, in Latin. Pure Latin masses, along with purely German ones, were still being held in Wittenberg in 1536. Toward the end of the 16th century, after the initial popularity of vernacular worship, the use of Latin in worship experienced a renaissance in many places, and throughout the century and beyond such Lutheran composers as Johann Walter, Sixtus Dietrich, Balthasar Resinarius, and Michael Praetorius continued to provide polyphonic settings in great abundance of the Latin ordinary and proper texts together with Latin settings of the canticles, antiphons, responsories, and hymns used in Matins and Vespers.

The *DM* of 1526, while retaining a recognizable outline of the traditional mass structure, more radically altered parts of the service and made provision for a greater participation of the people through vernacular hymns with a corrresponding reduction of the material, if any, to be presented by the choir. The performance of this order rested largely in the hands of the priest. Almost nothing is said about the choir, although it is clear that where one existed it was expected to take part in the service. The order itself was simple and direct: a German Psalm or hymn; a threefold Kyrie (the Gloria in excelsis was omitted); a Collect; Epistle; singing of "Nun bitten wir den Heiligen Geist" or another hymn[3]; Gospel; singing of the German Creed "Wir glauben all an einen Gott"; sermon; exhortation to Communion; Words of Institution; Luther's German Sanctus "Jesaia, dem Propheten, das geschah"; singing of such German hymns as "Jesus Christus, unser Heiland" during the distribution; the German Agnus Dei "Christe, du Lamm Gottes" or another hymn; Collect; Benediction.

Luther's musical suggestions in the *DM* involved the development of new forms of the reciting tones for the Introit, several of the old Kyrie melodies were preserved with some alterations, and, most importantly, the substitution of German hymns for such portions of the service as the Creed, Sanctus, Gradual, and Agnus Dei. The reciting tones for the lessons and collects were reworked to suit the German language. Luther included a number of musical examples in his *DM* to indicate rather clearly how different parts of the service were to be chanted. This was consistent with his desire that careful adaptation of the Gregorian melodies be made to suit the nature of the German language.

Both in his *FM* and the *DM* Luther encouraged the continued use of the medieval "hours" that were possible and practical under the circumstances, especially Matins, Vespers, and Compline. The daily services of Matins and Vespers were especially recommended by Luther for use in cities with schools, the school boys themselves reading the lessons in Latin and then in German "for the benefit of any layman who migh be present." These services followed the general pattern of the medieval offices and consisted chiefly of psalms, lessons, hymns, and prayers. Luther was particularly concerned that the entire Psalter remain in use, and he suggested the use of three psalms for Matins and Vespers together with appropriate Responsories. "Let the entire Psalter, divided in parts, . . . be preserved in the ears of the church."

Luther's orders were offered as suggestions as to how worship might best be carried out. His words were intended as description, not prescription. In these orders two ideas predominate: the desire to retain, as much as possible, the historic practices of the church in order that worship might truly retain its catholic character and thus avoid a sectarian spirit; and the desire to enlarge the involvement of the people as much as possible and appropriate.

Lossius' Psalmodia Sacra (1553)

To see how Luther's ideas worked out in practice, it is instructive to look briefly at an order of service that received wide usage in the second half of the 16th century, namely the order of Lucas Lossius. Its observance was obligatory in many parts of northern Germany. It is in his *Psalmodia sacra* (see Table E), for which Melanchthon provided the Preface. Through a succession of editions (1553, 1561, 1569, 1579) this order was widely disseminated and is in many ways typical of liturgical developments of the time.

Lossius' order of 1553 was a Latin mass. It began with the de tempore Introit, followed by the Kyrie (chosen according to the season and rank of the service), the Gloria in excelsis ("Allein Gott in der Hoeh' sei Ehr'" could sometimes be substituted), the Epistle, followed by the Gradual and Alleluia together with the Sequence on feast days and a German psalm hymn on regular Sundays, and the Gospel. The sermon and Litany, with the probable use of several hymn stanzas before and after the sermon, was followed by the Latin Creed or its hymn form "Wir glauben all an einen Gott." The Exhortation and Preface, the Sanctus or "Jesaia dem Propheten das geschah," the prayers at the altar, the Words of Institution and the

Distribution, during which such hymns as "Jesus Christus unser Heiland," "Gott sei gelobet," and others could be sung, the Agnus Dei or "O Lamm Gottes unschuldig," the prayer of thanksgiving and for the church, the Benediction, and the hymn "Erhalt uns, Herr, bei deinem Wort," brought the service to a close.

The order of Matins, according to Lossius' order, consisted of an antiphon before and after three psalms (on high feasts this psalmody might be preceded by an Invitatory), the Gospel read *latine in choro* and repeated in German by a young boy *ante chorum* (on high feasts it might be chanted by the cantor with a short Responsory following), then most likely the sermon, although it is not specifically mentioned by Lossius, followed by the Te Deum in Latin, and the concluding Benedicamus Domino sung by the pastor or the choir. Vespers followed a similar pattern, with the addition of a Latin or German hymn after the Gospel and the use of the Magnificat as the canticle.

Provision for music for such services was made by Lossius in his *Cantica sacra veteris ecclesiae selecta* (1553), the greatest part of which consisted of plainsong settings for the Sundays and feasts of the church year. Lossius' zeal for preserving the plainsong chant reflects a part of the 16th-century Lutheran musical practice that is often overlooked.

When the congregation sang the growing body of vernacular hymns, it did so in unison and unaccompanied. The choir's function in connection with the hymns was to present polyphonic settings (such as those in Johann Walter's collection of 1524) in alternation with the stanzas sung by the congregation. The organ did not accompany the congregation as is customary today, but presented intonations to the liturgical chants and often alternated with the singing in the presentation of certain chants such as the Introit, Kyrie, and Magnificat.

The development of Lutheran church music in the Scandinavian countries at the time of the Reformation followed roughly the same pattern as that in Germany. Many leaders of the Reformation in the Nordic countries (Laurentius and Olavus Petri, Hans Tausen, and Michael Agricola, to name a few) had studied in Wittenberg, and it was natural that the practices of the German Reformation would be strong also in the Scandinavian countries. Translations of German hymns and liturgies were widely used. A large body of hymnody, polyphonic works, and other worship material was held in common among the various Lutheran countries. As in Germany, significant efforts were made in the Scandinavian countries in the 16th century to continue the use of Gregorian chant, which ultimately gave way before the growing popularity of vernacular hymnody.

The bases for the developing worship practices of 16th-century Lutheranism might be summarized as follows. Basic to everything was Luther's view of the union of theology and music: music, first of all, was praise and worship *per se;* it could also serve as an aid to piety and devotion; and it was an important educational tool (in the most comprehensive sense of the term) for spreading the Gospel. There was a conscious attempt to preserve, as much as possible, the tradition received from the church of the past as a safeguard against the dogmatic impoverishment reflected in the worship practices suggested by many of the more radical reformers. There was a consciousness that the Lutheran chorale was a presentation of the Biblical Word itself, an essential part of the liturgy and in no way merely an appendage. There was a constant and continuous involvement of practicing church musicians in the developing of a usable tradition. (One can point to the close involvement of such men as Johann Walter, Conrad Rupsch, Georg Rhau, and many others.) Sixteenth-century Lutheranism based the organization of its church music on liturgical unison singing after the pattern of Gregorian chant, especially as it developed in the form of the Lutheran chorale. And finally, there was the freedom, within liturgical propriety, of congregations to develop church orders (Kirchenordnungen; plural acronym: KOO) most suited to their own needs and traditions. That freedom ("It is not necessary . . . that ceremonies, instituted by men, should be observed uniformly in all places," AC VII 3), however, was tempered by Luther's clear view that the church of the Reformation was part of the one, holy, catholic, and apostolic church, and that in its worship it dare never become sectarian.

Ironically, it was this freedom, encouraged at least in part by Luther's hesitation to become prescriptive, that contributed toward the loss of a distinctively Lutheran worship practice in the 17th and 18th centuries. Under increasing pressures of pietism and rationalism in the centuries following the Reformation, Lutheranism succumbed more and more to the temptation to forget its catholic character and heritage. The new spirit was one with which Lutheranism would have to reckon both on the Continent as well as later in the New World. This new viewpoint was to have decided implications for both theology and music.

The 17th Century
Paul Gerhardt and Christmas Matins in Berlin (1659)

By the 17th century, times and tempers had changed. The religious questions that had been left unanswered by the Peace of Augsburg (1555) concerning Lutherans, Catholics, and Reformed festered and grew until all of Europe was involved in one of the longest and bitterest of religious wars. The Thirty Years' War (1618-48) was not, however one long continuous struggle. It was rather many smaller wars, about a dozen all together, fought at different times and in different places and interrupted by years of relative peace in particular areas. While religious questions were certainly involved, political questions became increasingly important.

The strength and power of German towns that for centuries had been the center of German banking, industry, and trade were slowly giving way to the growing power of the territorial princes. By the early 1600s German economic life had fallen to a disastrously low point. Towns were destroyed, people were uprooted and killed, and in the wake of battle there followed starvation, typhoid, and the plague. There were years of devastation, deprivation, and human suffering on a massive scale.

> It was a time when men's hearts failed them for fear. State hurled itself at the head of state, army at the head of army, and those who fell not in battle perished before the still deadlier scourges of plague and famine. The very abomination of desolation seemed to be set up; rapine and pillage, outrage and slaughter, reigned unchecked and unconfined. In vain, to all outward appearance, did the saints cry: How long? yet of their cries and tears, and of the amazing tenacity of their faith, the hymns they have left us bear irrefragable witness.[4]

The arts in 17th-century Germany were largely influenced by Italian models. Music, painting, sculpture, and architecture reflected the new styles of the emerging baroque, which was centered in Italy. It was the time when Johannes Kepler discovered the laws of the planets and when Martin Opitz' *Buch von der teutschen Poeterai* of 1624 set the pattern for a new style of Christian hymnody. For many people of the time, however, it was a time of war and personal desolation, the time of Gustavus Adolphus, of Tilly and Wallenstein, of Christian IV of Denmark, of Cardinal Richelieu, and the Hapsburgs.

The Lutheran preacher and poet who above all represented the new tenor of the times was Paul Gerhardt (1607—76). Born a few miles south of Wittenberg in the little town of Graefenhainichen, it was there that Gerhardt spent the first 15 years of his life. From 1622 to 1627 he went to school at Grimma. In 1628 he entered the university of Wittenberg, where he came under the influence of August Buchner, one of the most esteemed members of the faculty and intimate friend of Martin Opitz. The influence of Opitz on the budding poet Gerhardt was to be a most profound one. Poetically his hymns reflect clean, smooth ideals; theologically they reflect a soft, warm attempt to bring objective faith into close relationship with life situations.

Gerhardt's friends included also Johann Crueger, the renowned organist and choirmaster of the Nicolaikirche in Berlin. It was Crueger who first brought Gerhardt's hymns into common use by publishing 18 of them in his *Praxis pietatis melica* (1644), among them "A Lamb Goes Uncomplaining Forth." This unique combination of poet and church musician, continued by Gerhardt in his association with Georg Ebeling, Crueger's successor, helped to popularize Gerhardt's hymns. Such hymns of Gerhardt as "All My Heart This Night Rejoices," "O Sacred Head, Now Wounded," "Commit Whatever Grieves Thee," and "If God Himself Be for Me" continue to be sung by Lutherans around the world.

Gerhardt did not escape the scars of war. In 1637 the Swedes came to his home town of Graefenhainichen demanding a ransom to save the city. The people scraped together 3,000 gulden and thought themselves removed from danger. But within 24 hours the town was a heap of ashes. The Gerhardt home, the church, and 400 buildings were ruthlessly destroyed. Later that summer the plague carried away over 300 of the townspeople.

In 1651 Gerhardt was ordained to the office of the ministry as provost at Mittenwalde, where he remained until called as deacon at the Nicolaikirche in Berlin. From the years in Berlin there is a unique description of Lutheran worship that tries to adhere to tradition but also incorporates folklike elements felt to be fitting and proper. The year is 1659, the city Berlin. The preacher is Paul Gerhardt, and the celebration is Christmas Matins.[5]

"The church is cold. Candles are being lighted. The people are coming and taking their places. A group of schoolboys is at one side of the gallery and a choir of mixed voices at the other side. Below the pulpit we see a *Collegium musicum,* a voluntary musical society composed of tradesmen and craftsmen, who perform on violins and wood-wind instruments, gathered around a small movable organ. Then there is a male quartet, also a military band with trumpets, kettledrums, and drums. After the organ prelude a choral is sung in the following manner: Stanza 1 is sung by the congregation, Stanza 2 is sung as a solo by the cantor, Stanza 3 is performed by four girls a cappella, Stanza 4 is sung by a male quartet together with the wind instruments, Stanza 5 is sung by the congregation, Stanza 6 is sung a cappella by the schoolboys in the choir, and Stanza 7 is taken by the congregation, the organ and all the singers. Now three clergymen with white clergymen's bands and black robes have appeared at the altar. The entire liturgy is sung in Latin, and all the responses and anthems are sung in Latin by the choirs and the schoolchildren. Next a college student, dressed as an angel with large white wings, sings from the pulpit an Old Testament prophecy, accompanied by the *Collegium Musicum* below the pulpit. More chanting from the altar, and then the principal door of the church opens, and in comes a procession of girls, headed by the teacher, all dressed as angels. They proceed to the high altar, where the teacher sings Stanza 1 of 'Vom Himmel hoch, da komm' ich her,' and Stanza 2 is sung by the girls in two-part counterpoint. The third stanza is taken by the organ and the choir in the gallery as a 'beautiful five-voiced motet.' While the procession has been marching down the aisle, one of the ministers chants a 'Gloria,' answered by the electoral court-and field-trumpeters with fanfares and drumrolls. After the sermon there is more chanting by the liturgist, and the instrumentalists play a boisterous *Te Deum*. The follows another Latin anthem by the school-children. Things now begin to happen in the organ-loft. Over the railing is raised a cradle with a doll, while some boys with incessant mooing imitate the animals in the Bethlehem stable. The choir and the congregation sing a hymn, and at this point high up on the organ facade a Bethlehem star, illuminated and supplied with small bells, is turned round and round. By the aid of a mechanism, operated by an organ-stop, three wooden images, representing the three Wise Men, with their traditional attributes, solemnly move forward and bow before the doll in the cradle. At the same time we notice two puppets, representing Moors (Negroes), standing on each side of the central group. One blows a trumpet, and the other beats a drum. Throughout this scene on the gallery railing the *Collegium Musicum* plays a ritornello. A boy soprano intonates *In Dulci Iubilo,* which is continued by male voices, accompanied by schalmeis (shawms) and bombards. The song is scarcely over before a sight 'exceedingly beloved to the children' appears in the center aisle. It is Old Father Christmas himself in his white beard, with pointed cap on his head and a large sack on his back, soon surrounded by 'angels' and children, who vie with one another for the good things that are to be given out. When the large sack is empty and Old Father Christmas has disappeared behind the sacristy door, then is sung as closing chorale *Puer natus in Bethlehem.*"

The traditional elements are all there: the Latin liturgy and Latin anthems and responses, the alternate singing of hymns between congregation and choirs, the liberal use of various instrumental groups, the importance of the children and the cantor. All these reflect the continued importance and continued influence of the Lutheran tradition in 17th-century worship. Yet these elements are interspersed with, enlarged on, and expanded by whimsically naive practices and developing customs: the use of the *Zimbelstern,* the costuming of the participants in the Christmas story, the *Weihnachtsbescherung* (the distribution of the Christmas gifts). That the sermon could have been preached by none other than Paul Gerhardt, a preacher so loyal to the Lutheran Confessions that only a few years later he would resign his ministry rather than submit to a Prussian ruler who sought to limit his freedom, may surprise some. Perhaps what this description shows above all is the extent to which a Lutheran congregation of the time could go in matters of liturgical freedom— possibly even exceeding the boundries of "good taste"—and still remain Lutheran both in spirit and substance.

The 17th century encompasses the lives and work of such great Lutheran church composers as Michael Praetorius, Johann Hermann Schein, Samuel Scheidt, and, above all, Heinrich Schuetz. In the music of these and many lesser masters can be seen the changes and accommodations to the newer musical styles of the day. Yet in spite of these changes, together with the increasing influences of pietism and later of rationalism, the worship of the church was to provide an anchor, even though an increasingly tenuous one, to which the people could hold.

Thirteen years after the death of Heinrich Schuetz in 1672, Johann Sebastian Bach was born in the town of Eisenach. Pietism and, increasingly, rationalism, were the important theological currents of the time. They were to have a crucial impact on the music of the church. In the 18th century it was Johann Sebastian Bach, who, among others, would have to wrestle and work in that new context. And it is to Lutheran worship at his time that we now turn.

The 18th Century

Leipzig Church Orders at the Time of Bach (c. 1725)

When Johann Sebastian Bach arrived in Leipzig in 1723 to take up his duties as cantor, the third choice of the selection committee, which expressed the hope that he would avoid "cheap theatricality" in his music, he found a busy and bustling city of about 30,000 people with streets surprisingly broad and clean for a medieval town. Hundreds of oil lamps lit the city at night, and throughout its four wards night watchmen sounded the hours and chased away marauders. The university buildings, on the eastern edge of the town, while neither ornate nor imposing, were nevertheless extensive and a source of pride to the city.

Leipzig boasted a number of churches, the most important among them being the churches of St. Thomas and St. Nicholas (the two most closely associated with Bach's name), the "New Church," and the church of St. Peter. The church of St. Nicholas, situated on the west edge of the town was large, venerable, but not particularly beautiful. In Bach's day it boasted of a new altar, and its pulpit contained an interesting adornment, an ornate, carved snuff box. The church of St. Thomas was situated on the opposite side of the city from that of St. Nicolas. Bach and his family lived at the Thomasschule, adjoining the church, in eight rooms provided for his household. As cantor, Bach was one of a circle of four *superiores* who supervised the schoolboys, also giving instruction in singing and a few lessons in Latin.

The boys of the Thomasschule were divided into four "Sunday choirs" to provide the music each Sunday in the four principal churches. The beginners and weaker singers were assigned to St. Peter's where only chorales were sung. The rest of the boys were divided among the other three churches, although at the "New Church" only chorales and motets were sung under the direction of a subordinate. The music at the St. Nicolas and St. Thomas churches received the greatest attention and was under Bach's direction.

Important changes in theology and worship life had taken place in the century and a half after Luther's death. The late 16th and 17th century especially was marked by religious controversy. As Lutheran Orthodoxy, as the theology of these years is usually characterized, involved itself in endless polemics and theological debate, its increasingly rigid dogmatism was no longer satisfying to many pious people who yearned for an

The church of St. Thomas, Leipzig, and the old *Thomasschule*. From the title page of the "Ordnung der Schule zu S. Thomae 1723."

opportunity for a more personal expression of their faith. Out of this situation there developed two powerful movements that were to have a significant impact on the direction and thrust of Lutheran thinking about worship. These movements were Pietism and Rationalism.

Partly as a result of the trials of the Thirty Years' War and partly as a result of attempting to bring the hymnody of the day closer to life situations, Pietism, in the late 1600s and early 1700s released a flood of religious poetry and hymnody of almost unheard of proportions. The dry, dogmatic, didactic, and often bombastic verse, born in the wake of the earlier controversies of the time, gave way to a kind of hymn that was softer and warmer in its theology, and also rhythmically smoother and poetically more polished. The hymns of Freylinghausen, Zinzendorf, Neander, Neumeister, and Schmolck are typical. Pietism also reacted negatively against the operatic tendencies of the music of the time, and sought instead a music that had no pretensions to art.

Already as a child, Bach had witnessed the conflict between Orthodox and Pietistic elements in Ohrdruf, at that time a stronghold of Pietism. During his early years as a church musician in Muehlhausen, Bach met such pietistic opposition head on. Convinced that church music as an art could not flourish in such an environment, Bach left after hardly a year.

Rationalism, on the other hand, fed by the Enlightenment and indebted at least in part to the rigid dogmatism of Orthodoxy, tried to reduce the content of the faith to an irreducible minimum of common sense in line with human reason. Rationalism was most comfortable with the forms and expressions of worship that were directly applicable to the moral needs of people. At the same time, its pedagogical approach aimed at transforming the human spirit by exposing the senses to what was high and ennobling in the artistic expressions of mankind. Both Pietism and Rationalism stood in stark contrast to Bach's piety, which, rooted in confessional orthodoxy, sought to praise God with the best craftsmanship that his talent and skill would allow. Bach's greatest contributions to church music in Leipzig continued to be marked with frustration and controversy, in part, at least, because of the significant differences in theological approach between himself and the rector of the Thomasschule, Johann A. Ernesti.

Leipzig had retained the older and richer worship forms and practices longer than most other German cities. Latin polyphonic motets continued to be sung well into the 18th century, many of them taken from Bodenschatz' *Florilegium Portense,* a collection from the early 1600s containing a large selection of motets in the *stile antico* from the old Roman, Venetian, and German schools. Latin continued to be used for many parts of the liturgy. Congregational singing of the chorales remained unaccompanied by the organ until the late 1700s, the organ serving chiefly to introduce the chorales as well as in the long-established practice of alternating, stanza by stanza, with the choir and congregation in the presentation of the chorales and certain parts of the liturgy.

While the churches of Leipzig had various weekday services, the Sunday services are of particular interest. At St. Nicolas, for example, there were four: Matins, the Morning service with Holy Communion, a brief midday service, and Vespers.

Matins, which began at 5:30 a.m. on regular Sundays and at 5 a.m. on festivals, was conducted in Latin according to the old liturgical order of Matins by 10 specially selected students under the direction of the cantor at St. Nicolas. Each of these students received a special stipend from the city council. Ordinarily there was no one else in attendance. The service began with the singing of from one to three Psalms by the students. The Lesson from the Old Testament was then read by a student, after which the Benedictus with an Antiphon appropriate to the day or festival was sung or, on occasion, the German Te Deum might be sung. The Versicle "Da pacem," or another suited to the season, was sung, followed by the Collect, the service concluding with the Benedicamus Domino.

The chief morning service of Holy Communion (see Table G) began promptly at 7 a.m. at both St. Thomas and St. Nicolas and often lasted, when the number of communicants was large, until 11 a.m. After an organ prelude, the Introit, usually in the form of a polyphonic motet in Latin, was sung (it was omitted in Lent or times of mourning). After a short intonation on the organ, the Kyrie was sung, alternating Sunday for Sunday between Latin and German in the two chief churches: in Latin, where the first choir was singing, as the chant "Kyrie fons bonitatis;" in German, where the second choir was functioning, according to the hymn "Kyrie, Gott Vater in Ewigkeit." After the Kyrie the Gloria was intoned with the response "Et in terra pax" by the choir if in Latin, or as the hymn "Allein Gott in der Hoeh' sei Ehr'" if sung by the congregation in German. As the last stanza of the Gloria was being sung, the pastor approached the altar and chanted the Salutation in Latin, with the choir giving the response. The Collect followed, also in Latin.

Between the chanting of the Epistle and the Gospel, the congregational hymn suited to the Gospel was sung, some stanzas by the congregation in unison and unaccompanied, others by the choir in polyphonic settings, other stanzas—at times—"sung" by the organ, the people following the text. Occasionally at this point the Litany was chanted by four specially appointed boys, the responses being sung by the choir. At this point the cantata (*Stueck* or Concerto) was performed, after which the congregation sang Luther's German Creed "Wir glauben all an einen Gott." During the last stanza of the German Creed the pastor went to the pulpit for the sermon, which was usually preceded by a short hymn (e.g., "Herr Jesu Christ, dich zu uns wend"), to prepare for a proper hearing of the Word, and a silent Lord's Prayer. The sermon, usually lasting from about 8 am. to 9 a.m., was carefully timed with a sand hourglass and followed by prayer, thanksgiving, intercessions, and announcements. After the Votum the pastor descended from the pulpit while several stanzas of another suitable hymn were sung or, on certain Sundays, the second part of the cantata was sung.

The Holy Communion formed the principal part of the service at Leipzig. On festivals the Latin Preface was chanted alternately by the deacon and the choir. The musical high point was the Sanctus, sung in parts by the choir. Then followed the Lord's Prayer, the Words of Institution, and the Communion itself. After the Words of Institution and during the distribution of Holy Communion, German hymns were sung by the congregation, and at times also Latin motets by the choir. Hymns that seem to have been used very often for the distribution include "Jesus Christus, unser Heiland," "Gott sei gelobet und gebenedeiet," "Nun freut euch, lieben Christen gemein," "Wo soll ich fliehen him?" "Es wolle Gott uns gnaedig sein," "Nun lob, mein Seel, den Herren," and "Der Herr ist mein getreuer Hirt." After the concluding Collect, which was intoned, the service closed with the Blessing.

A simple service consisting of a sermon preceded and followed by hymns began at about 11:45 a.m., lasted about an hour, and did not involve the choir.

The Vesper service began at about 1:15 p.m. with a motet by the choir and a congregational hymn, The deacon intoned a Psalm from the lectern, followed by the Lord's Prayer, Collect, congregational hymns, and the sermon. The sermon at this service was usually on the Epistle (in Advent it was the custom to preach on the Catechism and in Lent on the Passion history). After the sermon the Magnificat was sung, the service concluding with a Collect, Blessing, and the hymn "Nun danket alle Gott."

The worship life of Leipzig in the first half of the 1700s offered a rich fare for the worshiper on Sundays and festivals as well as throughout the week. It was a worship practice that retained to a surprising degree, and in a way that apparently was not the case in many other parts of Germany, a close connection with historic Lutheran practices. It was not to last much longer, however. Pietism and Rationalism, increasingly divorced from historic Lutheran understanding of worship and confession, began to take their toll.

The currents of thought separating continental Lutheranism from its historic understanding of its worship life and church music practice were also to be felt as Lutherans from Germany and the Scandinavian countries made their way to the New World. The 1700s saw the first large numbers of Lutherans emigrate to America, though some had arrived already in the 1600s.

America
The 17th Century

The Dutch and the Swedes

The earliest Lutheran settlers in the New World came as part of the Dutch colony of New Netherlands, the Swedish Lutherans along the Delaware, and the Germans who settled later in Georgia and Pennsylvania.

Among the settlers who came from Holland during the 1620s under the supervision of the Dutch West India Company were some Lutherans who found the practice of their faith difficult under the official religion of the New Netherlands colony, that of the Reformed Church. While there were many Lutherans in Holland, with strong congregations at such cities as Amsterdam, Rotterdam, and Leyden, in the New World they were few and were obligated to have their children baptized and instructed by Reformed pastors. Though the church constitution drawn up in 1734 by the Swedish pastor William Berkenmeyer was staunchly Lutheran, and though he frequently warned the Lutherans under his charge against unionistic practices with their Reformed neighbors, the worship order that he made obligatory in the congregations under his charge was essentially Reformed in character. Worship was characterized by hymn singing, Scripture reading, free prayer, sermon, and benediction. A consciousness of historic Lutheran liturgy and practice was conspicuously absent.

Swedish Lutherans had settled along the Delaware River in the mid-1600s as part of a Lutheran settlement planned by Gustavus Adolphus, Swedish Lutheran hero of the Thirty Years' War. Their worship followed that of the order of "High Mass" from the Swedish Psalm-Book of 1614. They carefully observed the church festivals, especially Christmas, Easter, and Pentecost, and celebrated the sacraments according to traditional Lutheran custom. They received their ministers from the state church of Sweden, and—in what was the first regular ordination in the New World, Pastor Andrew Rudman, representing the archbishop of Uppsala, ordained Justus Falkner on November 23, 1703, in a full Latin service with choir at "Old Swedes Church" in Philadelphia.

The Lutheranism of New Sweden, however, failed to endure. By the end of the Revolutionary War the Swedish missionaries had been recalled, and the younger members left for churches that used the English language. The Swedes who remained, unable to find pastors to serve them in either Swedish or English, began a transition that eventually took most of them into the Protestant Episcopal Church.

The 18th Century

The Germans: Muehlenberg's Church at Trappe, Pa. (c. 1751)

The German immigrants who came to the New World in increasing numbers during the early and middle years of the 1700s shaped the character of Lutheranism in the New World in the 18th century.

In Germany, as the century moved toward its midpoint, Bach was in his last years at Leipzig. In America, the New World had seen the founding of the last of the 13 English colonies, and—across the largely unexplored continent—Vitus Bering had discovered Alaska. The Salem Witchcraft trials had been held little more than 50 years ago, and in 1752 Benjamin Franklin was to fly his kite in a thunderstorm. In these years and to this new land came the German pastor who was to be chiefly responsible for shaping that early Lutheran tradition. He was Heinrich Melchior Muehlenberg.

Muehlenberg, a German pietist from the Halle school—Halle was less than 20 miles from Leipzig, where J. S. Bach served during Muehlenberg's term as teacher at the Halle school and for almost a decade after he arrived in America—arrived in the New World in 1742 and found a fledgling Lutheranism confused and divided. In a few short years, by 1748, he had

An interior view of Heinrich Melchior Muehlenberg's church at Providence (Trappe), Pa. Erected in 1743, the church still stands as a historical site.

united a small group of German congregations into the Ministerium of Pennsylvania, the first permanent Lutheran synod in North America.

Muehlenberg's background and experience combined deep personal piety with knowledgeable appreciation of music; his journals often mention the role of music in the life and worship of Lutheranism. He had studied the organ in Germany, and in his newly adopted land often "had to be precentor, organist, and preacher all in one." We are told that he sang accurately and admirably, that he played the organ in an unusually charming fashion, as well as the harp, cittern, and violin, and that he participated in a variety of informal music-making.

On arrival in America, Muehlenberg was confronted with a bewildering array of hymnals, brought by the early Lutheran settlers from their homeland. Among them were Freylinghausen's *Geistreiches Gesangbuch* or "Halle hymnbook," as it was often called, as well as hymnals from

Marburg, Wuerttemberg, Wernigerode, and Coethen. The confusion that followed attempts to use such a variety of books in public worship was soon evident, and Muehlenberg determined to see that a liturgy and a hymnal were provided that could unite the various congregations with which he came into contact.

The organizing meeting of the Pennsylvania Ministerium in 1748 made the establishment of an Agenda or liturgy for use by the "United Congregations" a chief order of business. Adopted at this first convention held at St. Michael's Church, Philadelphia, it was used for over 40 years by German-speaking churches. (See Table H.)

Muehlenberg's church at Providence (Trappe) is an example of Lutheran worship in America in the mid-18th century. Though relatively small, it regarded worship with utmost seriousness. According to the Agenda of 1748, they celebrated Holy Communion only infrequently: on Christmas, Easter, Pentecost, and "at other times, as the necessities of the congregation might demand." Several Sundays before such a celebration, the pastor would announce from the pulpit when Holy Communion would be celebrated, and indicate the time when those who wished to commune should report to him and have their names recorded in the register of communicants kept by the congregation.

The day before Holy Communion would be celebrated, the communicants would gather at the church for a service of confession and absolution. Beginning with the singing of a penitential hymn by the congregation, the pastor, speaking from the pulpit, exhorted his people to repentance. After the Lord's Prayer, the pastor read aloud the names of all who had announced their desire to commune. Those who for good reason were unable to announce previously did so then during the singing of a hymn stanza, the pastor writing down their names.

Then calling first on the male communicants to come forward, he addressed several questions to the congregation regarding their confession and intent to lead a holy life. As the communicants knelt, one of them led the congregation in repeating aloud the words of the confession, the pastor adding a few words of prayer. After the absolution by the pastor and the singing of another hymn verse, the service closed with the Benediction by the pastor.

The following day, Sunday, as one joined the congregation gathering to worship, one could not help being struck with the church building itself, built of local brown stone in 1743 shortly after Muehlenberg's arrival. On entering the church, the worshiper felt his eyes drawn straight ahead to the prominent red walnut pulpit with overhanging sounding board, and, in front of the pulpit, the white-painted altar. The roughly planed, high-back pews were of poplar and oak. The men and women sat separately on opposite sides of the church, the boys, apprentices, and servants mounting the high-tiered seats in the gallery under the watchful eye of the sexton. The gallery, newly built in 1751, held the newly installed organ built by John Adam Schmahl in Heilbronn. Under the gallery were the pews reserved for the elders and the "Vorsteher" (a general term for church officers).

The service began with the singing of the hymn "We Now Implore God the Holy Ghost;" on other Sundays the choice was often "Come Holy Ghost, God and Lord." The singing was led by Gottlieb Mittelberger from the new organ. Not every congregation was so fortunate as to possess an organ, although there were others in the vicinity, notably those at Lancaster, Germantown, New Hanover, and Tulpehocken. The organist played from the hymnals available, sometimes from the "Halle hymnbook," sometimes from Koenig's, Stoerl's, or other hymnbooks brought from Germany. These books contained only the melody with figured bass, the organists supplying the missing parts.

The organist serving at Providence was also schoolmaster. This combination was common, since most of the congregations had parochial schools for the education of their children. It was not unusual for the children to assist in the church music. The Providence school had opened in 1743. Since teacher-organist salaries often were low and it was often difficult to raise the necessary funds, it was the custom in Providence that the collection from the services on Easter and Pentecost were given to the organist to supplement his modest income.

After the opening hymn, the pastor invited the congregation to join in a confession of sins.

> I, a poor sinner, confess unto God, my heavenly Father, that I have grievously and in various ways sinned against Him. . . . But I do sincerely repent, in deep sorrow for these my sins; and with my whole heart I cry for mercy from the Lord, through His dear Son Jesus Christ, being resolved, with the help of the Holy Ghost, to amend my sinful life. Amen.
>
> Lord God the Father in heaven, have mercy upon us. Lord God Redeemer of the world, have mercy upon us. Lord God the Holy Ghost, have mercy upon us and grant us Thy peace. Amen.

After the singing of "All Glory Be to God on High" and the pastor's greeting, "The Lord be with you," and the congregation's reply, "And with thy spirit," the Collect for the Day was read from the Marburg hymnbook. There followed the reading of the Epistle and the Gospel for the Day, the two readings separated by the singing of the principal hymn, "Now Thank We All Our God," sung "choirwise" (*Chorweise*), a way of singing in which one part of the congregation answers another stanza by stanza. This method of singing was popular and often used in German congregations in the New World.

After the Gospel, the pastor devoutly read the Creed in versified form, and, as a preparation for the sermon, the congregation sang several stanzas of the hymn "Lord Jesus Christ, Be Present Now." The sermon was the high point of the service; at least it was the longest, often lasting almost an hour. The sermon concluded with the General Prayer, which was never omitted except occasionally when it was replaced by the Litany, special supplications for the sick, announcements, and the words "The peace of God, which passeth all understanding, keep your hearts and minds, through Christ Jesus, unto eternal life. Amen."

When the service included Holy Communion, the pastor went to the altar, placed the bread and wine in order, and after several versicles and responses, addressed the congregation with Luther's paraphrase of the Lord's Prayer and his exhortation to the sacrament in the *DM* of 1526. Then, turning to face the bread and wine, he repeated the Lord's Prayer and the Words of Institution. Turning again to the congregation, he said:

> Now let those who are found to be prepared, by the experience of sincere repentence and faith, approach, in the name of the Lord, and receive the Holy Supper.

As the congregation communed, such hymns as "Jesus, Lead Thou On," by Count Nikolaus von Zinzendorf, a prominent Moravian leader, whose hymns were popular among the Germans, were sung. After the Communion the pastor announced "O give thanks unto the Lord, for He is good. Hallelujah," to which the congregation replied "And His mercy endureth forever. Hallelujah." The service ended with a short collect from Luther's *DM,* the Benediction, and the Trinitarian Invocation.

As the congregation left the church, some gathered briefly outside the building to visit and exchange the news of the day. Looking toward the rear of the church, one could catch a parting glimpse of the church cemetery, the graves in the oldest part facing East, where the departed members of the congregation awaited the resurrection.

The worship of the Pennsylvania Lutherans reflected pietism rooted in the orthodox liturgy and hymnody of the 16th century. By the end of the 18th century, new cultural and religious winds were blowing that would sever those roots and take American Lutheranism on as yet uncharted ways.

The 19th Century

The Inroads of Unionism and Rationalism:

Even before Muehlenberg's death, forces were at work that would lead American Lutheran worship to its lowest point. Between 1748, the year of the first authorized Lutheran liturgy in America, and 1786, which marked the appearance of the first printed liturgy and the *Erbauliche Liedersammlung*, the first American Lutheran hymnal, the decline was already in evidence.

The Lutheran liturgy of 1748 followed the general outlines of historic Lutheran worship as filtered through the healthy pietism of its compilers. The revision of 1786 (see Table H), with its decreasing emphasis on the church year, its greater informality, and its emphasis on extempore prayer, was typical of the direction the future would bring. The "liturgical" part of the service was shortened, in order that the sermon might receive more time. All these changes were indicative of a pietism increasingly divorced from a confessional Lutheran practice.

But two other forces in the early 1800s were to have even greater impact on the worship life of American Lutheranism: unionism and rationalism. The impact of these developing movements was to lead to a marked toning down and relaxation of sound Lutheran worship practices.

Unionism developed in part because of a spirit of religious indifference nourished by the inroads of rationalism, in part because it was often the line of least resistance, but also because it often appeared to be the most prudent course in the cause of a common evangelism. In Pennsylvania the trend was toward union with Reformed churches; in New York toward union with Episcopalians.

The attraction between Lutheran and Reformed churches in the early 1800s was accentuated by a number of circumstances. In Prussia, homeland of many German Americans, union was the offical policy between Lutherans and Reformed. In Germany, Frederick Wilhelm III was preparing to proclaim the Prussian Union. In America, many Lutheran, Reformed, and other Protestant churches were making joint plans to celebrate the 300th anniversary of the Reformation. In addition, Lutheran and Reformed churches in America often shared the same church building, a fact attested to by many "Union" churches still dotting the rural countryside in Pennsylvania. Given such circumstances, the request for common worship materials could not be far behind. Hardly a decade after its formation as the second Lutheran synod in America, the New York Ministerium took note of the "intimate relation between the English Episcopal and Lutheran churches, the identity of the doctrine, and the near approach of their discipline," and efforts were begun—though never completed—looking toward the eventual union of the two churches. The tide of opinion favoring at the least a variety of united endeavors, and, as some hoped, union, was too great to be ignored.

Likewise, rationalism affected America as a result of close contact between America and France in the Revolutionary period. It had found its way into German universities, even into Halle, and the American church was not to escape its influence. As early as 1792, for example, the Pennsylvania Ministerium had deleted all reference to the Lutheran Confessions from its constitution. In 1803 the constitution of the North Carolina Synod, the third Lutheran synod to be organized in North America, made no reference either to the Lutheran Confessions or to Lutheranism. In 1807 the New York Ministerium elected as its president Rev. Frederick H. Quitman, an avowed disciple of John Semler, the "father of Rationalism" at Halle.

The ideals of unionism and rationalism found embodiment in congregational books of worship among the Lutherans. For unionism it was the *Gemeinschaftliche Gesangbuch* ("Common Hymnbook") of 1817, issued "for the use of Lutheran and Reformed congregations in North America"; for rationalism it was *A Collection of Hymns, and a Liturgy, for the use of Evangelical Lutheran Churches*, published in 1814. Both books were widely used in German and English Lutheran congregations that found them compatible with their ideas.

St. Matthew, New York, N. Y. (c. 1825)

By 1825 the oldest Lutheran church in America—and the largest and most important of the New York churches—was worshiping in two buildings: Christ Church for the German members and St. Matthew Church for the English members.[6]

The liturgy of Christ Church was apparently fashioned from the earlier German liturgies of 1748 and 1818, the New York Ministerium having decided as early as 1796 "to arrange our services according to the same." No longer was the pastor directed to face the altar or the people. The Gloria and the Creed were dropped, and in place of the Collect for the Day an extempore prayer "from the heart" was often substituted. Scarcely a trace of a responsive service remained.

For its hymnbook Christ Church used the *Gemeinschaftliche Gesangbuch,* having resolved to 1818 to introduce it into its German service. Apparently it was felt that the use of this book would indeed help to "break down the partition wall between Lutheran and Reformed," and that in G. Schober's words

> This meritorious undertaking [the "Common Hymnbook"] paves the way to universal harmony, union, and love among our Lutheran and Reformed Churches, removing all the obstacles which hitherto prevented that happy effect.

The organ at Christ Church is of some interest, having been built for $1,194.90 in 1799 by John Geib, a German piano maker who came to America in 1797 . Its specification, as described by Geib himself, is as follows:

1. Opdiapasson throughaute from treble GG, to F in alt—
2. Stopdiapason do-do-do
3. Principal—do-do-do
4. 12th do &c
5. 15th do &c
6. Tiers do &c
7. Cornet. treble ⎫
8. Sesq. Bass   ⎬ 3 rankes
9. Trumpet—throughaute as befor

Swell from Fidle G
1. opd or Dulciana
2. Stopd
3. Principal
4. Hautbois

Two pair of bellowes, an ellegant best mahogany case, gild front and ornaments—9½ by 15 feet. Duble GG in front, and a set of keys in great organ, and one set from fidle G in Swell—a trimland—the cost 1000 in this place.

The organ was played by the schoolmaster, who also sang at funerals and served as precentor in the regular services. The "Note Book" of sacred music, purchased by the congregation for use by the organist in accompanying congregational singing, was probably either the *Choralbuch fuer die Erbauliche Liedersammlung* of 1813, published to accompany Muehlenberg's hymnbook, or possibly Jacob Eckhard's organ book of 1816, which had been compiled, at least in part, with the New York hymnbook of 1814 in mind. In either case, the music in both of these collections was essentially melody with figured bass.

If the German service at Christ Church reflected the unionistic spirit of the day, it was the English service at St. Matthew Church that showed most clearly the inroads of the rationalistic thought of the time.

As the congregation gathered for worship, it was apparent that each person had brought with him his own copy of the "Quitman hymnbook" of 1814. Additional copies, bought by the congregation, were on hand for guests and visitors.

The service followed the "usual morning service" consisting of parts of the liturgies of 1748 and 1818 in English translation by George Strebeck. But even these minimal forms were "left entirely to the discretion of congregations and ministers, the Synod having no design to make them binding upon any." After several stanzas of the hymn "Ye Humble Souls, Approach Your God" the congregation was led in a public confession of sins by the pastor, the confession ending with the words of the Kyrie as a sort of absolution. The pastor and congregation exchanged the familiar words: "The Lord be with you, And with thy spirit." This was followed by a prayer, "the Gospel, Epistle, or any other suitable selection from the Scripture," and the sermon hymn—Eternal God, Almighty Cause of Earth, and Seas, and Worlds Unknown"—the pastor meanwhile entering the pulpit for a discourse on the "Duties of Piety."

After the sermon the pastor read from the 1814 liturgy a lengthy prayer that began:

Almighty and most merciful God, we desire to lift up our hearts unto Thee, the Hearer of Prayer, from whom alone cometh our help. We adore Thee as the great Parent of the Universe, from whom all things proceed . . .

The celebration of the Lord's Supper began with the pastor standing at the communion table addressing the communicants with an abbreviated form of the Sanctus: "Holy, holy, holy is the Lord of hosts; the whole earth is full of his glory." Then began his exhortation with the words:

Dearly beloved, as you intend to come to the Holy Communion, which our Lord ordained to be a memorial of his sufferings and death, and a means of improving his disciples in their attachment and obedience to his divine religion . . .

The exhortation was followed by the Lord's Prayer, another lengthy prayer, the Words of Institution, and the invitation:

In the name of Christ our common and only Master, I say to all who own him as their Savior, and resolve to be faithful subjects: Ye are welcome to this feast of love.

As the congregation communed they sang hymns, especially of Christ's suffering and death and hymns of the sacrament. Typical was the following:

> Ye foll'wers of the Prince of peace,
>   Who round His table draw!
> Remember what His spirit was,
>   What His peculiar law.
>
> The love which all His bosom fill'd.
>   Did all His actions guide:
> Inspir'd by love, He lived and taught;
>   Inspir'd by love, He died.
>
> And do you love Him? do you feel
>   Your warm affections move?
> This is the proof which He demands,
>   That you each other love.
>
> Let each the sacred law fulfill'
>   Like His be ev'ry mind;
> Be ev'ry temper form'd by love,
>   And every action kind.
>
> Let none who call themselves His friends,
>   Disgrace the honour'd name;
> But by a near resemblance prove
>   The title which they claim.

For the most part, the Communion hymns in the New York collection of 1814 contained nothing that would distinguish them from a Presbyterian or Methodist collection of that time. Hymns or hymn verses offensive to the Socinianism of the times were omitted. While the divinity of Christ was sometimes expressed quite clearly, more often it seemed to be kept carefully in the background. Doxologies were conspicuous by their absence. There were few hymns that could not be sung with satisfaction by a Unitarian or Arian.

As the pastor gave the bread and wine to the communicants, he spoke such words as "Come unto Me all ye that labor and are heavy laden," or "For My yoke is easy and My burden light," or similar passages suggested in the liturgy. With a concluding statement by the pastor, a prayer, another hymn verse, and the benediction, the service was over.

With the rise of unionism and rationalism at the beginning of the 1800s, even Muehlenberg's tenuous link with the 16th century began to give way before these new forces that sought to rework American Lutheranism's worship and hymnody. Rationalism sought to bring the forms of Lutheran worship in line with human reason; unionism sought to dilute those forms and practices in order to facilitate organic union. Both forces were, for a time, successful . But both ultimately gave way before a new movement that was to herald a return to confessional concerns.

The Beginnings of the Confessional Revival

The unionistic and rationalistic tendencies of the early 1800s presented American Lutheranism with a serious challenge. At stake was a distinctively Lutheran confessional point of view regarding its worship. Even the organization of the General Synod (1820), a loose federation of independent Lutheran synods, did little to do away with the rationalim and unionism of that day. Samuel Simon Schmucker, leader of the movement called "American Lutheranism," which attempted to make Lutheranism more palatable to the American scene by, among other things, revising the Augsburg Confession, exemplified this drift from traditional Lutheran beliefs and practices.

In the 1820s and 1830s especially, the influence of the Second Great Awakening began to be felt as many Lutheran churches appropriated the worship style, "new measures," hymns, and songs of the revivalism that was sweeping the country. "Gospel call" hymns, hymns for revivals, temperance hymns, all found a place in the Lutheran worship books of the time. Thus the General Synod's *Hymns, Selected and Original* (1828) could include hymns such as the following:

> Round the temp'rance standard rally,
>   All the friends of human kind;
> Snatch the devotees of folly,
>   Wretched, perishing and blind:
>   Loudly tell them
> How they comfort now may find.

In Germany, meanwhile, a confessional movement reacting against the rationalism of the time was beginning to assert itself. This movement would be transferred to America with the immigration of various groups during the 1830s and 1840s firmly committed to a strict confessional position: the Prussians, who settled in and near Buffalo, N. Y., and in parts of Wisconsin, led by Johann Graubau; the Bavarians, who settled in Michigan and were guided from Germany by Wilhelm Loehe; and the Saxons, who settled in Missouri under the leadership of Martin Stephan and, later, C. F. W. Walther.

The Bavarian Communities in Michigan (c. 1852)

The Bavarians came to America as a result of an appeal for help (*Notruf*) from Friedrich Wynecken that so impressed Wilhelm Loehe, pastor in Neuendettelsau, Germany, that he organized efforts to establish a mission colony in America. Such a colony could not only serve the scattered Lutherans on the frontier, but it was hoped that it could also be an effective way of bringing the Gospel to the heathen Indians. Loehe was a leader of the confessional movement in Bavaria, which also sought a return to the hymns and worship practices of the 16th-century Lutheran Reformation. The training of Loehe's "missioners" (*Sendlinge*) included drilling in the hymns and liturgical forms that he was trying to restore. In 1844 Loehe published an *Agende* (see Table I) with his "brethren in North America" in mind, and dedicated it to Pastor Friedrich Wyneken of Ft. Wayne, Ind. This agenda was to be used by the Bavarians in America.

The pastor who was to shepherd the Bavarian immigrant colony in its early years was Friedrich Craemer, a German pastor, who had been ordained by Theodor Kliefoth, a leader in the confessional movement and in the movement for liturgical reform in Germany. A bachelor when the emigrants set sail for Germany, Craemer was married the day after the colonists first set foot on American soil in New York. The wedding, which took place on June 10, 1845, was held in the oldest Lutheran church in America, mentioned above, St. Matthew, in New York, N. Y.

The Bavarian immigrants traveled via steamer up the Hudson river to Albany, by train to Buffalo, across Lake Erie to Detroit, and finally through the forest some 15 miles south of Saginaw, Mich., where they established a series of colonies in the fertile Saginaw Valley: Frankenmuth (Courage of the Franks or Bavarians), the first and most important of the settlements; Frankenhilf (Help of the Franks); Frankentrost (Consolation of the Franks); and Frankenlust (Joy of the Franks).

By the fall of 1852, the main colony at Frankenmuth was worshiping in a new frame church built that year and dedicated on St. Michael's Day. Seventy-four feet long, 40 feet wide, and 24 feet high, the building had three windows on each side but lacked a tower or even a chancel. It looked like a large Quaker meeting house. Two bells, brought from the homeland, hung in a modest structure near the church.

The general pattern of worship in the Bavarian colonies, in addition to the Sunday morning services and the Sunday afternoon catechisation services, was to hold brief morning and evening services every day. During the summer months services were held at six in the morning and six in the evening. After St. Michael's Day (September 29), during the winter half-year, the custom was to hold the services at seven in the morning and five in the evening. Some of the congregations in the colony discontinued daily services during the winter, holding weekday services every Wednesday and Friday instead.

Attendance at the daily service was often poor. The typical service began with the singing of several verses of a German hymn, followed by the reading of a lesson by a young boy from the school. (The school, maintained by the congregational for their own children as well as for Indian children who could be persuaded to attend, was an important part of the mission strategy of the Bavarians.) The school teacher then read a brief exhortation; if the service was led by the pastor, he might preach briefly. In the morning, the congregation sang the German Te Deum ("Herr Gott, dich loben wir"), in the evening, the Magnificat. Then kneeling, the school children, together with all present, said the Kyrie and Lord's Prayer, followed by any special prayers. An antiphon, collect, Benedicamus, and Benediction concluded the service.

Craemer noted with approval the participation of the Indian children in the school, and "how full-throatedly they join in the German morning hymns and prayers." It must have been interesting to hear the German children sing the Lutheran chorale "Liebster Jesu, wir sind hier" in the German language, or even in the Chippewa dialect as translated by one of the missionaries:

Oma sa nindaiamin,
O Tebeningeion Jesus
Chidodamang eshiang
Ima kitikitowining
Maba abinoji kidodisig
Iu sa chiwiwangomod.[7]

One of the pastors of the colonies, Johann Graebner, described this early morning service in the following words:

Behind the desk, which takes the place of a pulpit, there is a large chair, and about the altar there are grouped nine benches for the congregation. I can assure you that I experience, at times, great happiness as I kneel or stand at the altar at six in the morning and chant the Kyrie or Te Deum with my congregation. Then, as I see the morning sun rising above the green forest and shedding its benign and gentle light through the windows, the thought comes to me that our dear Savior would indicate how well He is pleased that His praises are sung and a tabernacle erected to His name in this wilderness where but a little while ago only the dreadful howling of the wild beasts was heard.[8]

The Sunday morning service at Frankenmuth was well attended and Holy Communion was celebrated almost every Sunday. In Frankenmuth the congregation was called to worship by the ringing of the bells, which hung outside the church. In the colonies that had no bells, e.g., Frankentrost, the call to worship was given by the pastor who, one-half hour before services were to begin, blew on a tin horn of the kind used by the housewives to call their husbands from the fields. The signal was then passed from house to house.

The service itself followed Loehe's *Agende* as prescribed in the congregation's constitution. The opening hymn was usually either "Komm, heil'ger Geist, Herre Gott" or a German translation of the medieval sequence *Veni, Sancte Spiritus* ("Komm heiliger Geist, erfuell'"). The singing was unaccompanied. It would be several years before the Bavarians would have their first organ. After a brief confession and absolution, the

Introit and Gloria Patri were spoken by the pastor, after which pastor and congregation alternately sang or spoke the Kyrie. After the words "Glory to God in the highest" the congregation responded either with the concluding words of the Gloria in excelsis or, more frequently, with the singing of the hymn "All Glory Be to God on High." There followed the salutation and response, the collect for the day, and the reading of the Epistle, to which the congregation responded "Hallelujah."

The collection was taken during the singing of a hymn based on a text appropriate to the day. Once more the salutation and response was repeated before the reading of the Gospel, after which the congregation sang Luther's versification of the Nicene Creed, followed by the sermon. While the sermon, according to Loehe's *Agende,* was not to exceed three quarters of an hour, the pastor frequently lost track of time.

After the sermon, the congregation sang the "Create in me a clean heart, O God," followed by the responses of the traditional Preface, the Sanctus (sung by the congregation and followed by "a short but deep silence"), the Words of Institution, the Agnus Dei (sung as the German hymn "O Christ, Thou Lamb of God"), the Lord's Prayer, to which the congregation responded with "Amen," and the Pax. Rising from kneeling, the congregation—the men first—gathered about the altar for the distribution.

As the congregation communed, it sang hymns; three of the most used were "Jesus Christ, Our Blessed Savior," "Isaiah, Mighty Seer in Days of Old," and "O Lord, We Praise Thee, Bless Thee and Adore Thee." The distribution ended, the congregation sang the Nunc dimittis or sometimes the hymn "In Peace and Joy I Now Depart." With the salutation, collect, Benedicamus, and Benediction, the service drew to a close. Announcements were made at the close of the service.

Though the worship of the Bavarians was conducted under quite primitve conditions, several items they brought from their homeland served to enrich and beautify the service. These included red altar and pulpit paraments, an altar crucifix that had at its base a serpent with a crushed head, two candlesticks, the Communion vessels, and a large pulpit Bible. Another item of special interest was a black funeral procession cross. It was the custom in Frankenmuth that the processional cross was carried from the cemetery entrance to the grave site by a young male relative of the deceased. At the grave site there was no committal service, only the singing of a hymn by those who had gathered.

The use of Loehe's *Agende* by the Bavarian immigrants was an attempt to root their worship in the historic practices of their Lutheran tradition. In accord with that tradition, private confession and absolution was practiced, and the minor festivals of the church year were observed on the appropriate weekdays. It was remarkable practice for its time. It was even more remarkable that such were the practices of a group of Bavarian immigrants in the mid-19th century in the primeval forests of northern Michigan.

The Saxons in Missouri: Old Trinity, St. Louis, Mo. (c. 1860)

The Saxons arrived in America in 1839, six years before the Bavarians, and made their way up the Mississippi River from New Orleans to Perry County, Mo., some 100 miles south of St. Louis. They left Germany because of harassment from the authorities in Germany and also because of poor economic conditions in Germany at the time. Their leader, Martin Stephan, had a high view of church and ministry and was minded much like Wilhelm Loehe. Shortly after their arrival, however, Stephan was deported from the settlement, and the young Carl Ferdinand Wilhelm Walther became their leader.

Confronted by the same array of hymnals that existed wherever German immigrants gathered to worship, Walther saw the necessity for a single hymnal for the Saxon congregations. At his instigation, the St. Louis congregation ("Old Trinity" as it is now popularly known) published a German hymnbook (1847) compiled by "several Lutheran pastors in Missouri" of whom Walther was undoubtedly the most influential. The criteria used in the selection of the hymns reflect Walther's concerns;

> . . . the chief consideration was that they be pure in doctrine; that they have found almost universal acceptance within the orthodox German Lutheran Church . . . ; that they express not so much the changing circumstances of individual persons but rather contain the language of the whole church.[9]

Equally important to the leaders of the Saxon immigrants was a concern for the restoration of the original melodic forms of the Lutheran chorales, which had become corrupted in the centuries since the Reformation. The deterioration of many melodies from their original rhythmic form to that of all equal-note melodies, together with the filling out of melodic steps with passing tones, and the slow dragging tempos had made congregational singing a dull and uninspiring affair. Against all of this Walther and his fellow pastors reacted strongly.

Already in the mid-1840s the St. Louis parishes had scheduled *Singstunden* (either a kind of "choir rehearsal" or possibly practice sessions for the entire congregation) for the purpose of practicing the old melodies. In 1849 the congregation resolved to introduce these old melodies gradually, and by mid-century they were on their way to becoming standard for congregational singing among these parishes.

Another deterrent to effective congregational singing was the custom among the Saxons, as it was in Germany, of playing interludes (*Zwischenspiele*) on the organ between the lines of a stanza of a hymn as well as between the stanzas themselves. Typical of this practice is an example of such interludes from a *Choralbuch* in use in one of the Saxon congregations.

Harmonization with *Zwischenspiel* from the *Choralbuch fuer Evangelische Kirchen*, Guetersloh, 1840, used by the Lutheran congregation in Horse Prairie (rural Red Bud), Ill.

The continual interruption of the lines of a chorale with such interludes had a deleterious effect on congregational singing. By 1851 the St. Louis congregations had resolved to do away with such interludes between the lines of a hymn. The practice of playing interludes between the stanzas, however, continued in many places for many years.

Worship in the St. Louis congregation ("Old Trintiy") reflected the simpler liturgical practices of the Saxons. (See Table J.) As the service began, the congregation sang the "Kyrie, God Father in Heaven Above," followed by the pastor's intoning of "Glory to God in the highest," followed by the singing of the hymn "All Glory Be to God on High." Thereafter followed the salutation and response, antiphon, collect, Epistle, principal hymn for the day, the Gospel, the Creed (sung to Luther's versification), and the sermon. At the end of the sermon, the pastor led the congregation in a short confession and absolution, a general prayer, special prayers, the Lord's Prayer, announcements, concluding with the votum— all from the pulpit. After the sermon, the congregation sang a brief hymn followed by an antiphon, a collect, the blessing, a concluding hymn verse, and a silent prayer.

When Holy Communion was celebrated—and it was celebrated only infrequently—after the sermon the congregation sang the "Create in me a clean heart, O God," followed by the traditional Preface, Sanctus, Lord's Prayer (to which the congregation responded "For Thine is the kingdom

. . .'"), the Words of Institution, and the Agnus Dei sung to the chorale "O Christ, Thou Lamb of God."

During the distribution of the elements the congregation customarily sang hymns, at the conclusion of which was a brief post-Communion versicle, collect, and benediction, the service concluding with the singing of "O Lord, We Praise Thee, Bless Thee, and Adore Thee."

Walther himself, on occasion, played the organ for certain services. An early student of Walther wrote:

> He was also a master at the organ. On the high festivals he usually played the organ at Old Trinity, and it was a rare treat to listen to the wonderful improvisations, which admirable served to create in the audience the proper devotional spirit.[10]

Another student of Walther's later years, Theodore Buenger, remarked:

> On high festivals, when he was not preaching, he would take the organ bench, and worshipers in Holy Cross Church had no need to look who was playing when he sounded the prelude and *Auf, auf, mein Herz, mit Freuden* pealed forth in Easter joy.[11]

With the publication of the "Saxon Agenda" in 1856, this simpler, more rudimentary order, less reflective of the richer traditions of the 16th century, became the norm for the Saxon Lutheran immigrants. Even the Bavarian Lutherans in Michigan abandoned Loehe's richer order for this simpler one, which, they felt, would be more appropriate for the American scene.

The Saxon immigrants led the way to a revival of congregational hymn singing through their enthusiastic adoption of the old Lutheran chorales in their original rhythmic form, but their ultimate adoption of a relatively impoverished order of service left much to be desired. It was a situation that remained unchanged until their descendants, about the end of the 19th century, began to make the transition to the English language, and adopted the results of the movement led by the descendants of Muehlenberg toward a Lutheran liturgy for America based more closely on the models of the Reformation.

The Norwegians in the Midwest (c. 1850)

One other group of Lutheran immigrants to America in the 1800s was to help swell the tide of confessionalism. These were the Lutheran

The interior of the old Muskego church, built by the early Norwegian immigrants and completed in 1844. The building is now on the campus of Luther Theological Seminary, St. Paul, Minn., where it serves as a museum.

immigrants from the Scandinavian countries, Norway, Sweden, Denmark, and Finland. The earliest to come were the Norwegians, who began to settle in northern Illinois in the 1830s; others, who began to settle in southern Wisconsin, soon followed. Among the earliest of these settlements were those at Fox River, Ill. (1834), Jefferson Prairie, Wis. (1838), Rock Prairie, Wis. (1839), Muskego, Wis. (1839), and Koshkonong, Wis. (1840).

The two streams of religious thought that dominated Lutheranism in Norway at the time were the Haugean spirit of personal piety and lay activity following Hans Hauge, and the other emphasizing Biblical doctrine and confessional Lutheran theology. Both viewpoints were transferred to America. These two emphases are nowhere seen more clearly than in the contrasting personalities and activities of Elling Eielsen and J. W. C. Dietrichson, two pioneer Lutheran religious leaders who were to have a profound impact on Norwegian Lutheranism in America.

Eielsen, a Norwegian lay preacher and evangelist, arrived in America in 1839, the year the Saxons arrived in America, and represented the Lutheran Low Church point of view with its emphasis on pietism, puritanism, the concept of the congregation as a body of the "awakened," and the firm belief in lay preaching. For many of the early Norwegian immigrants, it was generally lay preaching or no preaching at all. However, these immigrants were not entirely dependent on lay preaching for their spiritual edification. Family devotions were the rule, and small groups, both men and women, often met together on Sundays and listened to the reading of a sermon, sang the old hymns, and took part in prayer and testimony. Eielsen and his followers remained firmly anticlerical, however, and regarded the use of vestments and liturgy as "an irrefutable proof of the flight of the Holy Spirit."

Dietrichson arrived five years later as an ordained pastor with the firm conviction that the way to save the Norwegian immigrants in America was "to transfer the Church of Norway to the woods and prairies of Wisconsin and Illinois." Arriving in New York, Dietrichson held two services for the Scandinavians of that city, one aboard a Swedish ship in the harbor, the other in St. Matthew, the oldest Lutheran church in Manhattan. On his way west, Dietrichson visited in Buffalo, where he heard Pastor Grabau, leader of the Prussian immigrants, preach. Dietrichson was much impressed with Grabau's emphasis on ecclesiastical order and discipline, and the brief friendship that developed between the two men brought an invitation for Dietrichson to preach to the German congregation there.

Among the books that Dietrichson brought with him was a copy of the *Danmarks og Norgis-kirke-ritual,* the prescribed ritual of the Dano-Norwegian church dating from 1685. It was this ritual to which Dietrichson required subscription in the congregations under his care and influence. (See Table M.)

Typical of the Norwegian settlements in the west was the settlement at Muskego, some 20 miles to the south and west of Milwaukee, Wis., the third- or fourth-oldest of the larger rural Norwegian colonies established in America. The Muskego church, finished in the fall of 1844, stood on Indian Hill, the "most beautiful site in the whole development." The hill sloped away evenly in all directions from the highest point, where the church stood. It could be seen from near and far, dominating the surrounding countryside.

The church building itself, built by members of the congregation, was made of unpainted red oak. The logs were hand hewn and smoothly finished, fitted so tightly together that mortar was neither needed nor used. In contrast with the smooth interior walls were the black walnut pillars supporting the gallery, the pillars, including the two pillars on either side of the pulpit, the altar and the pulpit likewise made of black walnut. The interior measured about 45 feet in length, the main part of the church being some 30 feet wide, the chancel 20 feet wide. There were two rows of windows on either side. The double doors at the entrance were also of black walnut. One side of the church had seven pews, the other side eight, seating 90; the gallery, in addition, seated about 100. At the front and side of the church was the small enclosure from which the *klokker* or *forsanger* led the singing of the congregation.

The *klokker* was an important person in every congregation. He had to know the most used tunes, or be able to pick out—at home—unfamiliar melodies on a primitive stringed instrument called the *Psalmodikon*. Generally the *klokker* had received special training in Norway for the office of teacher, and, when congregations were able, they gave him full-time employment as parachial school teacher, *klokker,* and *forsanger.*

The first pastor of the Muskego congregation, Claus Clausen, was strongly influenced by Dietrichson's ideas of church order, and soon issued a manifesto to the congregation the purpose of which was to organize the congregation more along the lines of the church in Norway, including even the introduction of private confession. The opposition to his ideas was so strong, however, that Clausen eventually modified many of his demands. He ultimately accepted a call to the Rock Prairie congregation.

While the Dietrichson-inspired experiment of ecclesiasticism at Muskego was thus brought to an end, the use of the Danish-Norwegian Ritual of 1685, modified somewhat to meet the conditions in America, prevailed in most of the Norwegian churches.

Many of the unusual and quaint customs that continued in many places for many years are of particular interest. Much to the disgust of Elling Eielsen and those who were attracted to him, the majority of the Norwegian pastors wore the traditional clerical garb in the conduct of worship. This consisted of a long black gown hanging almost to the floor, a satin-covered stole or yoke hanging around the neck and down both sides of the front of the gown, and a fluted collar or ruff, about three inches wide and one inch thick, worn Sir Walter Raleigh-fashion over the pastor's wing collar. On the three major festivals of the church year, it was customary for the pastor to wear also a white surplice over the black gown. Those who followed Eielsen's ideas, however, refused to wear the Norwegian clerical garb.

The *hoeimesse,* the high mass or morning service, was generally preferred to the *aftensang* or vesper, regardless of the time of the day the pastor might arrive in a particular community from his travels. In those churches where there was a bell to call the congregation to worship, it was rung first on Saturday evening about sundown in the rural communities. On Sunday morning, the church warden or *kirkevaerge* would toll the bell at three half-hour intervals, the congregation assembling at the third tolling of the bell. Inside the church building, the men took their places on one side, the women on the other. As the pastor proceeded to the altar, the bell was tolled three times, symbolizing the Holy Trinity.

The service began as the *klokker* read the opening prayer, the pastor, meanwhile, kneeling at the altar. The pastor faced the congregation during the singing of the opening hymn under the leadership of the *forsanger* who was responsible for setting the pitch of the hymn as well as leading it. After the proper pastoral salutations and responses of the congregation, the pastor chanted the Collect for the Day and read the Epistle while the congregation stood. After the singing of a second hymn, the pastor read the Gospel, the congregation standing, after which the Creed was spoken together by pastor and congregation. After a third hymn the pastor ascended the pulpit and offered a free prayer, read the text for the day, and delivered the sermon.

The sermon was the most important part of the service, and it was expected that the pastor would preach on the appointed text for each Sunday. Thus not only would the congregation be assured that in the course of a year the sermons would touch all of the cardinal points of the Christian's faith and life, it would also facilitate the reading and meditation on the texts in the home. While in the Norwegian synod the emphasis in the sermons tended to be on purity of doctrine and the leading of holy lives, in the Haugean circles the emphasis was more on conversion and sanctification.

The sermon concluded with the Lesser Gloria and, while still in the pulpit, the pastor read the General Prayer and made any necessary announcements. After another hymn, the pastor chanted the Collect for the Word and the Aaronic blessing, followed by the fifth and final hymn, after which the *klokker* read the closing prayer, the pastor kneeling at the altar.

While the Lord's Supper was, theoretically at least, a part of every Lutheran service, it was customarily celebrated among the Norwegians only at certain times of the year. Pastor Clausen, at the urging of

Dietrichson, insisted that the people at Muskego announce for communion on Saturday in the event that someone had to be denied the Sacrament on account of his sinful life. Both men and women communed at the same time, the men on one side of the semicircular altar rail, the women at the other.

Coming from a tradition of a state church, the collection of money proved a problem for many. Since the treasuries in Norway had been filled through taxation, it easily seemed a form of beggary to ask for "voluntary" contributions. For this purpose special congregational business meetings were called, even though in the same building, and it took several generations before most people felt it proper to combine the *hoeimesse* with the ordinary Sunday offering.

It was Dietrichson's ideas about doctrine, worship, and church polity, however, that were embodied into the church life of the Norwegian Lutherans in America. With the organization in 1853 of The Norwegian Evangelical Lutheran Church in America under the leadership of Herman Preus, a strict orthodoxy was to become the rule, an orthodoxy determined to root out all traces of both Haugeanism and the Danish reformer Grundtvig. The Low Church emphasis of Eielsen, emphasizing lay leadership, free prayer, an antagonism to clerical garb and chanting in worship remained, however, especially in the Eielsen Synod.

Movement Toward a Common Service

By the closing decades of the 19th century it was apparent that a new movement was making a slow but steady impact on the worship and hymnody of Lutherans in America. That movement was a confessional revival, a reawakening of interest in and commitment to the historic creeds and confessions of the Lutheran church and, together with that commitment, a reawakening of interest in the traditional worship forms and practices of the Reformation. The confessional revival was provoked, in part, by a climate of theological laxness, a condition that drove many back to a serious study of the writings of Luther and the Confessions of the church. While the gradual change from freer and more informal services to more ordered worship was clearly evident among many mid-century immigrant groups that brought with them a committed confessionalism from the continent and from Scandinavia, the confessional revival was a force that was felt among all Lutherans, including those with deep roots on the American continent. It was significant that the leaders of the confessional revival in America—e.g., Charles Porterfield Krauth, Matthias Loy, and C. F. W. Walther—were among those who in various ways also contributed to the revival of worship.

In part the confessional revival among Lutherans in America was a reaction against the "new measures" of revivalism, an approach that continued to find a good deal of support among some Lutherans. But even such a prominent Lutheran clergyman as William A. Passavant, who had been brought up in a period of revivalism and was active in a variety of educational, missionary, social, and philanthropic endeavors, gradually abandoned it. Opposition to revivalism, as well as to the more liberal brand of "American Lutheranism" promoted by S. S. Schmucker from Gettysburg, was strengthed by the Lutheran immigrants from the German and Scandinavian countries, as well as by the arrival from Europe of new books and periodicals. Antiquarian copies of liturgical orders from the 16th and 17th centuries were eagerly sought out, as were older book of dogmatics.

Representing a broad spectrum of Lutherans, such men as C. Porterfield Krauth (who served on the committee of the General Council's Church Book of 1868—see Table K), Sigmund Fritschel (who contributed toward the efforts of the General Council's *Kirchenbuch* of 1877), C. F. W. Walther (who was chiefly responsible for the German hymn book of the Missouri Synod of 1847), Beale M. Schumucker in the East, and Friedrich Lochner and Ulrich Koren in the Midwest—each made notable contributions to the movement for liturgical reform. The confessional revival and liturgical renewal, begun in Europe and carried on from a different perspective in England through the Oxford Movement, found its parallel in America.

Probably the single most significant accomplishment of the years at the end of the 19th century was the work that led to the adoption of the *Common Service* of 1888. (See Table L.) The quest to unite Lutherans in America about a single liturgy had eluded Lutherans since Muehlenberg had first proposed the idea. With the multiplication of regional synods in the early and middle 1800s, and the apparent desire of virtually each group to have its own book, such a dream was effectively set aside.

The idea of a common liturgy was revived as early as 1870 by the Rev. John Bachmann of St. John, Charleston, S. C. But while the idea met with general approval, it provoked no action until several years later, when the General Synod (later the United Synod of the South) suggested that it explore the idea with the General Council and the General Synod (North). In the early discussion of the possibility among the various groups, the General Council, meeting in 1879 at Zanesville, Ohio, suggested a basis for the preparation of a common liturgy. The suggested basis was "The common consent of the pure Lutheran liturgies of the sixteenth century, and when there is not an agreement among them the consent of the largest number of the greatest weight."

That basis had, in effect, already been the foundation on which the General Council's *CB* had been based, a book that contained the best English liturgy and hymnal that American Lutherans had yet produced. It leaned heavily on the Lutheran practices of the 16th century and in many ways anticipated the principles and solutions effected in the *CS*. Leaders in the preparation of the *CB* were C. Porterfield Krauth, J. A. Seiss, B. M. Schmucker, and Frederick Bird.

With agreement reached on the basic principle guiding the effort, work on the *CS* began in earnest in 1884. The drafting of the *CS* was largely the work of three men: Edward Traill Horn, Beale M. Schmucker, and George U. Wenner. To them must be given the credit for formulating an order that has served American Lutheranism longer than any other.

The *CS,* embodying slight variations among the three editions published by the participating bodies, united the practice of the General Council, the General Synod, and the United Synod of the South in a closer liturgical bond than had ever obtained before. It provided American Lutheranism with a full set of services, the church year in a fuller and richer form, complete sets of introits, collects, and a variety of invitatories, antiphons, responsories, and versicles for the church year. The Litany, Suffrages, Bidding Prayer, complete Tables of Lessons, Epistles and Gospels—all these presented a richer liturgical resource than had been available to Lutherans in America. Within a few years such groups as the Iowa Synod, the Joint Synod of Ohio, the Missouri Synod, the Norwegian synods, and later the Augustana and Icelandic synods provided it for their English-speaking constituencies. An article by Edward Traill Horn in the *Lutheran Quarterly Review* in 1881 contended that there was a normal Lutheran service that was common to the best liturgies of the 16th century and that the time was propitious for its restoration. The acceptance and widespread use of the *CS* was testimony to the clarity and accuracy of his vision.

The interior of First English Lutheran Church, Pittsburgh, Pa., as it appeared in 1892.

First English Lutheran, Pittsburgh, Pa. (c. 1893)

Among the congregations whose leaders were active in one way or another in various aspects of the confessional revival, and whose worship practices reflected the developing pattern of the times, a unique example was the First English Lutheran Church of Pittsburgh, Pa.

In 1837, when First English was founded, the population of Pittsburgh stood at about 20,000. The city comprised five wards and was supplied with water from a reservoir on Grant's Hill. Pedestrians using the streets after dark had to light their way with lanterns. There were four or five stage lines, with daily arrivals from the east; others fanned out to the north, south, and west. The "Spread Eagle Tavern" was the headquarters for the huge, covered, six-horse wagons that transported the city's freight. Steamboats plied the rivers, but the rapidly developing system of canals was probably the more important means of transportation for both passengers and freight.

Some other Lutheran congregations in the East had been involved in bitter controversy over the transition into the English language, but this problem seemed not to have touched the early days of First English, a remarkable tribute to the farsighted courage of those who sought to establish an entirely English-speaking congregation at that time. The pastors at First English included a number of prominent men, including William A. Passavant (who, in addition to his missionary and social concerns, founded *The Lutheran* in part, at least, to present a more conservative position over against the currents of the day) and Charles Porterfield Krauth (whose *The Conservative Reformation and Its Theology*, 1871, and efforts toward a more liturgical and sacramental worship practice were important).

When the second meeting of the General Council was held at First English on Nov. 12, 1868, it found its own hymn book—the *CB*—in the pews, having been adopted by the congregation and used for the first time just four days earlier. The use of the full service contained in the *Church Book* was not introduced until 1872, it being felt that the congregation was not yet ready for a full liturgical service.

The year that saw the publication of the *CS* also saw the erection of a new house of worship for First English. The new building on Grant St., consecrated on Nov. 4, was a Gothic building of sandstone built in the shape of a Greek cross. The nave, which provided for a seating of about 500, was 74 feet deep, with an equal width in the transept. On the northeast corner of the building an impressive spire and tower rose 75 feet above the ground. The chancel was well-elevated, with the choir and organ occupying the western side of the north transept. The organ of three manuals and pedal, built by the Johnston Co. of Westfield, Mass., had been installed just before the dedication at a cost of $5,250.00. A short time later a marble baptismal font, an exact copy of Thorwaldsen's famous "Angel of Baptism," was set in place and dedicated. In the course of the 1890s the chancel and church were refurbished with the addition of oil frescoes, a new marble altar and marble wainscoting in the chancel, handsome brass candelabra were placed in the chancel with a brass pulpit and an eagle lectern, and the installation of electric lighting replaced the former gas system. In all, the newly refurbished First English represented the best of current thought as to the ideal environment for worship.

On Sunday, July 2, 1893, the newly revised *CB* containing the *CS* was introduced to the congregation. The following Advent the first full rendering of the Vesper service was given. The music for the service, which had been carefully rehearsed by the choir, was a manuscript setting of the traditional plainsong melodies. This setting, after years of continuous use in the congregation, was finally incorporated in the books of liturgical service music edited by Harry Archer and Luther D. Reed.

First English had an active musical tradition and, through various efforts, this congregation helped to point the way to a richer liturgical practice for many Lutheran churches in America. A series of Wednesday afternoon organ recitals, begun in 1894, containing special organ music, often with violin and cello, appropriate music by the choir, and hymns and the Litany by the congregation, were very popular. The Lutheran Liturgical Association was organized in the chapel of First English in October 1898, and their regular meetings held there for seven years featured papers and discussions by such men as E. T. Horn, J. F. Ohl, John Hass, and Luther D. Reed. These activities helped to make First English a center for development of a parish worship practice along the lines laid out by the *CS.*

By 1901 the *Choral Service Book,* edited by Harry G. Archer, then organist of First English, appeared in print. In a beautifully printed and bound edition Archer, together with Luther D. Reed, had produced the first serious effort to provide the historic Lutheran liturgy in English with the traditional music of the church. Later efforts by the same authors produced the *Psalms and Canticles* and the *Season Vespers,* which were used for many years in the congregation.

The 20th Century

Any description of worship in American Lutheranism in the 20th century faces the danger of any attempt to describe the present or recent past. In portraying what is so close to us the truly salient features and thrusts of worship in our own century may easily be lost in the prejudices and biases of the observer.

One thing, however, is certain. The 20th century in American Lutheran worship has been the century of the *CS.* That order has provided the essential framework for Lutheran worship in America from 1888 to the present. How all-encompassing this liturgical framework has been becomes clearer when one surveys the various Lutheran books produced in this century. From the *CSB* (1917), largely the product of Eastern Lutheranism, through the *American Lutheran Hymnal* (1930), the joint product of the united Iowa, Ohio, and Buffalo synods, to *TLH* (1941) of the Synodical Conference, and the *SBH* (1958), the product of eight cooperating Lutheran church bodies, it has been the structure of the *CS* common to all these books and based on the "consensus of the pure Lutheran liturgies of the sixteenth century," that has been the common bond that—wittingly or unwittingly—has united Lutherans in America in their worship since that time.

That individual groups or congregations have sometimes adapted, altered, added to, or subtracted from the *CS,* often in capricious ways, is evident from such summaries of conditions in Lutheran worship as Theodore Graebner's trenchant article "Our Liturgical Chaos" of 1935. Yet the overwhelming effect of the use of the *CS* by American Lutherans has been to enrich and enlarge their vision of worship in terms of both catholicity and confessionalism.

With the advance of the 20th century came the final transition to a completely English-speaking Lutheranism. In the course of this transition were to be found the efforts of many individuals to transmit to their children through English translations the Lutheran hymnic heritage of the Swedish, German, Norwegian, Danish, and Finnish groups. Though these translations were sometimes inelegant and lacking in certain literary graces, the attempt was made. And the labors of such men as Charles Schaeffer, William Reynolds, Carl Doving, E. W. Olsen, Matthias Loy, and August Crull bear eloquent testimony to the seriousness with which they took their task. And those who have enjoyed the fruits of their labors have been enriched by their efforts.

But what will Lutheran worship be like as we move into the 21st century? How will a sketch of Lutheran worship in the year 2025 A.D. read? Obviously none can say with any precision. But if one were to attempt to draw from the preceding descriptions of Lutheran worship some central strands that weave their way through the fabric of Lutheran worship as described in this chapter, perhaps three stand out.

First of all there is *the variety of forms, practices, traditions, and customs* that have constituted Lutheran worship in the past. No exclusive way of worship has seemed either desirable or possible. The umbrella under which Lutheran worship practices are carried out is broad. Variety and adaptation are important factors.

The second thread, in many ways providing the necessary balance for the first, is *the centrality of the historic catholic forms,* especially the structure of the mass, as a touchstone for Lutheran worship. Events, movements, and forces that sought to move Lutheran worship from this basic structural pattern were ultimately superseded by a swing back to the catholic tradition.

The third thread is *the continued importance of a strong and vital musical tradition.* Whether in the music of the congregation, the music of the choir, or the music of the instruments, Lutheranism has maintained—with varying emphases—a tradition of musical involvement that sees all of music, both its creation and its re-creation, as a gift of God both useful and necessary for corporate worship.

But to specifics. What of Lutheran worship of the future? What will the buildings, if any, be like? What will be the music of the liturgy, of the choir, of instruments?

That sketch is yet to be written. That will be another chapter.

See also the related articles in *Key Words in Church Music:* alternation practice; canonical hours; cantor; cantorei; chant, Gregorian; choir, history; chorale; church music history, Renaissance—the Reformation tradition; church music history, baroque; church music history, American Lutheran; de tempore hymn; gospel song; hymnody, German; hymnody, Scandinavian; hymnody, American; hymnody, American Lutheran; Leisen; mass; office hymn; organ, history; organ, literature; all articles on theology of church music.

CHAPTER III

The Music of the Congregation

Louis G. Nuechterlein

Introduction

The music of the congregation, like all the other music of the church, is God's own gift to His people. It is a gift mediated through the talents of composers, arrangers, and parish musicians; yet its true source is God's own Spirit, who inspires the exercising and sharing of musical talent for the glorification of God and the edification of God's redeemed family. The music of the congregation derives from the triangular shape of Christian worship in that it serves as a means through which

> a. God Himself communicates with His people in Law and Gospel;
> b. Christians communicate with God in prayer, praise, and thanks;
> c. Christians teach and admonish one another (Col. 3:16).

God's Spirit energizes not only those who provide music for the congregation; He provides the congregation itself with the devotional energy to make melody to the Lord in its weekly public worship. As Dietrich Bonhoeffer once put it: "The new song is sung first in the heart. Otherwise it cannot be sung at all."[1]

The music of the congregation need not be everywhere the same. As Article VII of the Augsburg Confession states: "It is not necessary (for the true unity of the Christian church) that human traditions or rites and ceremonies, instituted by men, should be everywhere alike."[2] Diversity of musical styles from one geographic area of the church to another within a single generation, coupled with the inevitable and necessary evolving of musical styles from one generation to the next, preclude even the possibility of designating any one specific musical style as "the ideal" for Christian worship. Whatever the style of music in which the congregation's prayer and praise is cast, it must be meaningful (or at least potentially meaningful through a systematic program of music education) for the worshiping community; it must enable and stimulate the people of God to do in the house of God what they come there to do—namely, to "sing with the spirit and with the mind also" (1 Cor. 14:15).

Keeping the music of the congregation within the intellectual-emotional reach of people does not imply, however, that it be reduced to the lowest possible cultural denominator so as to "keep the folks happy" or to assure the widest possible evangelistic outreach. On the contrary, since music is a means through which God reveals Himself in love and through which Christians respond to Him in faith and through which they support and encourage one another, the church is compelled to care enough to use the very best in musical art. And the congregation that remains open to new musical experiences can expect to be enriched accordingly, provided it is willing to forgo from time to time the pleasure of instant musical gratification in exchange for the promise of long-term spiritual growth.

The decisive factor is not whether this or that particular music will be immediately pleasing to, and accepted by, the worshiper, but rather: is it worthy of being incorporated into the corporate worship of almighty God? The ideal toward which the church in every generation strives is to provide music for the congregation that possesses genuine artistic merit and is "absorbable" (gradually if not immediately) by the broad spectrum of people (young and old, educated and uneducated, cultured and uncultured, etc.) who comprise the congregation at worship.

Finally, the music of the congregation must serve as testimony from week to week of the living faith of the dead (that is, the best music from the past) as well as of the living faith of the living (that is, the best of current creative contributions to the musical art). As the church is enriched by the music of past centuries, it builds on that heritage, reshaping it in keeping with the unique artistic insights that God's Spirit gives to each succeeding generation of music makers.

We have now come full circle, arriving back where this chapter began, namely, with the music of the congregation as a means for the worship of God. This being so, the church continually strives to provide for the congregation music in keeping with and appropriate for its goals and purposes in public worship. So long as these goals and purposes remain determinative, the music the congregation uses will be an acceptable and pleasing offering to God.

Psalmody in Congregational Worship

The psalms of the Old Testament Scriptures are the oldest hymnody in use in current congregational worship. They remain in the church's hymnic repertoire because of their inherent poetic value and because their subject matter covers the entire span of devotional expression from the depths of despair (Psalm 130) to the heights of exaltation (Psalm 150), from the praise of God as Creator (Psalm 104) to the confidence in Him as Shepherd (Psalm 23), from prayers of penitence (Psalm 32) to hymns of thanksgiving (Psalm 136).

Since all the psalms were composed centuries before the birth of the Savior, none of them are explicitly Christ-centered. Hence, the centuries-old custom in Christian worship of ending each psalm with the explicitly Trinitarian canticle, the *Gloria Patri*. (Hence, also, the church's encouragement to poets in each new generation to add their own "new songs" to those that have been inherited from ages past.)

The basic structural device of all the psalms is the principle of Hebrew poetry known as parallelism. Each verse or half verse is coupled with (paralleled by) an additional verse or half verse which either restates the original sentiment in a slightly different way,

> e.g., Ps. 95:1—O come, let us sing to the Lord!
> Let us make a joyful noise to the Rock of our salvation.

or which complements or contrasts with the original sentiment,

> e.g., Ps. 95:4—For great is the Lord, and greatly to be praised!
> He is to be feared above all gods!

This principle of parallelism is highlighted when the psalms are sung (or spoken) in an *antiphonal* manner between equal forces (for example, one half of the congregation alternating with the other half in the singing or speaking of verses or half verses) or in a *responsorial* manner between unequal forces (for example, between pastor and people, or between choir and congregation, or between soloist and choir).

Musical settings for the psalms are many and varied: ancient plainsong and psalm tone formulas, Anglican four-part (SATB) chants, and the more recent and extensive work of Joseph Gelineau, Paul Bunjes, and Charles Frischmann all deserve careful study.[3] Inasmuch as all of this music requires prior rehearsal, it must of necessity be assigned to the choir; the congregation, however, may participate by responding to the choir's singing periodically with an easily learned musical refrain or antiphon.

Another musical possibility for the congregation's singing of psalms is to use the many rhymed versions of them, coupled with a metered melody already known or easily grasped. Examples of this type of psalmody are

Isaac Watts' version of Psalm 90, "Our God, Our Help in Ages Past"; Henry Baker's paraphrase of Psalm 23, "The King of Love My Shepherd Is"; and Martin Luther's adaptation of Psalm 46, "A Mighty Fortress Is Our God."

In the liturgy of the Lutheran Church the psalms are used in various ways: as the initial thematic material for the day, as intervenient material between Scripture readings, as Offertory material at the beginning of the Holy Communion, and as prayer and praise material during the distribution of the Sacrament. An Index of psalms, or portions thereof, appointed for the Sundays and Feast Days of the Christian Year is provided for Lutheran congregations in the ILCW's *Contemporary Worship 6: The Church Year Calendar and Lectionary*; other indices of psalmodic material can be found in *TLH*, *WS*, and *SBH*.

Christian Hymnody[4]

Hymn Tunes as Music Literature

The music for Christian hymnody is by definition the music of the people. Its closest musical relative in the secular realm is the folk song rather than the art song. It is democratic in spirit as well as in intent; it is music of the people and for the people, even if not always by the people. Eric Routley colorfully describes hymn tunes as "music domesticated, if you will, but not debased."[5]

Because hymn tunes are written for popular usage, they must of necessity be simple and uncomplicated. They are strophic rather than through-composed. Their melodies are usually restricted in range to an octave, or, at the most, a tenth; unusual melodic skips and sophisticated rhythmic patterns are avoided. Nevertheless, the best hymn tunes are miniature works of art, standing on their own artistic merit as *tunes*, without need for a harmonic undergirding to make them attractive.

The relationship between text and tune in Christian hymnody is much the same as it is in other forms of sacred and secular music: the tune most often determines the fate of the text. An appealing tune can sustain poetry of poor quality; an unappealing tune, however, is rarely able to give much help even to a first-rate text. This is not to suggest that the tune is to be regarded as more important than the text; the text remains as the reason for the existence of the hymn.

Yet it must be acknowledged that the tunes of the hymns are generally a more dominant factor than the texts. That is, a hymn is liked or disliked most often because of its tune rather than because of its text. Care must therefore be taken never to judge a text solely on the basis of its association with a given tune. Rather, it must be judged on the basis of its intrinsic *artistic* and *spiritual* worth. Only if it passes these tests is it ready to be considered for a place in a hymnal. If it is matched with a tune that sustains, heightens, and intensifies its theological message as well as its poetic mood, one can expect to sing a truly great hymn.

In centuries past, the musical styles of hymn tunes tended to vary widely from one generation to the next and from one branch of the Christian church to another. Hymnals published in the 20th century have increasingly reflected the influence of the worldwide Christian ecumenical movement. As a result, hymnals have been incorporating the best of tunes from every cultural source on the basis of artistic merit rather than longtime denominational associations. Hence a Lutheran hymnal will include the original plainsong version of the ancient 9th-century *Veni, Creator Spiritus*; and in a Roman Catholic hymnal one will find Martin Luther's Reformation hymn *A Mighty Fortress Is Our God*. Likewise, composers writing hymn tunes today do not design them for any particular denominational usage; they offer their creative work to "the whole Christian church on earth" for its musical-spiritual enrichment.

Metrical Patterns of Texts

An understanding of the structure of hymn tunes requires a prior knowledge of the structure of the metrical patterns of the hymn texts. All rhymed verse is organized into metrical "feet." A "foot" consists of a group of two or more syllables, with one accented and the others unaccented. The most common foot in English verse is the iambic, which consists of an unaccented syllable (˘) followed by an accented syllable (´). The following verse line,

Praise God/ from whom/ all bless/ings flow!

contains four iambic feet, totaling eight syllables. The trochaic foot is the reverse of the iambic, beginning with an accented syllable (´) and ending with an unaccented syllable (˘). The following verse line,

Oh, re/joice, ye/ Christians,/ loudly!

contains four trochaic feet, totaling eight syllables. Additional foot patterns are the dactylic (´˘˘) and anapaestic (˘˘´), although the pure dactylic is a rarity in hymnody because of its two unaccented syllables.[6]

The metrical patterns of hymn texts are categorized according to the number of syllables in each line, or verse, of each stanza.[7] The most common patterns are as follows:

6.6.8.6—commonly called *Short Meter*
8.6.8.6—commoned called *Common Meter*
8.8.8.8—commonly called *Long Meter*
7.7.7.7.
and
7.6.7.6. D

The "D" in the last of the above patterns means "double," indicating that the stanza is comprised of eight lines, the last four having the same metrical pattern as the first four. In addition to the more common patterns, a glance at the Metrical Index to the Tunes in any hymnal will reveal the large number of other patterns, including many that are "irregular," that is, each pattern being the only one of its kind.

Historical Survey of Tunes

The oldest hymn tunes included in hymnals today are the free-flowing, mystically flavored plainsong tunes that date from the 6th to the 12th centuries. Originally assigned to be sung as part of the divine office in monastic communities, many of these haunting melodies are easily within the performance capability of the average congregation today, provided they are introduced in an intelligent manner into the congregation's hymnic repertoire. As can be observed in Example 1, their distinctive charactertistic is their even-note pattern (as contrasted with the regular

Ex. 1   *Veni, Creator Spiritus*

pulsation, in duple or triple meter, of later hymn tunes). Light-textured accompaniments are provided for them in the hymnals of today; however, they are intended to be sung in unison, in an unhurried, undulating manner.

The music most closely identified with the Lutheran Church is that of the 16th-century chorale melodies of Martin Luther and his contemporaries. Luther himself spent much time and energy in writing hymns and in supervising the preparation of new hymnals. In addition, he adapted for Lutheran congregational use various melodies from Roman Catholic Latin hymnody as well as from the folk-song literature of his day. These melodies are characterized by a rugged rhythmic vitality, a modest melodic range, a variety of metric patterns, and a distinctly modal flavor. Example 2, *Es ist das Heil uns kommen her,* , is one of the four melodies provided in the *Achtliederbuch* (1524), the first of Lutheranism's hymnals.

Martin Luther's creative contribution to the music of Christian

Ex. 2   *Es ist das Heil uns kommen her*

Ex. 3   *Ein' feste Burg ist unser Gott*

hymnody is best exemplified in his rousing melody for his paraphrase of Psalm 46, shown in Ex. 3 in its original rhythmic version. The isometric (metered) version that appeared in many 19th- and early 20th-century hymnals is a later, 18th-century, "flattened-out" adaptation that makes less physical demand on the singer but is far less musically interesting and exciting to sing. Happily, the trend among music editors of hymnals published today is to incorporate the original rhythmic version of *Ein' feste Burg ist unser Gott* and of other 16th- and 17th-century chorale melodies.

The composition of the energetic, rhythmic type of chorale melody continued throughout the remainder of the 16th century. In 1599 Philipp Nicolai brought this development to a grand climax with the tunes that hymnologists have labeled the King and Queen of chorale melodies: *Wachet auf, ruft uns die Stimme* and *Wie schoen leuchtet der Morgenstern*. Example 4, however, does reveal a shift to a more shapely and refined melodic style; also, a shift away from the modal flavor of many of the earlier tunes to a distinct tonal flavor.

Ex. 4   *Wie schoen leuchtet der Morgenstern*

Ex. 5   *Auf, auf, mein Herz, mit Freuden*

Johann Crueger (1598—c. 1662) is the dominant figure of the music of 17th-century Lutheran hymnody. He was the initial editor of what remains to this day a classic source for Lutheran chorale tunes, his *Praxis pietatis melica* (1644). The tunes *Jesu, meine Freude*; *Nun danket alle Gott*; *Herzliebster Jesu*; *Schmuecke dich, o liebe Seele*; and *Auf, auf, mein Herz mit Freuden* (Ex. 5), are among his many masterful melodies. The rhythmic drive of the older chorale melodies from the 16th century is still present; the same AAB structural design is followed; but the multiple (that is, duple *and* triple) rhythmic patterns that identify many of the older tunes are now replaced by a single (in the case of Ex. 5, triple) pattern throughout.

The bulk of our English hymn music today has come from two traditions, the Lutheran and the Reformed (or Genevan), differing markedly from each other in development. The chorale tunes of the Lutherans were ecstatic and often "untamed"; the psalm tunes of the Calvinists were more refined and restrained. The latter were also, from the very beginning, almost entirely syllabic (that is, one note per syllable of text), whereas it was not unusual for the former to contain melismatic (that is, two or more notes per syllable) passages. In addition, the melodic range of the psalm tunes was generally more limited than that of the chorales. Psalm tune rhythms, however, were often as sophisticated as those of their Lutheran "cousins." Illustrative of the type of tune in the *Genevan Psalter* of 1551 is Example 6, a melody either composed or adapted by Louis Bourgeois, the musical editor of that publication. It is a representative blend of the Lutheran approach to rhythm and the Genevan approach to shape.

Although the name of Johann Sebastian Bach is closely associated with the history and development of the Lutheran chorale, his contribution was

Ex. 6   *Freu dich sehr, O meine Seele*

not that of a writer of new chorale melodies, but rather that of an arranger of earlier 16th- and 17th-century melodies in his own 18th-century harmonic, rhythmic, and contrapuntal idiom. Bach's exquisite, gem-like harmonizations of the chorales were not intended for congregational singing; they are choral pieces, ingenious four-part choral writing of the highest caliber intended for part-singing by the choir.

This chapter pertains primarily to the *music* of Christian hymnody, but it must note a significant development in the history of English hymn-texts. In the 16th and 17th centuries one of the significant differences in the weekly public worship of the Lutherans and the Calvinists was that Lutherans felt free to, and did, add hymn texts of their own to the hymnic heritage given to them by previous generations. This, in turn, gave impetus to the composition of an ever-enlarging repertoire of new tunes for these new texts.

The Calvinists, on the other hand, regarded the Old Testament Psalms as the only hymnody suitable for public worship, since the psalms were part of God's inspired Word, whereas "hymns of human composure" were not. Since all 150 Psalms are pre-Christian poetry and hence lacking in any explicit witness to the New Testament Gospel, Calvinist Christians of this era never experienced the thrill of singing the Good News of the Savior's birth, ministry, death, resurrection, and ascension. It was a predicament deplored by many Calvinists themselves; yet their weekly public worship remained entrenched in their "psalms only" tradition for nearly 200 years.

Others tried unsuccessfully, but Isaac Watts (1674—1748) managed to legitimatize the singing of "hymns of human composure" alongside the Biblical psalter in the Calvinist churches of England as well as in Europe and America. With the publication in 1719 of *The Psalms of David Imitated in the Language of the New Testament and Applied to the Christian State and Worship*, Watts clothed many of the psalms with an indelible New Testament interpretation. Three examples of his artistic handiwork in this genre are Psalm 72 ("Jesus Shall Reign Where'er the Sun"), Psalm 98 ("Joy to the World! The Lord Is Come!"), and Psalm 103 ("Oh, Bless the Lord, My Soul!").

We are also indebted to Watts for his classic poetic versifications of other psalms, such as Psalm 23 ("The Lord My Shepherd Is") and Psalm 90 ("O God, Our Help in Ages Past"), and for many more original texts based on passages of the New Testament, the most beloved of which is "When I Survey the Wondrous Cross." "To Watts more than to any other man is

115

due the triumph of the hymn in English worship. All later hymn writers, even when they excel him, are his debtors; and it is possible to hold that his work for hymns is greater than Charles Wesley's, even if as a writer of hymns we place him a little lower than Wesley."[8]

The Wesley brothers' utilization of hymnody was one of their most effective tools in supplanting cold, legalistic Calvinist worship in England with their own warm, evangelical approach to the Christian religion. They learned early in their pastoral ministries, as Martin Luther had learned 200 years earlier, that "a message that is to be forced home to individual men can be immensely strengthened by simple, melodic music. This is especially true of a message which proclaims certainty and safety rather than the answers to sophisticated intellectual problems. Exuberant melody is the natural accompaniment and expression of that ecstatic individualism which was the popular reaction to Luther and Wesley."[9]

Unfortunately, the folklike quality of these tunes for the Wesley hymns soon deteriorated in the 19th century into an undisciplined exercise in emotional fervor for its own sake. The essential balance in the compositional art between head and heart was ignored. Melodies became more and more florid, with texts degenerating into mere vehicles for them. In the later 19th-century decades John B. Dykes, W. H. Monk, Arthur Sullivan, and others wrote tunes almost totally devoid of melodic content of interest, depending instead for their popularity on the exploiting of their harmonic possibilities. The increasing use of chromaticism gave them a sweetness which made them immediately popular, but they were lacking in inherent musical substance.

At the beginning of the 20th century Ralph Vaughan Williams appeared on the hymnological scene, insisting that the barrenness of the Victorian style of hymn tunes must be replaced with something more distinctive and virile. His solution: for the secular idiom of the 19th century he substituted the secular idiom of the 16th century, the traditional English folk song; and in *The English Hymnal* (1906) he turned the tide in England in favor of sturdier hymn tunes.

In addition to its strong emphasis on plainsong hymns, *TEH*'s major contribution was its large number of old English folk songs in 20th-century harmonic dress; their freshness and vitality helped greatly to break the long stranglehold of the Victorian idiom on the English and American churches. Example 7, Ralph Vaughan Williams' restoration of an old English carol entitled *Kings Lynn*, is an example of his work as musical editor of *TEH*.

Ex. 7   *King's Lynn*

Melody collected by Ralph Vaughan Williams (1872—1958)
From the *English Hymnal* by permission of Oxford University Press.

Before the 20th century little creative work in hymn writing was done among Christians in the mainline Protestant churches of the United States. Emigrant ethnic groups brought their hymnody here from Europe, and most of them were far too busy settling the New World to give much attention to new music for their worship. American blacks were, of course, singing their spirituals; but these were reflective and expressive of the social and economic plight of 18th- and 19th-century black Americans. Not until the 20th century did some of these spirituals find a place in some of the hymnals of both black and white American Protestants.

Another strand of melody was quietly being formed in the backwoods areas of the ever-expanding 19th-century American western frontier. Although many of these melodies were originally secular in association, they seem well-suited for religious verse as well; and a number of them have been incorporated in recently published hymnals. The tune *Jefferson*, Ex. 8, first appeared in William Walker's 1835 songbook *Southern Harmony*; it bears a strong resemblance to the old English folk melody (Ex. 7) resurrected for 20th-century use by Ralph Vaughan Williams from his country's musical folk lore.

An effort to enlarge the American repertoire of new hymn texts and tunes is associated with the publication of the *The Hymnal 1940* (EpH), which contained 109 tunes bearing a 20th-century date of composition. Of these, 44 were written specifically for the volume itself. These tunes bear the marks of no one single musical style. The only feature many of them share in common is a rhythmic elasticity within the bar line, a characteristic of much music of the 20th century. Their poetic meters have not been altered; instead, the tunes have been shaped to correspond more

Ex. 8   *Jefferson*

Ex. 9   *Wittenberg New*

From the *Worship Supplement* © 1969 by Concordia Publishing House. Used by permission.

directly with the word accents of conventional meters. Their harmonies are mostly conventional, except for the occasional thickening of texture in order to achieve a greater richness of sound and effect.[10]

The search for new and fresh hymn tunes bore further fruit in the publication of *Worship Supplement* (*WS*)[11] in 1969. Of its 84 tunes, 16 come from the 20th century; and of these 16, at least two seem destined to live a long and useful life in the church: Jan Bender's energetic setting for a text by Martin Franzmann, Ex. 9, and Carl Schalk's lilting *Now* for a text by Jaroslav Vajda, Ex. 10.

The ILCW, organized in the mid 1960s and consisting of representatives from most of the Lutheran churches of North America, stimulated continuing creativity through two of its *Contemporary Worship* (*CW*)

Ex. 10   *Now*

Melody © Carl Schalk
Used by permission.

Ex. 11   *Earth and All Stars*

Reprinted from *12 Folksongs and Spirituals* by David N. Johnson © 1968
By permission of Augsburg Publishing House.

booklets: *CW1—Hymns*, and *CW4—Hymns for Baptism and Holy Communion*.[12] Along with the 51 hymn texts in these two booklets, 16 new tunes made their first appearance in print. A lively tune by David N. Johnson taken from *CW1*, Ex. 11, with an equally lively text by Herbert Brokering, illustrates the rhythmic "drive" characteristic of many currently written hymn tunes.

In recent years, especially during the 1960s, the churches of America were flooded with a seemingly endless stream of so-called folk texts and folk tunes for which people claimed the ability to relate to worshipers with more relevance than the classic hymnody of most denominational hymnals. The bouncy tunes and folksy verse of men such as Ray Repp, Peter Scholtes, Paul Quinlan, Ian Mitchell, Richard Avery and Donald Marsh, and others found their way into the congregational worship of almost every denomination.

For the Roman Catholic Church these composers undoubtedly filled a temporary need in the years immediately after the Vatican II Council's decision to make congregational hymn singing a more important part of worship; Roman Catholics seemed not to be aware of the treasures of hymnody already theirs as Christians. In Protestant churches the most probable explanation for the wave of popularity of this type of substandard music literature was the lack of capable leadership from both parish pastors and musicians in leading their congregations through the years to "higher hymnic ground." To paraphrase the familiar maxim, "where there is no leadership, the people flounder."

There is only one sure, evangelical way to stop the inundation of second- and third-rate hymnody into the repertoire of worshiping congregations. To borrow the title of a famous sermon by the 19th-century Scotch preacher Thomas Chalmers, it must be stopped by "The Expulsive Power of a New Affection." Chalmers was referring in his sermon to the power of a new love for God as the only power strong enough to expel the love for the world and the things in it. His point is equally valid regarding the music of the church: the inherent strength of the finest in hymnody (and in liturgical music as well), systematically, perseveringly, and winsomely introduced into the worship life of the congregation, is the only power strong enough to expel a love for that of inferior quality. The church is ever in need of, if not always immediately grateful for, this kind of artistic leadership among its clergy and parish musicians; the same is doubly true with regard to the colleges and seminaries that train parish musicians and pastors for such service.

Suggestions for the Use of Hymns

Choosing Hymns. Hymns are an integral part of the congregation's worship; they are not to be scheduled merely as congregational busy work or as time fillers. The pastor must therefore discipline himself to know in advance what the hymn-texts say, lest he become guilty of requesting the congregation to sing words and phrases that may be liturgically and pastorally ill timed. For example, the following harvest hymn stanza:

> What our Father does is well:
> Blessed truth His children tell!
> Though He send, for plenty, want,
> Though the harvest store be scant,
> Yet we rest upon His love,
> Seeking better things above.

would be altogether inappropriate for a Thanksgiving Day Service following a bountiful autumn harvest, although quite appropriate following a "scant" one.

Similarly, many of the "Cross and Comfort" hymn-texts can serve as effective pastoral aids at the bedside of the sick and dying, but they make only a minimal spiritual impact on healthy, prosperous, prime-of-life Christians. Hymn texts must be vehicles through which worshipers can sing to the Lord and to one another with integrity as well as with truth.

A practical suggestion: it is often best to schedule only hymns with familiar tunes as "Entrance" or "Opening" hymns and during the Distribution (provided, of course, that their texts are also liturgically appropriate). Keep the challenge of the unfamiliar and more demanding hymns for use between the Scripture readings or immediately before or after the sermon.

The choice of hymns sung during the Distribution need not be restricted to those included in the hymnal's section dealing with the Sacrament of Holy Communion. Hymns sung during the Distribution may also amplify the church year accent for the day as well as reflect the joyful character of the Meal itself. For example, "O God, Our Help in Ages Past" and "The Church's One Foundation" would be fitting Distribution hymns for a parish anniversary festival service; "From Heaven Above to Earth I Come" for a Christmas communion; "As with Gladness Men of Old" for an Epiphany Feast; and "Jesus Christ Is Risen Today!" for an Easter Eucharist.

No hymns need to be scheduled at all after the Distribution; as soon as all have communed, worship is best concluded without unduly prolonging the service. A hymn stanza after the Benediction is unnecessary and, at this point in the service, redundant.[13] If, after the Blessing, the pastor moves from the chancel to the narthex in order to greet the departing worshipers, the organist ought not be asked to provide "traveling music" along the way. Several moments of silence after the Blessing and its congregational response are much to be preferred; the organist may then play a postlude of his choosing if it is local custom for him to do so.

Cultivating a Core of Congregational Hymnody. Either the pastor or someone else designated by him should keep a cumulative record of the hymns sung by the congregation from week to week and from year to year. Having this information at hand can pay healthy dividends in congregational hymnic growth, for it enables the pastor to build systematically on that which has gone before. A core of 125 to 150 hymns is the maximum number many congregations can or will absorb. So let these same 125 to 150 hymns—hopefully reflecting a judicious and enriching balance, both theologically and artistically—keep reappearing year after year. Through such continuing exposure the unfamiliar hymns will inevitably become familiar—and loved.

But whenever a totally unfamiliar hymn tune is being introduced, be sure to precede it with some advance preparation. Rehearse it with the congregation immediately before (rather than during) the service in which it is to be sung. Alert the congregation to its place in the service and to the reason for its being there; challenge the worshipers to a willingness to make the "new" hymn their very own. A rehearsal of even a few minutes duration, conducted by the pastor or the parish musician in an informal and winsome manner, can work wonders in transforming a "silent majority" into a "singing majority."

Selectivity in Choosing Hymn Stanzas. No liturgical law compels the congregation to sing every stanza of every hymn. The pastor is therefore encouraged to be selective, especially with hymns of six or seven or more stanzas. The attention span of today's TV-oriented worshipers is extremely limited; hence, every moment in every service should be carefully measured.

It is especially important to keep the opening hymn short, lest the worshipers gain the impression that the service is having difficulty in "getting off the ground." The bulletin may indicate which stanzas of the opening hymn are to be sung. This assumes, to be sure, that the pastor has taken sufficient advance care to see to it that the abbreviated arrangement of stanzas is theologically logical, cohesive, and complete.

Splitting Hymns into Groups of Stanzas. If the bulletin regularly lists every item in the service in its proper sequence,[14] the worshipers will experience no difficulty noting which hymn stanzas are to be sung at various points.[15] For example, Martin Luther's Easter hymn "Christ Jesus Lay in Death's Strong Bands" (*TLH* 195) might be sung immediately before (stanzas one to three) and immediately after (stanzas four and five) an Easter sermon. Or the hymn "Hallelujah! Let Praises Ring!" (*TLH* 23) might be sung in single stanzas, each stanza introducing a specific portion of a Trinity Sunday sermon and then the final doxological stanza summarizing the entire sermon at its conclusion.

Bodily Postures in Worship. The congregation ought to stand for the singing of most if not all the hymns. At the very least, the service ought to begin with the congregation standing for the opening hymn. The matter of bodily posture *is* significant; the body plays an important role in worship. Standing to sing is as meaningful as is kneeling to pray and sitting to learn.

Suggestions for the Organist

Chapter V in this handbook offers technical assistance to the organist as hymn player. The following paragraphs in this chapter provide nontechnical suggestions that the congregation itself might offer if it were able to verbalize its needs.

1. Introduce each hymn in *exactly the same* tempo in which it is to be sung. Keep the tempo constant from phrase to phrase; and when the singing itself begins, keep the instrumental support firm and steady. Remember that the organist's assignment is to lead, not to trail behind, the congregation.

In introducing the hymns, use only as much time as is necessary to "say" what needs to be "said." If the tune is a familiar one, play only as much of it as is necessary to give the people time to locate the hymn in the hymnal. If the tune is unfamiliar, introduce it in its entirety, thereby emphasizing to the people their need to be doubly alert and ready to learn. Finally, if the introduction is in the form of an extended composition (a chorale prelude or fantasy) on the tune, move immediately from prelude to hymn, without any further introduction, except when a modulation is required.

2. Give the congregation time to catch its breath at the end of each stanza. With most tunes this can be done by inserting an additional half or whole measure of time between stanzas by holding the final chord of each stanza for a designated number of additional beats, followed by a beat of

silence. With some tunes the final chord of the stanza itself provides sufficient pause; with other tunes only the rule of experience is ultimately applicable. The important consideration is that an opportunity for breathing be provided and that it be done in a way that the congregation feels to be natural. The interval should be identical between all stanzas.

3. Sing, or at least hum, along with the congregation when accompanying their singing. Doing so helps prevent jerking, dragging, or racing, or any other idiosyncrasies that the organist may develop.

4. Do not succumb to the temptation to use all of the organ all of the time, a warning that is doubly applicable if the organist is blessed with the varied tonal resources of a large and well-designed instrument. As the artist uses the many oil colors in his palette judiciously and contrastingly, so the organist disciplines himself to become thoroughly acquainted with his palette of tonal colors and learns to mix them in a musically imaginative and aurally satisfying manner. He reserves full organ for climactic moments only; he uses mixtures with discretion, especially if they are highly assertive and penetrating. He resists the urge to "shoot the works" with every hymn. In short, his performance practice is governed by his knowledge of basic principles of organ registration and controlled by his desire to *serve* the congregation even as he *leads* it in singing.

Both the pastor and the parish musician must be alert at all times to the possibilities for hymn singing as a means for praising God and for the mutual encouragement of Christians in the faith. Let them lavish as much care on the choosing and playing of hymns as in their preparation of preludes, voluntaries, postludes, and sermons. Their artistic-liturgical care from week to week will result in worship that is both cogent and vibrant in all it parts.

The Music for the Liturgy

The Christian liturgy, with its centuries-old interlocking system of *proper* (changeable textual parts of the service) and *ordinary* (unchangeable parts of the service), is a weekly action in which pastor and choir and congregation share either as a *drama* (all roles by all participants spoken), as an *opera* (all roles by all participants sung), or as an *operetta* (some parts spoken, others sung). Few services of worship are totally devoid of all music since even the musically-insensitive worshiper senses the power of music to give "wings to the Word" as that Word is proclaimed and shared.

Nor are many services of worship set to music in their entirety since not all parts of the liturgy are equally suited for the musical "wings" (e.g., the Scripture Lessons, the Prayers, although these have also been sung throughout certain parts of the church's history).

Consequently, the liturgy is at most times and in most places set within the structural framework of an operetta, with some of its parts sung and others spoken. This being the case, it is aesthetically desirable that the parts that are set to music bear a stylistic relationship to each other. Furthermore, the bits of dialog that occur throughout the liturgy (e.g., "The Lord be with you." "And also with you") should be exchanged "in kind." That is, if the minister speaks, the congregation responds by speaking; if the minister sings, the congregation responds with singing.

For the past several generations there has been considerable discussion among Roman Catholic, Anglican, Lutheran, and Episcopalian liturgiologists regarding the wisdom of retaining the historic Ordinary of the Mass (*Kyrie, Gloria in excelsis, Nicene Creed, Sanctus,* and *Agnus Dei*) as the foundational unchangeable textual material for the celebration of the Holy Communion. As of the mid-1970s, Lutherans have decided that in the Lutheran orders these historic elements are to be retained. Thus there remains the need for congregational settings of these great songs (with the possible exception of the Nicene Creed) that are musically satisfying *and* durable.

As substitutes for these musical settings, the congregation may choose from time to time to *speak* the entire liturgy. Or the choir may be assigned to sing the portions of the Ordinary settings that lie beyond the ability of the congregation. Still, the weekly offering of the liturgy is retained by the entire congregation as *its* normal function since worship itself must always remain the work of *all* the people of God. Finally, it is also important that any keyboard accompaniment for the music of the liturgy be light-textured, lest it overwhelm the congregation with too much sound; it is imperative for the congregation to be compelled to "move along" in singing, lest the music become a funeral pall for the Holy Communion instead of the cover of rejoicing that it is designed to be.

The Importance of Acoustics for Congregational Worship

A live acoustical environment is an absolute necessity if the music of the congregation is to come alive. This is a basic principle that needs to be emphasized again and again, not for the sake of the parish musician but *for the sake of the congregation itself* as it renders its musical offerings to the Lord from week to week. Well-intentioned as many worshipers and many church building committees may be in wanting to make their church interiors as comfortable and luxurious as their homes, the plush and intimate atmosphere of the living room is altogether incompatible with the participatory demands of the liturgy of the people of God. Carpeting on the floor and acoustical tile on the ceiling absorb not only the sounds of shuffling feet and nervous coughing; they also dampen the enthusiasm and drain the vitality of the congregation's vocal energy as it tries to sing.

A nave that is sufficiently reverberant for spirited singing can easily be adapted for effective public speaking as well. However, a nave that has been acoustically treated so as to favor the speaking voice and achieve a "hushed" atmosphere has unfortunately also been ruined for effective music making. Since music of one kind or another is an ingredient during more than half of every hour worshipers gather together, it is incumbent on the public speaking voice to accommodate itself to acoustics that are sufficiently "alive" for music making as well. The interior of the nave, chancel, and gallery are instruments that need to be designed and constructed in such a way that the praise of God, whether with voices or with instruments, is a thing of beauty; and there is yet no known substitute for hard ceiling, wall, and floor surfaces.

Conclusion

The music of the congregation is not that which is sung by the clergy or choir on the congregation's behalf, with the congregation as an attentive and appreciative audience. Nor is it music scheduled for all the people to sing, but in which only a faithful few participate while the majority stand with hymnals open but with mouths shut. The music of the congregation is that in which *all* those gathered for worship take an active part, regardless of their native musical ability or vocal skill. Even those very few who cannot carry a tune join unabashedly in the singing, using their limited vocal resources in the praise of God. And whatever its aesthetic shortcoming may be, such music making *is* a work of divine art since God's own Spirit is its source and its prime mover.

See also the related articles in *Key Words in Church Music*: alternation practice; canticle; chorale; de tempore hymn; gospel song; all articles on hymnody; Leisen; metrical psalmody

126

CHAPTER IV

The Music of the Choir

Carlos R. Messerli

The Choral Heritage

Church choirs—groups of dedicated people trained to sing in services of worship—can trace their distinguished history in the Judeo-Christian tradition for nearly 3,000 years. King David, that often embattled leader of Israel during a turbulent and exciting period in its history, founded one of the first bodies of organized "church" musicians when he commissioned the leaders of the Levites "to appoint their brethren as the singers who should play loudly on musical instruments, on harps and lyres and cymbals, to raise sounds of joy" (1 Chron. 15:16). The Levites appointed Heman, Asaph, Ethan, and others to lead in singing and playing. Chenaniah, leading musician of the Levites, was chosen to "direct the music, for he understood it" (1 Chron. 15:22). The occasion for this activity was the joyous procession, led by David, of the Ark of the Covenant to Jerusalem.

As David made preparation for worship in the temple his son was to build, he continued to help organize the Levitical musical forces. At least 288 musicians were to participate in 24 choral groups, singing various liturgical works. These singers and instrumentalists, augmented by other musical Levites, prepared for months for the services that were to initiate temple worship.

The consecration of Solomon's temple provided one of the most spectacular and awe-inspiring events in which any choir has ever participated:

All the Levitical singers, Asaph, Heman, and Jeduthun [Ethan], their sons and kinsmen, arrayed in fine linen, with cymbals, harps, and lyres, stood east of the altar with a hundred and twenty priests who were trumpeters; and it was the duty of the trumpeters and singers to make themselves heard in unison in praise and thanksgiving to the Lord; and when the song was raised, with trumpets and cymbals and other musical instruments, in praise to the Lord, "For He is good, for His steadfast love endures forever," the house, the house of the Lord, was filled with a cloud, so that the priests could not stand to minister because of the cloud; for the glory of the Lord filled the house of God. (2 Chron. 5:12-14)

Subsequently, the many full-time choirs served in rotation, preparing and performing ritual music, including various psalms for temple worship.

The place of women in liturgical worship is not clearly identified, but it appears that they also participated. Heman, the singer noted above, had 14 sons and 3 daughters: "They were all under the direction of their father in the music in the house of the Lord." (1 Chron. 25:6)

The liturgical choirs of the Christian era fulfilled a function in worship no less significant than that of their ancient counterparts. The venerable papal *Schola cantorum* has existed continuously since the sixth century. Almost every European royal house in the later Middle Ages and the Renaissance supported an entourage of musicians (a "chapel") to whom was delegated the responsibility of performing liturgical worship music at court. Most flourishing monasteries, especially those of the Benedictine Order, maintained choirs that provided elaborately chanted music for the various liturgical observances.

In the large churches of the Lutheran Reformation *Kantoreien* (choirs) were formed to assist the congregation in worship with liturgical performance of the new chorales and the polyphonic literature. The German tradition of liturgical choirs was to be continued in the 17th and 18th centuries in many cities by outstanding musicians, the most famous of whom is Johann Sebastian Bach, cantor at the St. Thomas Kirche in Leipzig.

The renowned English cathedral choirs of men and boys, formed to sing liturgical music, perpetuate their ancient tradition by performing the finest historical and contemporary liturgical music in more than 20 English cathedrals today.

The leaders and members of the church choirs of Western Christianity have included at one time and place or another the majority of the greatest musicians of all periods up to the beginning of the 19th century. A representative list would include: Guillaume de Machaut, John Dunstable, Josquin Desprez, Giovanni Pierluigi da Palestrina, Claudio Monteverdi, Henry Purcell, Michael Praetorious, François Couperin, Dietrich Buxtehude, Johann Sebastian Bach, Ludwig van Beethoven, and Franz Schubert.

As various aspects of the role and function of the church choir today are examined below, it will be helpful to remember the examples of excellence provided by our predecessors in the church's choirs, for the problems facing our age are neither novel nor insurmountable. We must be comforted and stimulated by the magnitude of the accomplishment of our fathers in faith and music and be ever grateful to them for the heritage of music and liturgy bequeathed to us.

The Function of the Choir in Worship

Lutheran worship flows within an essentially liturgical channel that it shares with much of past and present Christianity. Lutheran worship moves in the rhythms of the church year, which effect a felicitously thorough emphasis on the essential truths and themes of Holy Scripture and Christian life with an annual review of the chief events in Christ's earthly ministry. Liturgical worship provides the security and stability fostered by the regular repetition of certain songs and prayers, but at the same time it allows variety through changing texts. Liturgical worship encourages the enthusiastic and wholehearted involvement of all Christians; its liturgical plan allows for the ordered participation of the entire priesthood of all believers. Finally, liturgical worship is run through with the strong, sure strand of doxological praise.

Traditional Lutheran worship grew out of centuries of Roman Catholic practice. Although Lutherans revere the worthy elements of the past, they have not uncritically accepted all of its traditions. Rather, they gratefully receive their rich heritage in order to develop meaningful and worthy worship practices for the present. The past becomes a foundation on which to build, and a vast reservoir from which to draw for the renewal and invigoration of worship today.

The function of the choir in Lutheran worship is most easily defined as both liturgical and congregational.[1] It is liturgical in that its musical contribution is made within a prescribed and ordered framework that offers a great variety of opportunities for participation. It is congregational in that its musical efforts are directed with, for, and on behalf of the congregation it serves. The choir serves as the musically trained partner of the worshiping congregation for the purpose of helping its worship, singing with the congregation to the glory of God and the edification of man.

The specific tasks to be undertaken by the choir in fulfilling its proper function may be ranked in order of importance:

1. The choir encourages hearty and devout participation by the people in the liturgy and hymns that are assigned to the congregation.
2. The choir sings the texts of the liturgy assigned to it; it may also, upon occasion, sing the texts that are now usually given to the people or the pastor but for which liturgical precedent made choral provision.
3. The choir sings such music attendant to the liturgy as may be appropriate and possible.

Each of the specific tasks cited above will now be viewed in relation to the major Lutheran services of worship: The Eucharist or Holy Communion, the Offices of Matins and Vespers, and other orders of worship. No particular attention is devoted to differences in worship resources between small or large congregations, to small or large choirs, or to choirs of children or choirs of adults. Such differences are not generally important, for sufficiently numerous musical possibilities are present in all congregations, and literature exists for all sorts and conditions of choirs. The ability to translate the above assignments into reality depends largely on the wisdom and competence of the choral and pastoral leadership.

None of the foregoing should be interpreted as a discouragement of congregational song. Quite the opposite is the intent; the extensive and perhaps elaborate choral participation to be articulated below is proposed to enliven the worship experience of both congregation and choir. Much of the choir's effort (e.g., in The Hymn of the Week) is to be aimed directly at improving and intensifying congregational participation.

1. *In order to encourage hearty and devout participation by the people in the liturgy and hymns, the choir must take an active part by learning to sing these songs of the people well.* Not all of the familiar chants are sung by the people with equal skill, accuracy, and enthusiasm. Not all hymns are sung well by the congregation. Though the organist may try to improve the phrasing or attack in hymns and liturgy, a choir of human voices can often clarify the confusing passages more easily, efficiently, and gracefully. A choir, either by demonstration on a given Sunday, or by sheer persistence in the proper singing of the passage, can subtly improve congregational singing calcified by years of neglect or indifference. Remedial work on the familiar liturgy and hymns demands a commitment by the choir to serve the congregation, to assist the people in their song.

The choir can also encourage congregational singing by performing sections of the liturgy in alternation with the people. Ever since the ancient Jews sang psalms antiphonally (alternating phrases between two groups) or responsorially (alternating phrases between a leader and a group), church musicians have taken advantage of the stimulation offered by such performance. Certain songs and canticles of the liturgy, such as the Gloria in excelsis and the nine-fold Kyrie, lend themselves to performance in alternation between congregation and choir. When such alternation is introduced with proper explanation and performed with skill, the attention and interest of the congregation in the familiar liturgical song can be greatly heightened.

One of the greatest musical contributions of the Lutheran Reformation was the development of the practice of alternation (*alternatim praxis*) in chorale singing, in which the choir sang certain stanzas of a hymn to settings of a more elaborate or artistic nature in alternation with the singing of simpler settings of stanzas by the congregation. The choir is able to add special emphasis to a hymn-text by performance of a setting or harmonization of the melody that is different from that of the hymnal, and the congregation can meditate on the text sung by its partner, the choir, while it gathers strength to sing the following stanza. The performance of each partner is improved by hearing the challenge of the other. While the practice must not be distorted to the point that the choir dominates hymn singing, the use of available polyphonic or concerted chorale settings by the choir can be both stimulating to the congregation and satisfying to the choir.

Both hymns and liturgical songs can from time to time be embellished in various ways, e.g., with vocal and instrumental descants, effective use of handbells, and varied organ accompaniment. The effect of singing liturgical songs in the same way in both penitential and joyous seasons can be deadening to meaningful worship. The choir can play an important role in reflecting the significance of the day in the type of embellishment selected for the liturgy.

With increasing frequency congregations are seeking the stimulation and refreshment offered by the introduction of new settings of the familiar liturgical texts as well as new hymns and new melodies to old hymns. The choir that seeks to encourage participation by the people will naturally lead in the introduction in easy stages of any new song intended for the people. After demonstration of a new setting, perhaps spread over several weeks, the congregation may be asked to join in all or part of the new music, while the choir will remain alert to any developing insecurity on the part of the congregation. If entirely new orders of worship are introduced, the leadership role of the choir becomes even more crucial.

Every congregation ought to experience the joy that comes from learning to sing a new hymn well. Our present hymnals have outstanding hymns from all periods of history; yet many congregations have not learned some of the oldest—or newest—and best hymns. The responsibility for remedying this neglect belongs in large part to the choir.[2]

2. *In Lutheran worship the choir sings the texts of the liturgy assigned to it.* For several centuries the church has assigned to its choirs the texts that change with each Sunday or festival. These texts, called the propers, vary according to the particular theme of the day. The propers traditionally used in Lutheran worship include the Introit (or Introit Psalm) at the beginning of the Holy Communion service, the Gradual (or Gradual Psalm), Alleluia or Tract, and Sequence Hymn, all placed between the Scripture readings. It is also appropriate for the Lutheran choir to sing two other propers with changing texts: the Offertory at the time of the gathering of the offerings, and the Communion, sung during the distribution of the Sacrament. The choir that does not sing the propers loses by default its historic privilege of underscoring the theme of the day with special music.

The choir may also occasionally sing the texts that now are usually given to the people or the pastor but for which liturgical precedent has made choral provision. Foremost in this category are settings of the unchanging ordinary (Kyrie, Gloria in excelsis, Credo, Sanctus, Agnus Dei). Christian choirs can be grateful that, with certain exceptions, the body of liturgical texts has remained quite constant through the ages—not only in outline, but also in detail. Many of the texts in the liturgical portion of the major hymnals are of considerable antiquity and have had international currency. Choral settings of the ordinary include music by a host of eminent composers. From the 14th to the 18th century a composer's worth often was judged by the quality of his composition of the ordinary of the mass. As a result, thousands of Kyrie, Gloria in excelsis, Credo, Sanctus, and Agnus Dei settings are available for performance by contemporary church choirs. While it is true that many of these compositions are hard to prepare and perform, many present no great technical problems and could be prepared as easily as many anthems. By singing these important compositions, especially on festival occasions, the choir can lead the congregation to ponder anew the spiritual truths expressed in the timeless texts, which will then assume new meaning for singer and listener alike.

3. *The choir also has the opportunity to present music that is attendant to the liturgy,* though not a designated part of it. The large body of nonliturgical choral literature that has developed since the 16th century is often called, in the aggregate, "anthem." The purpose of the anthem has varied over the centuries. From earliest times in the Church of England it had a quasi-liturgical function,[3] but by the 19th century it was far removed from the liturgy in function and in spirit. Then, as now, it served a function not unlike that of the nonliturgical sermon.

At best, the aim of the anthem is to present to worshipers an uplifting musical discourse on a sacred text closely related to the theme of the service. It may stimulate, inspire, ennoble, and please the hearer, and as such be of considerable value. But quite often an anthem chosen to fill no other role than to please the hearer fails to do more than that. Because such music is first chosen for its "beauty," it often does little more than "beautify" the service. In contrast to the liturgical music and hymns discussed above, the anthem often exists solely unto itself, even when it speaks to the theme of the day. The greatest danger in the excessive singing of anthems by the church choir, therefore, is not the possible selection of unworthy music—though it must be admitted that that danger is great. The chief peril encountered in the anthem repertoire is that beguiling music will lead the choir astray from its reason for existence; that service, the noblest goal of church choral performance, will be debased into mere choral pleasure and pride.

The music of the anthem has a rewarding and respected position in choral literature. Every choir should have the pleasure of preparing and performing anthems, and every congregation should hear anthems from time to time, but choirs that emphasize this attendant repertoire must always remain sensitive to the more critical needs of the worshiper and the more rigorous discipline of the liturgy. In a very real sense the choir must remain the servant of the liturgy in order to render its greatest service to the congregation.

The Participants

For much of its life the church has supported its musicians by payment of money or goods, usually combined with educational opportunities. In royal chapels supported by the nobility, as well as, in cathedrals and establishments supported directly by the church, the musicians were generally engaged in full-time service and would today be called "professional" musicians. In the course of the 18th and 19th centuries support from these two sources gradually declined, until today, with some noteworthy exceptions, many church choirs, particularly those in the United States, are composed of amateur musicians who volunteer their service to the church. While the loss of patronage for church musicians has resulted in an apparent decline of musical quality, the accompanying change of emphasis has been largely salutary for the faith-life of the church. Choir membership once again requires, as it did in the ancient church, primarily a desire to serve the Lord and His people in song.

The image of the choir member as servant is seen clearly from the perspective of the goal of the church choir, which is to provide support, encouragement, and enrichment for the worship of the congregation. This goal has two components, one musical and the other devotional.

The musical component is foremost, demanding the most perfect choral performance possible, given human limitations of time and talent. The devotional component is also significant, but it flows naturally from a proper understanding of Christian faith and worship, as well as the acceptance by the choir of its position as servant of the people of God at worship.

The success enjoyed by the church choir is not measured by the difficulty of its repertoire or the number or loyalty of its members, but rather by its continual demonstration of willingness to serve, that is, to help inspire the congregation to sing and worship at the highest level of devotion and praise.

The leader of the church choir should be the most qualified person available for the position. While it is not easy to identify the ideal director, certain qualifications suggest themselves as essential:

1. A strong Christian faith that expresses itself naturally in word and action.

2. A positive personality that enables easy working relationships with the church's pastor and members; that is optimistic and buoyant, yet modest and sincere; that inspires confidence by being friendly, yet fair and decisive; that reflects a sense of humor.

3. A sensitivity to the needs and limitations of the choir and the

congregation, and to the requirements and possibilities of liturgical worship.

4. A thorough understanding of the art of choral directing and all that it entails, especially musical fundamentals, literature, history, analysis, interpretation, and vocal technique. The ability to perform acceptably on some solo instrument (preferably keyboard and voice) is most desirable.

5. A capacity to grow in knowledge and skill in all matters—liturgical, musical, and personal—relating to choral leadership.

The choral ensembles that comprise a good music program vary from church to church. Ideally, every parish member who is seriously interested in singing and is able to rehearse regularly should have the opportunity to participate in a choir. The multiple-choir program, which can make this goal a reality, should be developed by every congregation as an extension of its worship and education functions. In addition to increased involvement, one of the chief advantages of the multiple-choir program is the possibility of the appearance of at least one choir in every worship service. The burden of an unrelieved schedule of performance every Sunday by a single choir is thus lightened as others share the opportunities to sing. The specific groups to be formed can be chosen from the suggestions given below as adapted to the membership and resources of the congregation and the skill and ingenuity of its leaders.

Almost any group of children, teenagers, young adults, or mature adults can be fashioned into an effective church choir, provided they are willing to work to develop their abilities. The task will be easier if some sort of homogeneity of membership can be achieved, but it is important that one not begin with the fixed assumption that a certain disposition of singers (e.g., eight sopranos, six altos, six tenors, and eight basses) is the only true church choir, and that any group less perfectly "balanced" than this will produce inferior results. A repertoire that will fulfill the true purpose of a church choir already exists, or can be created, for almost any combination of voices that might appear. The standard adult mixed choir is but one of many groups that can serve as the musical partner of the congregation.

In planning choral organizations for a church, it is most productive to concentrate on groups of people of similar age, education, marital status, and employment who often have similar interests and free hours for rehearsal. Following is a list of some typical groups that may be considered. Listed after each is the likely range of vocal possibilities that might be expected:

Children, grades 2—5	(S to SA)
Children, grades 5—6	(S to SA)
Children, grades 4—8	(S to SSA)
Children, all boys, grades 4—8	(S to SSA(T))
Children, all girls, grades 4—8	(S to SSA)
Teenage, grades 7—9	(S to SAB)
Teenage, grades 10—12	(S,B to SATB)
High school, grades 8—12	(S,A,B to SATB)
Young adults	(S,B to SATB)
Young couples	(S,B to SATB)
Adult	(S,B to SATB)
Family choir	(S,B, to SATB)
Men	(B to TTBB)
Women	(S to SSAA)
Senior ladies	(S to SSAA)
Senior couples	(S to SATB)
Midweek school	(S to SAB)
Saturday school	(S to SAB)
Choir school	(S to SSA)
Confirmation class	(S to SAB)
Summer choir	(S to SATB)

Some choirs may be best identified by a specific repertoire, although most of the groups suggested here, except possibly the first, would sing music in four or more parts:

Chant choir (*Schola cantorum*)
Motet choir (*Figural* choir)
Chorale choir
Cantata choir
Contemporary choir (Folk-music choir)
Festival choir

While choirs are ideally formed to fulfill a yearlong singing schedule, it may be necessary to form groups for shorter periods of time if potential singers prefer a short-term commitment. The time periods suggested here correspond generally to the church year divisions:

136

Advent-Christmas	6 weeks
Epiphany	up to 9 weeks
Lenten	6 weeks
Lenten-Easter	14 weeks
Easter	8 weeks
Early Pentecost	early summer, 7—9 weeks
Mid-Pentecost	midsummer, 7—9 weeks
Late Pentecost	fall, 7—9 weeks

The plan requires a great amount of organizational effort by the director, but it provides for flexible individual membership and may have strong appeal in some situations. It is also an attractive means of initiating choral activity in small or newly formed parishes where no choral program exists.

Any of the adult groups listed above that grow in size to over 30 members may contain enough competent singers to form a modern *favorit*, or core choir of from four to eight voices, patterned after the 17th-century Lutheran groups of especially skilled singers who performed in double-choir works with the larger choir (*capella*) and even taught vocal techniques to less experienced singers. A modern *favorit* could be expected to participate in performance of works from the polychoral repertoire.[4] It could also sing some of the liturgical items beyond the limitations of ability or time of the full choir. Certain sections of the liturgy can be performed effectively by an inner choir of voices singing in alternation with the full choir. The singing of a selected chorale stanza by the *favorit* provides a delightful contrast when placed between the sections sung by the full choir.

Not all of the "choirs" of the church need be large. Small ensembles of gifted and willing singers can also perform the function of helping the congregation at worship to sing the hymns and liturgy. Trios, quartets, quintets, and similar combinations of voices can develop sufficient skill and confidence to make an important contribution to worship.

While choral performance of music in the church service is generally to be preferred because of its supportive role in congregational worship, solo song also has a legitimate place in the church music program. In the first place, correct liturgical performance of some texts, such as the Introit or responsorially chanted psalms, calls for soloists (cantors) to sing a portion of the chant. Also, solo performance of an entire chant, such as the

Introit or the Psalm for the day, is appropriate when the choir is unavailable. Some standard choral works, such as baroque cantatas and Passions and English verse anthems, require the performance of soloists. Solo singing of individual stanzas of chorales or hymns with organ accompaniment in alternation with the choir can be a pleasing contrast to the sound of the full chorus. And finally, certain pieces can be selected from the vast repertoire of sacred solo song that will assist the congregation in worship. These should be focused on the theme of the day, should be musically worthy, and should be performed in a way that will not draw undue attention to the singer.

The choir director must also encourage the formation of auxiliary instrumental ensembles to support a variety of choral functions. Since instruments can also support and accompany congregational song (usually designated as the specific responsibility of the organist), the organist and choir director will need to cooperate closely to utilize the available musicians effectively.

Specific responsibilities that may be assumed by instrumental ensembles include the doubling of some or all parts of Renaissance (and to some extent baroque) polyphony, such as music by Palestrina, Orlando di Lasso, or Michael Praetorius. Occasional doubling of all choral voices by woodwind or string instruments in familiar hymn or chorale settings is an excellent means of varying the choral timbre. If a voice is weak or missing altogether, an appropriate instrument may play that line. In music from the baroque period, for example, the soprano and the bass choral parts may be doubled by soprano or bass instruments, especially strings or woodwinds. Instrumental descants, published or specially composed, have an enlivening effect on the choral singing of hymns or chorales. Concerted music of the baroque type, such as cantatas or concerted chorales and motets, usually requires the participation of instruments, especially for the *basso continuo* (bass instrument with organ).

Choral Music for the Liturgical Service

Bases for Selection

Choral music chosen for performance in church should be evaluated according to the following criteria: liturgical propriety,[5] musical quality, and suitability for the performing group.

Choral music should be chosen for its capacity to contribute to a liturgical worship service for three reasons. First, the liturgical repertoire is of immense size and of high quality. Settings of the texts of the ordinary of the mass (e.g., Sanctus and Agnus Dei), the canticles (such as the Magnificat or Te Deum) or the Psalms, comprise an almost inexhaustible source of sacred choral music. This repertoire includes a large number of choral masterworks that could again find a congenial home in the liturgy.

Second, liturgical texts are a vehicle of contemporary musical expression. Masses, canticles, and psalm compositions are being published in settings in many musical styles for a variety of performers. Liturgical choral performance offers not merely a revival of the best and most useful of the past but also a utilization of the excellent work of contemporary musicians.

Third, the capacity of the liturgical text vividly and succinctly to encapsulate the essence of the divine proclamation of Scripture and the adoring response of the believer is unrivaled by any other body of Christian literature. In addition, few texts are as familiar as the liturgical texts of Christian worship. For example, nearly all Christian denominations have found some place in their worship for the Kyrie eleison or the great psalm texts. These texts evoke a host of familiar associations and serve as a reminder of the fellowship all Christians share as members of the body of Christ.

Music to be sung to the glory of God and the edification of man should reflect the high regard in which the Christian holds his Lord and his neighbor. Thus, every choral composition selected should give evidence of high musical quality, whether it is of simple or complex construction, whether it is intended for adults or children. If both choir and congregation are steadily confronted with excellent music, they will gradually develop powers of understanding and appreciation that will result in an enriched worship life.

Choral music should also be selected for its appropriateness to the performing group. Most choirs attempt music that is too difficult or that was intended originally for another type of choir (often from a misguided desire to "impress" the hearers). Small and inexperienced adult choirs, as well as children's choirs or youth choirs, should first consider performing unison hymn or liturgical arrangements with varied organ accompaniment. All choirs, even those composed of children, can enjoy the process of learning to chant well. Also suitable for small adult choirs or youth choirs are two-part mixed voice arrangements of hymns and liturgy. Large oratorio forms are not intended for performance by small choirs of untrained voices, no matter how enjoyable they may be to sing.

The ensuing discussion will present a few examples of liturgical choral literature in the context of the modern services of the church. The examples cited are but suggestions of an approach to choral literature that will encourage the choir to sing excellent music in its most natural setting.

The Holy Communion (Eucharist)[6]
Liturgical Texts Suitable for Regular Use

The Introit, the "entrance" text that traditionally marks the beginning of the service and notes the theme of the day, is to be sung in its entirety by the choir. The full texts consists of Antiphon, Psalm verse(s), Gloria Patri, and repeated Antiphon. Several excellent settings of the traditional proper Introit texts for the entire church year are:

Bunjes, Paul. *The Service Propers Noted.* St. Louis: Concordia Publishing House, 1960. Formulary Tone (chant) settings.

Burgess, Francis, ed. *The English Gradual, Pt. II: The Proper for the Liturgical Year.* London: Plainchant Publications Committee; U.S. selling agent, New York: H. W. Gray, [n.d.]. Simple Gregorian chant.

Buszin, Walter E., ed. *The Introits for the Church Year.* St. Louis: Concordia Publishing House, 1942. Simple Gregorian chant; Preface provides a good introduction to chant.

Christensen, Albert O., and Harold E. Schuneman, eds. *Proper of the Service.* New York: H. W. Gray, 1947. Moderately elaborate Gregorian chant; also includes proper Offertories.

Ensrud, Paul, ed. *Introits and Graduals for the Lutheran Service, Series A: Psalm Tone Settings,* 6 vols. Minneapolis: Augsburg Publishing House, 1960—64. Simple Gregorian chant.

Fryxell, Regina H. *Introits and Graduals for the Church Year,* 2 Vols. Philadelphia: Fortress Press, 1967—68. Easy settings for mixed choir.

Wetzler, Robert. *Introits,* 5 vols. Minneapolis: Augsburg Publishing House, 1964-65. Contemporary settings in various styles for mixed, unison, and solo voices; some have organ accompaniment; congregational (or choir) singing of SBH Gloria Patri settings possible.

Willan, Healey. *The Introits and Graduals for the Church Year.* St. Louis: Concordia Publishing House, 1967. Smoothly written mixed choir and chant settings.

The Introit psalm chosen for a given day was, in ancient usage, a complete psalm and Gloria Patri with a preparatory and concluding verse (Antiphon) to set the textual theme. The ancient practice may be revived by the choral singing of an "entrance" psalm. Such singing of complete psalm texts is often appropriate for liturgical processions on festivals.[7]

The occasional substitution of an appropriate motet or concerted arrangement of the Entrance Psalm is an option that must be exercised with care. Liturgical propriety suggests caution concerning frequent use of large or dramatic settings, even if the text is that of the full proper psalm. The singing of a single psalm verse in an anthem arrangement may also be questioned because of the hazards inherent in breaking off a fragment from a poetic whole.

The Intervenient Songs (Gradual, Alleluia or Tract, Sentence for the Season, Sequence Hymn). The appointed readings for the service form a trilogy from Holy Scripture presented for special attention on each Sunday or festival. Dividing the three Lessons are appointed proper texts, usually from the Psalms, which form a commentary on, or response to, the Lessons and the theme of the day. From several points of view—practical, dramatic, theological, and musical—the chants that come between the readings assume considerable importance. At the very least, the Lessons and the Gospel are given added emphasis by the connecting and complementary texts and music.

The Gradual, historically sung after the first Lesson, is usually composed of psalm verses. Several types of musical settings of the texts are available. Performance of the chanted forms will reflect the ancient responsorial practice if small and large groups within the choir alternate by half-verses. Except for that of Buszin, the collections cited above under "Introit" all contain the historic Gradual texts. The following collection contains Gradual settings in Anglican Chant:

> Buszin, Walter E., and Erwin Kurth, eds. *The Graduals for the Church Year.* St. Louis: Concordia Publishing House, 1944. Preface contains valuable information on the Gradual and on Anglican chant performance.

The Alleluia consists of the word "Alleluia" sung twice and a psalm verse, followed by a single "Alleluia." It is properly performed after the Second Lesson (Epistle), or immediately following the Gradual if only one Lesson is read. The collections of Graduals all contain the Alleluia as well, but in some cases the arrangements make separation of the two items difficult, if not impossible. The settings by Bunjes, Willan, Ensrud, and

Burgess have separable Alleluias. Where possible, the performance of the chant settings should reflect the responsorial nature of the text.

The Tract replaces the Alleluia in Lent or on penitential days. It consists of several psalm verses without Antiphon or response. All of the Gradual collections cited above include the Tract as a replacement for the Alleluia.

The Sentence for the Season consists of traditional phrases of Scripture, usually from the Psalms, applied for an entire season of the church year with an eye towards providing a liturgical text that would serve the choir for several consecutive services within a season. The related Gradual for the season (*SBH*) consists of a single Gradual elevated to the status of a seasonal text. The texts are quite appropriate and merit performance if the proper Gradual and Alleluia cannot be sung. Useful settings of the Sentence texts are:

> Buszin, Walter E., and Erwin Kurth, eds. *The Graduals for the Church Year.* St. Louis: Concordia Publishing House, 1944. Three sets of Sentences: Gregorian chant, Anglican chang, and four-part settings.

The Sequence Hymn is a Gregorian Hymn for the Day, which historically follows immediately after the Alleluia. From a very large repertoire of sequences for all seasons and festivals of the church year only a few designated for certain festivals remain in use today, but these few are of exceedingly high quality and have wide currency. An outstanding example is the Easter Sequence, "Victimae paschali," which not only appears in modern hymnals but forms the basis of several German and English hymns, of which "Christ lag in Todesbanden" ("Christ Jesus Lay in Death's Strong Bands") is probably the most famous. Gregorian sequences that appear in modern hymnals and are suitable for choral or congregational performance are:

> "Veni, Sancte Spiritus." (Pentecost) *TEH*[8] 155 "Come, Thou Holy Paraclete" (additional tune); *EpH*[9] 109 "Come, Thou Holy Spirit, Come!" (additional tune); *SBH* 121 "Come, Holy Ghost, in Love" (rev. text, other tune), *TLH* 227 (rev. text, other tune); Buszin and Kurth. *Graduals*, pp. 44-47 "Holy Spirit, Come, We Pray."
>
> "Victimae paschali." (Easter) *TEH* 130 "Christians, to the Paschal Victim;" also *EpH* 97; Buszin and Kurth. *Graduals*, pp. 32-35; *WS* 741 "The Victimae Paschali Celebration" (includes "Christ is Arisen").
>
> "Lauda, Sion, Salvatorem." (Maundy Thursday/Holy Communion) *TEH*

317 "Laud, O Sion, Thy Salvation;" *EpH* 193, 194 "Sion, Praise Thy Savior, Singing" (additional tune).

"Dies irae, dies illa." (Judgment, the Departed) *TEH* 351 "Day of Wrath and Doom Impending; " *EpH* 468 "Day of Wrath! O Day of Mourning;" also *TLH* 607 (other tune).

"Stabat mater." (Good Friday) *TEH* 115 "At the Cross Her Station Keeping" (two additional tunes); also *SBH* 84 (other tune), *EpH* 76 (additional tune).

Other sequence hymns that may be useful are in *TEH:* "Laetabundus" (Christmas), "Solus aeterna" (Advent), "Jerusalem et Sion filiae" (Dedication Festival), and "Sponsa Christi quae per orbem" (All Saints). After the choir has sung the simple Plainsong form of the Sequence, polyphonic or contemporary settings may be explored. Some of the Sequences in modern hymnals could be performed by choir and congregation in alternation, for example, following the plan involving "Victimae paschali" and its descendant "Christ is arisen," given in *WS* 741.

The Psalm of the Day may be sung in its entirety between the first two lessons as an Intervenient Song or Gradual Psalm. Various forms of chant or metrical psalmody are available for performance as well as polyphonic, concerted, or anthem compositions.[10]

The Hymn of the Day (Hymn of the Week, De tempore Hymn, Gradual Hymn). The Reformation practice of singing appointed hymns related closely to the theme of the day or festival developed in the course of time into a series of hymns as propers.[11] A number of Hymn-of-the-Week plans are now available, each of which reflects certain cultural inclinations of those proposing it.[12] Whichever plan is followed, the Hymn of the Day should be the first hymn to receive the attention of the choir for possible embellishment or for application of the practice of alternation. Fortunately, many of the historic selections are still popular hymns, and they have inspired choral and organ settings of great beauty by important composers.

The most effective method of choral participation in the Hymn of the Day is simply to sing alternate stanzas with the congregation. For its stanzas the choir may sing in unison to a varied accompaniment or may sing in parts to one of the available settings. Two examples illustrate the potential of the plan to use the choir as a partner of the congregation. In the first example the choir assists the people to sing a long hymn of outstanding quality:

"Salvation Unto Us Has Come" (*TLH* 377)
stanza	1	Congregation
stanza	2	Congregation
stanza	3	Choir, setting by J. S. Bach*
stanza	4	Congregation
stanza	5	Choir, setting by Hans Chemin-Petit*
stanza	6	Congregation
stanza	7	Choir, setting by J. S. Bach
stanza	8	Congregation
stanza	9	Choir, setting by Hans Chemin-Petit
stanza	10	Congregation

The second example is that of a magnificent chorale of three stanzas that might receive special choral treatment:

"Wake, Awake, for Night Is Flying" (*SBH* 7; *TLH* 609)
stanza 1	Congregation
stanza 2	Choir, setting by Bartholomaeus Gesius*
stanza 3	Congregation

Many other possibilities will suggest themselves to the imaginative director, but close attention must be paid to several practical and musical considerations: choir and congregation settings must be in the same or closely related keys, or a suitable modulation must be prepared. If congregation and choir join to sing together, the rhythmic and melodic features of both settings must complement each other. The hymnal texts of choir stanzas may need to be written into the choral scores to secure the proper progression of stanzas. The final stanza of the hymn should be assigned to the congregation; it may be best for the congregation also to sing the first stanza. The alternation concept should not be distorted by an excessively lengthy setting for the choir stanzas, although hymns with few stanzas can accommodate longer alternations.[13]

*The setting by Bach suggested in this example may be found in *The Hymn of the Week*, 5 vols., ed. Paul Thomas (St. Louis: Concordia Publishing House, 1961), V, 14—15; that by Hans Chemin-Petit in *The SAB Chorale Book*, ed. Paul Thomas (St. Louis: Concordia Publishing House, 1956), 14—15; that by Bartholomaeus Gesius, published separately by Concordia Publishing House, n.d.

Liturgical Texts Suitable for Occasional Use

The following suggestions concern musical settings not intended for regular performance in weekly services, but only for periodic performance on special days. The suggested texts include the ordinary of the mass, which comprises a large repertoire of liturgical music suitable for modern performance in church. At most, only one or two of the following items would be sung in any single service. Balance between choral and congregational assignments, as well as the continuity of the liturgy, must always be maintained. Many of the excellent and highly useful settings of the ordinary remain in Latin. When the original text is sung, the people should be provided with a parallel translation of the original, especially for the long texts (Gloria in excelsis, Credo, and Sanctus).

Kyrie. The modern three-fold or six-fold forms of the Kyrie are historic remnants of a longer, litany-type Kyrie. Normal practice through much of the church's history has been to sing a nine-fold Kyrie (a three-fold statement of each phrase: "Lord, have mercy upon us; Christ, have mercy upon us; Lord, have mercy upon us").

An element of variety and interest could be introduced into the singing of the Kyrie if the men and women of the choir were to sing the litany form or the six-fold form of the Kyrie in *SBH* or *WS* in alternation.

While the litany-type Kyrie text has much to commend it for regular use, the occasional singing of a Gregorian, polyphonic, concerted, or other setting of the three-fold or nine-fold Kyrie eleison text could provide a special emphasis for festival worship.

A traditional Lutheran chorale substitute for the Kyrie is "Kyrie, Gott Vater in Ewigkeit" ("Kyrie, God Father in Heaven Above," *TLH* 6), which forms in essence a litany-type, through-composed setting in the form of a *Leise*. Harmonized versions of this chorale for *a cappella* or concerted choir would be suitable alternates to congregational singing of the Kyrie.

Gloria in excelsis. Varied performance of the Gloria in excelsis text is surely one of the most effective means of heightening the special nature of a festival service. A simple plan that takes advantage of the three major divisions of the hymn and the antiphon-character of the initial phrase allows for antiphonal performance between men and women of the congregation, or between people sitting on one side of the church and those on the other, or between choir and congregation. The Antiphon could properly be repeated by all at the conclusion of the hymn:

Antiphon (Leader) (All)	Glory be to God on high And on earth, peace, good will toward men.
Stanza 1 (Men or Group 1)	We praise Thee, we bless Thee, we worship Thee, we glorify Thee, we give thanks to Thee for Thy great glory. O Lord God, heavenly King, God the Father Almighty.
Stanza 2 (Women or Group 2)	O Lord, the only-begotten Son, Jesus Christ; O Lord God, Lamb of God, Son of the Father, that takest away the sin of the world, have mercy upon us. Thou that takest away the sin of the world, receive our prayer. Thou that sittest at the right hand of God the Father, have mercy upon us.
Stanza 3 (All)	For Thou only art holy; Thou only art the Lord; Thou only, O Christ, with the Holy Ghost, art most high in the glory of God the Father. Amen.
Antiphon repeated (All)	Glory be to God on High, and on earth, peace, good will toward men.[14]

Another plan of alternation for the Gloria in excelsis involving more frequent exchange is found in Eucharist I of *WS*. The Gloria in excelsis sung by the congregation on festivals could also be embellished by special instrumental accompaniment, even though that be only the simple doubling of the melody.

Simple choral settings of the Greater Gloria are found in abundance. Various congregational settings are also available to choirs. Chorale settings of the Gloria in excelsis, such as "Allein Gott in der Hoeh' sei Ehr'" ("All Glory Be to God on High." *SBH* 132; *TLH* 237), or "All' Ehr' und Lob" ("All Glory Be to God Alone," *TLH* 238) have been popular substitutes for the liturgical texts since the early days of the Reformation. While they do not fully match the succinct grandeur of the original, the

146

chorales are valued for quality of text and music and because of the additional musical possibilities they suggest. A chorale version could be sung in alternation between choir and congregation, the choir singing its stanzas to any of the many available chorale settings.

Various Lutheran liturgies have allowed the singing of other canticles in place of the Gloria in excelsis. (In traditional penitential observances it is omitted altogether.) The ILCW *CW2 Services: The Holy Communion* suggests the canticle "Worthy Is Christ" as a substitute, especially in Eastertide.

Credo. The singing of the Creed by the people has an ancient heritage; yet, perhaps because of the length of its prose text, the Creed has not been sung as much in English as have other mass texts. The musical setting of the Creed has much to commend it, especially on festivals or in services that seek to stress the unity of the body of Christ, the doctrines of the church, or the persons and work of the Trinity.

Congregations that do not sing the Creed would find satisfaction and meaning in the introduction of Luther's hymn paraphrase of the Nicene Creed, "Wir glauben all' an einen Gott" ("We All Believe in One True God," *TLH* 251) or in a setting of the Apostles' Creed ("We All Believe in One True God," *TLH* 252, or "In One True God We All Believe," *TLH* 253). The sturdy chorale melody of *TLH* 251, second tune, is musically the most satisfying of the group and presents the greatest potential as a source for chorale-based compositions for the choir.

The choir or the congregation could sing the old Gregorian melody, which has appeared in the settings of the Holy Communion service by Healey Willan and Jan Bender. This "De angelis" chant has a long history of popular usage, perpetuated by many Christians in the 20th century. The third setting of the *SBH* Holy Communion service also contains a fine Credo.[15]

Chant or polyphonic Credo settings or settings with instruments could replace the text spoken or sung by the congregation on special days, thereby heightening the congregation's understanding and appreciation of the text.

Sanctus (and *Benedictus*). Always grouped together in the liturgy, though separated in some musical compositions, these two texts form a musical high point in the Eucharist. In the Sanctus the faithful join in song with the seraphim before the throne of God in Isaiah's vision and with the throngs welcoming Jesus into Jerusalem. The congregation's song at this point is to be sung with enthusiasm and verve. It could well be sung with a special accompaniment of instruments.

Luther's "Sanctus" chorale "Jesaia, dem Propheten, das geschah" ("Isaiah, Mighty Seer," *TLH* 249), an excellent song in its own right, is the least satisfactory of the liturgical chorales of the early Reformation when used as a substitute for the full liturgical text. It presents only a paraphrase of Isaiah 6:1-4 and ignores the Benedictus. Nevertheless, it is a significant chorale deserving consideration as an occasional substitute for the Sanctus. A similar melody by Lucas Lossius with the complete Sanctus text has been set for mixed choir by Paul Bunjes.[16]

Other Sanctus compositions in chant, polyphonic, concerted, or modern choral settings include some of the finest of all choral literature.

Agnus Dei. This ancient hymn of the mass may be regarded as the first hymn of the congregation during the Distribution. Its text form suggests performance in a variety of ways. Choir and congregation could sing the three stanzas of the Agnus Dei in alternation, using any of the variety of familiar harmonizations of "Christe, du Lamm Gottes" ("O Christ, Thou Lamb of God"). The congregation may also be introduced to the melodies of other settings of the Agnus Dei through choral performance of other worthy settings.

The 16th-century chorale "O Lamm Gottes" ("Lamb of God, Pure and Holy," *TLH* 146; "O Lamb of God, Most Holy!" *SBH* 70) presents an alternate text for the common Agnus Dei.

The place of the Agnus Dei at the beginning of the Distribution suggests that it could easily be performed in extended choral settings without lengthening the service at all. Settings originating in the Renaissance, such as those of Victoria, di Lasso, Palestrina, or Byrd, would be effective and concerted settings, such as those by Buxtehude, Charpentier, and Purcell or contemporary settings would probably match the spirit of festive days.

Offertory. Choirs may find a potentially congenial location for a musical "offering" at the position of the general gathering of the offerings of the people. Traditionally, the chant sung at this point in the mass consisted of psalm verses with an antiphon appropriate to the particular theme of the day in the church year. In the course of time the psalms were shortened until only the antiphon remained as a covering chant for the offering of the people.

In modern Lutheran practice the concept of the Offertory has changed, and the once practical and richly liturgical body has atrophied, assuming the nature of a mass ordinary.

Rather than search for performance possibilities to enhance the present texts, admirable as they may be, the church musician could well use another suitable Offertory based on the psalms and related to the theme of the day. The choir could regularly perform the Offertory Psalm according to one of the many settings listed below under "Psalms and Canticles": Gregorian or Anglican Chant, Metrical Psalmody, or Gelineau Psalmody. When the setting is appropriate, the Offertory Psalm performance could include participation by the congregation. From a practical point of view, texts and musical settings should be chosen that approximate the length of time ordinarily needed for the gathering of offerings.

Music Sung During Distribution of Holy Communion. It is particularly appropriate for congregation and choir to sing music for the day while the worshipers attend the Lord's Table. The traditional proper texts, called the Communion, are available in Gregorian settings for choir. However, these brief texts are not sufficiently long to cover the time required for the action.

Two additional types of musical composition suggest themselves for performance during the Distribution: hymn-based music for choir and congregation and independent choral music.

Hymns sung by the people during the Distribution provide an excellent vehicle for focusing on the theme of the day, the Holy Communion, the person and work of Jesus Christ, Christian service, witness, mission, praise, and thanksgiving. The choir can assist in the singing of hymns by the congregation through the practice of alternation. The choir can also introduce unfamiliar hymns to the people by singing them in their entirety.

Independent choir music can be performed, provided that the composition emphasizes the themes suggested above for hymns to be sung during the Distribution. Large choral compositions, including cantatas can be performed here without lengthening the service unduly. Care must be taken that the choral performance not distract the communing worshiper through excessively dramatic or subjective qualities.

Other Liturgical Texts for Occasional Use

A body of choral literature has developed that is attendant to several items in the liturgy not yet discussed. Each of the texts to be identified next was deemed appropriate for musical composition at some point in the history of the church; however, when the liturgical emphasis of an age changed, the tradition of setting that part of the liturgy to music also lost popularity. None of the texts suggested below are appropriate today for regular musical performance, but the musical settings of the texts can contribute to worship, and the sung texts are best understood in the environment of the liturgy.

The Collect. The Collect for the Day is that prayer which gathers together the thoughts of the congregation in relation to the theme of the day and expresses them in a few terse, significant words. The historic Collects are unmatched for beauty and concision, and a few excellent musical settings are available.

The Old Testament and New Testament Lessons and the Gospel. Many composers have set portions of the historic Scripture Lessons or Gospels for the day to music.[17] The settings, written mostly in the 16th and 17th centuries, were probably performed in proximity to the readings themselves. A large number were written on the Gospels in German and may have been sung just before or after the reading of the Gospel or perhaps between successive parallel readings in Latin and German. It is also possible that, since the entire Gospel was chanted as a normal practice, the few verses of the polyphonic Gospel motets were simply inserted at the appropriate position in the middle of the Gospel chant of the pastor, who then resumed the chant upon completion of the motet. The Scripture text settings are often memorable and provide fresh insights into the reading. Contemporary congregations should have an opportunity to share the experience of a sung Gospel or Lesson.

Some choral Gospel settings could be placed just after the reading of the Gospel, while others could be positioned before the Gospel reading or even during the Distribution. The best location for a few probably is in the course of the reading of the Gospel itself as described above.

Lord's Prayer. Numerous choral settings of the Our Father have appeared in print, many of them expressive, restrained, dignified, and worthy. Choral performance of such settings in the liturgy could help a congregation in worship, but the pitfalls of vocal display, exaggerated effects, and distraction of the worshiper are real. If used, such choral settings must not prolong the liturgy unduly at the moment the congregation awaits the consecration and reception of the Sacrament.

Nunc dimittis. After the people have received the Lord's body and blood, the Sacrament draws to a speedy conclusion with Simeon's Song of

Thanksgiving. The Anglican or Gregorian Chant settings in Lutheran hymnals provide adequate musical vehicles for the text. On occasion, these or other brief settings could be sung by the choir in unison or in harmony. Additional English-language settings of the canticle are available in great variety.

Liturgical Texts Least Suitable

The Confession, Benediction, and the brief Versicles and Responses have been performed by church choirs at various times and places and under certain unique circumstances. While theological or liturgical thought does not mark musical elaboration as reprehensible, each of these texts has specific drawbacks that tend to inhibit choral performance. Participation in the liturgical portions suggested earlier should always receive the initial consideration for choral performance.

The intimate nature of the Confession, even when made in a large assembly, does not seem to lend itself to choral embellishment. While many settings of the brief versicles and congregational responses appear in American hymnals, assignment of these to the choir in place of the congregation seems to interrupt the liturgical flow of the dialog between pastor and people. Above all, the simple, reverent pronouncement by the pastor of the Aaronic Blessing can hardly be improved on—even on days of high celebration—by the singing of a choral Benediction. The quiet statement of the Lord's blessing by the shepherd of the gathered flock exercising his pastoral privilege seems to preclude choral performance. The congregational "Amen" is also best retained by the people.

Matins and Vespers

The early Lutheran reformers retained two of the eight orders of worship comprising the Office and formed them into the vernacular services of Matins for morning and Vespers for evening. These orders were furnished with a plentiful supply of constant and variable liturgical texts following the similar principle governing the ordinary and proper of the Eucharist.

The liturgical texts of Matins and Vespers afford ample opportunities for choral participation in worship. The psalms, hymns, canticles, and responsories of the morning and evening services have been set to music by some of the greatest composers of the Western world. The two services will be treated together in the ensuing discussion because the orders and the opportunities for choral participation are similar.

Liturgical Texts Suitable for Regular Use

The Psalm. The singing of psalms is one of the chief features of the historice Office. While one psalm is all that is currently designated in Lutheran hymnal rubrics, more are allowed. The regular inclusion of at least three complete psalms (or portions thereof) would be a blessing to the worshiper and permit the psalms to regain their proper and historic role. A particularly desirable feature of liturgical psalm singing is the potential emphasis of the theme or topic of the day by means of the Psalm Antiphon. The absence of a Proper Antiphon (as in metrical psalmody), however, should not inhibit the use of any psalm setting. Hymnals and lectionaries provide helpful lists of liturgically appropriate psalms; some also suggest Antiphon texts.

The choir has the opportunity to choose from the many formulary patterns, Gregorian chant, Anglican chant, *et al.*, metrical psalmody, and the thousands of polyphonic, concerted, or anthem settings based on psalm texts.[18] Many of these compositions were specifically written for the Office, and they would fit naturally into the Matins or Vespers liturgy. While the singing of complete psalm texts is always to be preferred liturgically, choral settings of selected verses of a psalm could prove to be acceptable substitutes occasionally.

Three psalms can be sung conveniently in Matins or Vespers orders in plans such as the following:

First Psalm:	Choir—Gregorian or Anglican Chant
Second Psalm:	Congregation—Metrical Psalter
Third Psalm:	Choir—Gregorian or Anglican Chant

or

First Psalm:	Congregation—Metrical Psalter
Second Psalm:	Choir—Polyphonic setting
Third Psalm:	Congregation—Metrical Psalter

Responsory. The seasonal responsories that appear in Lutheran hymnals are but a fraction of the total number once appointed to be sung at the conclusion of the reading of a Lesson in the Office. They generally consist of several phrases of psalmodic texts in a prescribed form (which includes the first part of the Gloria Patri) and reflect or comment on the readings and the day. Present reponsories are intended to be sung after the concluding Lesson. Of all the choral opportunities in the Office, responsories seems to offer the largest collection of neglected texts in the entire liturgical corpus.

Of the comparatively few examples of liturgical responsories that have appeared in print, two of the best are:

Willan, Healey. *The Responsories for the Church Year*. St. Louis: Concordia Publishing House, 1964. Simple chordal and chant settings of eleven historic texts.

Hillert, Richard. *Seasonal Responses for Unison Voices*. St. Louis: Concordia Publishing House, 1972. Six texts with keyboard or guitar accompaniment.

It is possible to view the responsory function rather freely and insert other related choral texts at this point in the office. If the association between the musical composition and the Lesson or the theme of the day is very close, the substitution could form an acceptable "response" to the Lesson; however, retention of the original responsory text form is preferred.

The Hymn. In the course of centuries of monastic worship the Office was enriched by a large repertoire of Latin hymns. Many magnificent texts have been translated into English and appear in modern hymnals, often with original Gregorian melodies. Such office hymns are particularly appropriate as the chief hymn in Matins and Vespers, for the texts breathe the spirit of the church year.

Because of its close liturgical ties to the theme of the day, the designated Hymn of the Week (sung primarily in the Eucharist) could also be placed in Matins and Vespers. Other appropriate hymns could be selected to serve as office hymn.

Some of the great office hymns are:

(Where not otherwise indicated, the tune is Gregorian.)

Advent	"Conditor alme siderum." *WS* 703 "Creator of the Stars of Night;" also *TEH* 1, *EpH* 6 (additional tune).
Christmas	"A solis ortus cardine." *TEH* 18 "From East to West, from Shore to Shore" (additional tune); also *SBH* 20 (additional tune), *WS* 709 (other tune).

Christmas/Epiphany	"Corde natus ex parentis." *WS* 721 "Of the Father's Love Begotten" ("Divinum mysterium"); also *SBH* 17, *TLH* 98, *EpH* 20, Buszin and Kurth, *Graduals*, pp. 94-95; *TEH* 613 "Of the Father's Heart Begotten."
Lent/Holy Week	"Vexilla Regis prodeunt." *TEH* 94 "The Royal Banners Forward Go;" also *WS* 730, 729 (additional tune), *SBH* 75 (additional tune), *EpH* 63 (additional tune), Buszin and Kurth, *Graduals*, pp. 96-97, *TLH* 168 (other tune).
Lent/Holy Week	"Pange, lingua." *TEH* 95, 96 "Sing, My Tongue, the Glorious Battle"; also *EpH* 66, *SBH* 61 (additional tune), *WS* 728 (other tune).
Pentecost (Trinity) Season	"O Lux beata Trinitas." *TEH* 164 "O Trinity of Blessed Light" (additional tune); also *SBH* 133 (two additional tunes), *EpH* 171 (additional tune); *TLH* 564 "O Trinity, Most Blessed Light" (other tune).
Morning	"Nocte surgentes." *TEH* 165 "Father, We Praise Thee, Now the Night Is Over" (additional tune); also *EpH* 157 (additional tune), *SBH* 204 (other tune), *WS* 788 (other tune).
Morning	"Splendor paternae gloriae." *TEH* 52 "O Splendor of God's Glory Bright;" also *EpH* 158 (additional tune), *SBH* 206 (additional tune), *TLH* 550 (other tune).
Evening	"Te lucis ante terminum." *TEH* 264 "Before the Ending of the Day" (two additional tunes); also *WS* 790 ("Jam lucis"); *EpH* 164 "To Thee Before the Close of Day."

Liturgical Texts Suitable for Occasional Use

The following are texts that could occasionally be assigned to choirs or could be shared between the congregation and the choir. Many settings of these liturgical texts are available in the choral repertoire.

Invitatory—Venite (Psalm 95). The placement of Psalm 95 with its seasonal Antiphon in the form of a versicle and response (the Invitatory stimulates an enthusiastic entry into the Matins Order. Rubrics indicate that the Invitatory is repeated after the conclusion of the Venite. The Venite itself may be set to Anglican Chant (three in *SBH*, one in *TLH*) or to newly composed melodies (*WS*, where alternation performance is specified).

The choir and congregation can sing many of the given arrangements of the Venite in phrase-by-phrase alternation. The Invitatory could also be assigned to the choir with the caution that the performance preserve the versicle and response form. Choral settings of a portion of Psalm 95 may serve in the place of the liturgical text.

Office Canticles. In Lutheran tradition Te Deum Laudamus and Benedictus are assigned to Matins; Magnificat and Nunc dimittis appear in Vespers. Festival celebration requires singing of Te Deum and Magnificat, but the occasional substitution of other canticles is suggested. Proper antiphons may be sung before and after all canticles except Te Deum.

Although congregational performance of the canticles is preferred, the choir could assist the congregation through the singing of alternate phrases (a practice specified in *WS*) on certain days, or through the performance of alternate settings. The musical literature based on the canticles is vast, and it includes compositions for all kinds of choirs. Selections from the numerous polyphonic and accompanied settings of the major canticles would enhance festival services in particular.

Kyrie. The choral options presented in the discussion of the Eucharistic Kyrie also pertain to the Kyrie of the Office. The choir can assist the congregation in singing Kyrie settings, it can introduce new Kyrie settings, or it can sing choral settings. An office Kyrie setting should not overshadow the preceding canticle, which ordinarily is the musical high point of the service.

Other Liturgical Texts for Occasional Use

Lord's Prayer and Collect. Suitably restrained, objective, and succinct settings of the Our Father or the Collect could be performed in place of the congregational or pastoral recitation, but the choral setting must enhance and not unduly dramatize the liturgical text.

Liturgical Texts Least Suitable

Although it is possible for choirs to perform versicles, responses, Gloria Patri, Litany, and Benediction, it is more important that the choir function elsewhere and that the service begin and end with the uninterrupted liturgical dialog between the leader and the people.

Preaching Services

Services outside of the liturgical Eucharist or office structure that reflect the normal practice of many non-Lutheran Protestants have been published in *WS* as "Services of Prayer and Preaching" and in the ILCW *Services of the Word*. The liturgical possibilities these services present for choral participation are quite extensive. Because of the breadth of its plan, the ILCW *CW5: Services of the Word* will be examined for choral options.

The ILCW offering presents six seasonal services, each of which contains settings for two canticles and a response for the congregation, a Hymn of the Day, and provision for "A Psalm, Hymn, or Choir Selection" after the First Lesson. Altogether, nine different traditional and new canticles are included in the services.

Liturgical choir participation in these services is much the same as in other liturgical services. The choir leads in singing the canticles and the response. Alternation between choir and congregation is designated for some of the canticles. The choir is also encouraged to participate through the musical embellishment of the Hymn of the Day, especially by means of the practice of alternation.

Special choral attention should be directed to the "Psalm, Hymn, or Choir Selection" specified after the First Lesson. The rubrics indicate the intent of encouraging psalm singing in any form at this point. Many types of choral psalm performance are available: chant, metrical psalmody, polyphonic, concerted or "anthem" type choral settings. Some of these could also involve congregational participation.

Festival or special services provide opportunity for the occasional substitution of a more elaborate choral setting of one of the designated canticles, particularly those from traditional liturgical practice. Substitution of other canticles is also possible if the character of the original is reflected in the replacement.

Two other liturgical texts, the Apostles' Creed and the Lord's Prayer, may be performed by the choir on occasion as a welcome alternative to the normal congregational recitation. Such substitution should respect the congregational nature of the liturgical item through clear and restrained projection of the text.

Psalm and Canticles

The Book of Psalms has proven over the centuries to be an almost inexhaustible well of devotional refreshment for worshipers and a rich source of inspiration for musicians. The 150 Psalms have probably been sung more than any other texts in Christian literature, for they have inspired more choral composition than any other portion of sacred Scripture. Whole psalms and canticles are regularly assigned to Matins and Vespers, and encouragement is once again being given to the use of complete psalms in the Eucharist.[19]

The traditional canticles, with the exception of the Te Deum, consist of the major songs of the Bible found in books other than the Psalms. They are grouped with the psalms here because they resemble them in poetic form and imagery. Among the major canticles are the following: Magnificat (Song of Mary, Luke 1:46-55), Nunc dimittis (Song of Simeon, Luke 2:29-32), Te Deum (ancient hymn), Benedictus (Song of Zechariah, Luke 1:68-79), Beatitudes (Matt. 5:3-12), Dignus est Agnus (Rev. 5:12-13; 15:3-4; 19:5-6), Benedicite omnia opera (Apocrypha, Song of Three Children), Confitebor tibi (Isaiah 12), Exultavit cor meum (Song of Hannah, 1 Sam. 2:1-10), Cantemus Domino (Song of Miriam and Moses, from Exodus 15), Domini audivi (Song of Habakuk, from Hab. 3), Audite coeli (from Deut. 32), Ego dixi (Song of Hezekiah, Isaiah 38:10-20), Benedictus es, Domine (Song of David, 1 Chron. 29:10-18).

The church musician who wishes to take advantage of the rich psalmodic heritage should first investigate the major vehicles for performance of entire psalm texts: the formulary Gregorian chant, Anglican chant, or Gelineau psalmody, and the metrical psalter hymns. All four types may include a degree of congregational participation, depending on the interest, ability, and patience of pastoral and musical leadership.

Historic liturgical use requires the addition of a Gloria Patri at the end of a psalm or canticle, in order to place the New Testament seal on the songs of the Old. Liturgical practice also favors the addition of an antiphon at the beginning and end of the song to establish its relation to the liturgical theme of the day or season. In those settings where it is possible, as in the chanted psalm settings, the ancient musical performance practice of responsorial or antiphonal alternation ought to be considered.

The following forms provide the most suitable musical vehicles for carrying the text of an entire psalm:

Gregorian Chant. The setting of the Latin Psalms to the eight medieval modes has been adapted for English practice. In performance, a single melody, with a midpoint punctuation matching the division of the psalm verse, is repeated for each verse and for the Gloria Patri. A reciting note of variable length for each half-verse allows for the contraction or expansion of the melody according to the length of the text. While the matching of textual and melodic accents is not always as admirable in English as in Latin, Gregorian chant in English may be highly singable and can achieve a beautifully clear and fluid transmission of the text. Some, but not all, Gregorian psalm collections include at least a few canticles. Examples of collections of Gregorian psalms are:

Briggs, H. B., and W. H. Frere. *A Manual of Plainsong for Divine Service*, rev. and enl. by J. H. Arnold. London: Novello, 1951. A complete Psalter with several canticles; no antiphons; simplified Gregorian notation.

Frischmann, Charles, ed. *The Psalmody for the Day, Series A*. Philadelphia: Fortress Press, 1974. A liturgical Psalter using four simplified Gregorian tones with antiphons set to four-part harmony; the people sing the psalm text; the choir sings the antiphon; arranged for use with ILCW *Calendar and Lectionary*.

Willan, Healey, ed. *The Canadian Psalter, Plainsong Edition*. Toronto: Anglican Church of Canada, 1963. A complete Gregorian Psalter based on the Briggs and Frere *Manual*; no antiphons; also contains several canticles and liturgical chants, including Compline.

Lindemann, Herbert, and Newman W. Powell, eds. *The Sunday Psalter*. St. Louis: Concordia Publishing House, 1961. The Psalms with antiphons arranged for use in the historic church year. Optional performance of the psalm tones in the rugged harmony of several types of parallel organum is suggested.

The Plainsong Psalter. The Psalms of David according to the American Book of Common Prayer, Pointed and Set to Gregorian Chants . . . New York: H. W. Gray, 1932.

Anglican Chant. The English reformers adapted Gregorian chant principles to four-part harmony for the singing of psalms and canticles. As in Gregorian chant, a reciting tone may be held for longer or shorter periods to accomodate the varying lengths of the verses. Anglican chant can be an effective carrier of the English text, but both the original pointing and the performance must avoid any hint of metrical time values. Psalm collections in the Anglican tradition customarily include some canticles. Useful examples of Anglican chant psalters are:

The American Psalter. The Psalms and Canticles . . . Pointed and Set to Anglican Chants . . . , prepared by the Joint Commission on Church Music. New York: H. W. Gray, 1930.

Brown, Ray F., ed. *The Oxford American Psalter.* New York: Oxford University Press, 1949.

The Canadian Psalter; Psalms and Canticles Pointed and Set to Anglican Chants. Toronto: Anglican Church of Canada, 1963. A well-pointed, complete Anglican Chant Psalter with canticles and several liturgical chants.

Thalben-Bell, G. T., ed. *The Choral Psalter.* London: Ernest Benn, 1957.

Gelineau Psalms. A fresh translation of the Psalms that reflects the structure of the original Hebrew poetry more carefully than most available translations, is used by Joseph Gelineau in new melodic settings that are intended for choirs and soloists but may also be used by congregations. Each melody consists of a succession of notes proceeding according to a regular pulse, which is divided into the number of beats necessary to accomodate the syllables of the text assigned to that pulse. Thus, the melody moves in an unhurried manner, and the text is presented in a flow resembling quite closely that of natural English speech. The result is a charming and effective setting of the Psalms in "sprung" meter similar to folk verse. One or more attractive antiphons are suggested for use with each psalm melody in the small collections, while the complete Psalter is published without antiphons. Each of the collections includes a number of canticles. The complete edition contains four-part harmonizations that may be attempted after unison performance is mastered:

Carroll, J. Robert, comp. *The Grail/Gelineau Psalter.* Chicago: G. I. A. Publications, 1972. One-hundred fifty psalms and 18 canticles for singing in unison or four-part harmony with optional accompaniment; no antiphons provided.

Gelineau, Joseph. *Thirty Psalms and Two Canticles.* London: The Grail, 1958.

Selection of antiphons available for liturgical performance; accompaniment and harmony edition available.

———— . *Twenty-four Psalms and a Canticle.* Toledo, Ohio: Gregorian Institute of America, 1956. Selection of antiphons given for liturgical performance; accompaniment and harmony edition available.

———— . *Twenty Psalms and Three Canticles.* Chicago: G. I. A. Publications, 1967. Selection of antiphons given for liturgical performance; accompaniment and harmony edition available.

Gelineau psalm melodies may be sung by the choir or by soloists. The antiphons may be sung by the congregation or by the choir. Keyboard accompaniments are available. Accompaniment by handbells, melody bells, and percussion may be improvised.

Formulary Tones. This system of chant devised by Paul Bunjes is a modern adaptation of formulary principles to accomodate the English language. The system of 12 tones has been applied chiefly to the psalmodic proper chants of the Eucharist (Introit, Gradual, Alleluia, Tract), but it may also be applied in extended form to the entire body of Psalms. Although intended for choral performance with accompaniment, the formulary tones may successfully be performed by *a cappella* choir or by soloists. The method for applying the formulary tones to an entire psalm is illustrated in a theoretical treatise *The Formulary Tones Annotated.*[20]

Metrical Psalmody. Metrical paraphrases of the Psalms were created during the period of the Reformation in order to provide the people with a vehicle for singing psalms in their own language. Although these metrical texts were at first set to melodies only, harmonizations were quickly provided. Today almost every hymnal contains an assortment of metrical psalms in four-part harmony, and larger metrical Psalters are also available. The choir with a complete metrical Psalter in hand possesses the delightful capacity to perform any assigned psalm after relatively brief rehearsal. Examples of metrical psalm collections are:

Book of Praise; Anglo-Genevan Psalter, published by order of the Canadian Reformed Churches. Hamilton, Ont.: Committee for the Publication of the Anglo-Genevan Psalter, 1972. Unison melodies.

Schuetz, Heinrich. *Ten More Psalms from the "Becker Psalter,"* ed. and trans. Robert E. Wunderlich. St. Louis: Concordia Publishing House, 1968. Simple settings.

——— . *Ten Psalms from the "Becker Psalter,"* ed. and trans. Robert E.

Wunderlich. St. Louis: Concordia Publising House, 1958. Simple settings.

The Scottish Psalter, 1929; Metrical Version and Scripture Paraphrases. London: Oxford University Press, 1929. A horizontally split page format enables the singer to match the four-part music printed on the upper half of the page to any text of appropriate meter printed on the lower half of the page; also contains 67 paraphrases of other Scripture texts.

The metrical paraphrases that are chosen for performance should faithfully reflect the thought and text of the original. Many "psalm" hymns are in reality devotional songs or hymns—some of considerable merit—but not accurate renditions of the psalms. Examples of the best metrical psalm paraphrases are: "All People That on Earth Do Dwell" (*SBH* 169; *TLH* 14), based on Psalm 100; "The Man Is Ever Blest" (*TLH* 414), based on Psalm 1; and the settings of Psalm 23 (*SBH* 522, 526, 530; *TLH* 368, 426, 431, 436). Some paraphrases found in modern hymnals faithfully present several of the original psalm verses but omit others. Nevertheless, these often succeed in imparting much of the text and thrust of the original and should be considered for use. An example of an abbreviated psalm paraphrase is "O God, Our Help in Ages Past" (*TLH* 123; *SBH* 168), based on Psalm 90.

A union of chant and metrical Psalter forms for joint congregation and choir performance has been achieved by Carl Schalk in *Psalms for the Church Year*.[21] The choir, singing the psalm text set to Paul Bunjes' formulary tones, and the congregation, singing a metrical paraphrase of the psalm text set to hymn tunes, alternate to present the entire psalm. In some psalms the metrical paraphrase repeats, and thus reflects on, the chanted text; in others, the metrical paraphrase advances the text.

Individual Psalm and Canticle Settings. In the 15th and 16th centuries polyphonic settings of texts taken wholly or in part from the Book of Psalms formed a prime ingredient of the sacred music repertoire. Nearly all of the greatest masters of music of that period wrote compositions on psalm texts. The pieces were written in the so-called polyphonic-motet style, which is characterized by contrapuntal writing, often featuring imitative motives and the absence of any apparent accompaniment. (The lack of any printed instrumental score is deceiving, however; in reality most of the choral music of this "a cappella" period was performed with instruments of some sort that doubled the voices.)

English anthems of the 16th century often were based on psalm texts and resembled the polyphonic motets. In the course of the 17th and 18th centuries psalm settings were written in the so-called concerted style. Psalm-based and canticle-based compositions since the baroque era defy easy categorization. Some recent contemporary settings offer the opportunity for vivid realization of the psalmist's injunction to "sing to the Lord a new song" with hand-clapping, shouting, and a variety of instrumental activities. Individual psalm settings are published in profusion, but canticle settings (with the exception of the Magnificat) are less common.

Hymns and Chorales

Choral literature based on the hymn and chorale repertoire is extensive and varied, providing a rich musical treasury enjoyed by choirs and worshipers alike. Many small or inexperienced choirs will probably first explore the basic resource in the field: the hymnal, which is also a valuable collection for mature choirs. While it must be admitted that not all harmonizations are of equal musical quality, the major hymnals generally provide serviceable arrangements, and many are superior to those hymn settings published separately. To perform hymnal settings in unison or in parts with doubling instruments revives the colorful practice of the 16th and 17th centuries, while providing support for choir (or congregational) song.

The second category of hymn or chorale setting is that ranging from the simple, four-part harmony arrangement to settings for unison, two-, three-, and four-part choir with simple accompaniments that appear in a great variety of collections for choirs. The following are some of the most useful hymn and chorale collections:

Bach, Johann Sebastian. *101 Chorales*, comp. and ed. Walter E. Buszin. Minneapolis: Schmitt, Hall, and McCreary, 1952. Comprehensive collection.

Drischner, Max. *Make a Joyful Noise*. St. Louis: Concordia Publishing House, 1965. Twenty-five hymns and carols for unison voices, descanting instrument, and keyboard accompaniment.

Johnson, David N. *Gloria Deo*, 2 vols. Minneapolis: Augsburg Publishing House, 1967. Thirty-three simple accompanied settings for SAB choir, some with optional part for melody instrument.

Pooler, Marie, arr. *Festival Hymns with Descants*. Minneapolis: Augsburg

Publishing House, 1963. Eight simple accompanied settings for unison voices with descant.

————, arr. *Unison Hymns with Descants*. Minneapolis: Augsburg Publishing House, 1959. Accompanied settings of 10 hymns for unison voices with simple descants.

Schalk, Carl. *Chorales for Lent*. Minneapolis: Augsburg Publishing House, 1966. Eleven settings for unison or solo voices with instruments.

————. *The Crown Choir Book*. St. Louis: Concordia Publishing House, 1964. Simple unison and two-part accompanied settings of 13 chorales and an original Nunc dimittis for mixed voices.

————. *A Second Crown Choir Book*. St. Louis: Concordia Publishing House, 1969. Ten simple unison and two-part accompanied hymn settings and an original Offertory sentence, for mixed voices.

Schein, Johann Hermann. *Eight Chorale Settings from "Opella Nova, Pt. 1, 1618,"* ed. Ludwig Lenel. St. Louis: Concordia Publishing House, 1966. Moderately complex, two-part, concerted settings for treble voices.

Thomas, Paul, ed. *The Hymn of the Week*, 5 vols. St. Louis: Concordia Publishing House, 1961. Comprehensive collection of old and new settings intended for *alternatim praxis*.

————, ed. *The Hymn of the Week, SAB*, 5 vols. St. Louis: Concordia Publishing House, 1965. Simple contemporary settings intended for *alternatim praxis*.

————, ed. *The SSA Chorale Book*. St. Louis: Concordia Publishing House, 1960. Thirty-four simple settings, most by contemporary composers.

————, ed. *Sing Glorias!* St. Louis: Concordia Publishing House, 1971. Twenty-four hymns and chorales from Christmas Cycle of *Worship Supplement*; simple settings useful for *alternatim praxis*.

Elaborate hymn or chorale settings have been published in great profusion. Some of these extended settings are *a cappella* arrangements in one or more stanzas; others call for accompaniments of various kinds. Sixteenth-century polyphonic settings often resemble contrapuntal motets with a chorale *cantus firmus*. In 17th-century concerted chorale settings, the chorale melody is often treated quite imaginatively. The *basso continuo* accompaniment is sometimes enriched by paired treble instruments (flute, oboe, violin, etc.). Three examples from a very great number of such large-scale compositions of this type, often called "cantatas," are:

Buxtehude, Dietrich. *Lord, Keep Us Steadfast in Thy Word*, ed. Fritz Oberdoerffer. St. Louis: Concordia Publishing House, 1960. Extended setting for two violins and *b.c.* of "Erhalt uns, Herr, bei deinem Wort."

Schuetz, Heinrich. *From God Shall Naught Divide Me*, ed. Otto Gombosi. St. Louis: Concordia Publishing House, 1956. Extended concerted setting (two violins, *b.c.*) of "Von Gott will ich nicht lassen" for SAB solos or choir.

Wienhorst, Richard. *Christ Jesus Lay In Death's Strong Bands*. St. Louis: Concordia Publishing House, 1955. Accompanied contemporary setting of five stanzas of "Christ lag in Todesbanden" interspersed with settings of liturgical texts for Easter Day.

Recent publications have shown the musical and worship possibilities inherent in congregational participation in choral music based on hymn melodies. These works generally involve the congregation as singing partner with the choir. The music usually features instrumental accompaniment with descants for voices or instruments, particularly in the concluding stanza, which sometimes is a doxology. In the most liturgically satisfying of these arrangements, often published under the name "concertato," the participants sing alternate stanzas, the goal being the achievement of a balance between the impressive simplicity of unison singing by all and the potential musical embellishment possible by a variety of choral and instrumental performers. Examples of this type of setting are numerous, and some of the most useful are associated with the names of such composers as Paul Bunjes, S. Drummond Wolff, Walter Pelz, Carl Schalk.

The performance possibilities for choral settings of hymns and chorales reside chiefly with the Hymn of the Day, although other locations are available. The simple choral arrangements of hymns and chorales can be sung by the choir as alternate stanzas with the congregation (*alternatim praxis*). Several settings of a given hymn may be sung in turn by the choir, thus forming an improvised concertato. So that the flow of the joint hymn performance is not impeded, complex or lengthy motet and concerted settings should be used with discretion. If hymn-based compositions prove to be too long or complex for alternation use, they could be sung at the Offertory or as music for the Distribution. The hymn and chorale collections listed above contain much music suitable for alternation.

Cantatas and Passions

The cantata, a genre that includes some of the largest and most glorious compositions written for church services, was born a secular form during the 17th century. It was soon adapted for use in the Lutheran Church and became a major form of service music in the later 17th century and the 18th century.

Traditionally, the church cantata consists of a series of recitatives, arias, and choruses, based on a given topic in Scripture—often related to the texts of the propers for the day. Many Lutheran cantatas served a liturgical function and were positioned in the service near the sermon. Some German cantatas include or briefly quote chorales. Most cantatas require instrumental accompaniment, including the *basso continuo*.

Several factors must be considered when a cantata is to be selected for performance: the large amount of rehearsal time necessary for the preparation of one large work in proportion to total rehearsal time available, the desirability of introducing a single large musical element into the service, the amount of solo material to be sung as opposed to music for full choir, and the necessity of reducing the time allotted to other elements of the service in order to remain within time limitations.

Each of these factors must be considered in view of the total liturgical responsibility of the choir. A satisfactory answer to the final consideration involves cooperative service planning with the pastor, which may result in the placement of the sermon at the end of the cantata. The sermon may even reinforce the Scriptural theme of the cantata, assuming that the latter is based on the Gospel or one of the Lessons or the Hymn of the Week. If the cantata is long, it could enframe the sermon, half being sung before and half after the sermon. In no case should the cantata become a vehicle for display of the ability or virtuosity of either choir or soloist. Chorale cantatas should receive special consideration, because the generally perceptible chorale *cantus firmus* can be a familiar landmark for the people in what otherwise may be strange and alien territory.

Some cantata arias can be beautifully and securely performed by an entire section of the choir singing in unison, thereby encouraging the development of vocal skills and providing additional opportunity for participation.

The accompanying instrumentalists must be rehearsed carefully and thoroughly to ensure a reliable performance. Competent instrumentalists are well worth the extra expense for rehearsals and services. Nothing can ruin the worshipful effort of a well-prepared choir more surely than struggling or incompetent instrumentalists. Cantata texts should be printed for the people. Useful cantatas by such composers as Buxtehude,

Hammerschmidt, Luebeck, Telemann, virtually every baroque composer, culminating in J. S. Bach, are readily available from many publishers.

Performance of musical settings of the Passion story has formed an important part of Holy Week observance in Christian churches for hundreds of years. Worshipers had the opportunity to hear all four of the Passion accounts each year: Matthew's version was sung on Palm Sunday, Mark's on the following Tuesday, Luke's on Wednesday, and John's acount on Good Friday. Modern practice has retained at least the retelling of the St. John Passion on Good Friday.[22]

At first, Passions were sung entirely in Gregorian chant; later, the choir was added to sing parts of the crowd or certain individuals; still later, the choir sang the entire story as one long motet. In the 17th century instrumental accompaniment was added, and all individual parts were sung by solo voices; the chorus sang the words of the crowd.[23]

Choral performance of the Passion history is not only possible for church choirs, but it is an important service they can render in the worship life of the congregation. While reading the account of the Passion is salutary, the musical presentation of the story can provide another dimension to the events described, giving the worshiper additional insights into the Scriptural text. It can lend an aura of solemnity to the narrative and cast it into a properly impressive ceremonial setting. Furthermore, the establishment of an annual tradition will deepen congregational appreciation of the Gospel accounts as the interpretations of various composers are heard. Representative Passion accounts suitable for congregational presentation are:

Bender, Jan. *The Passion According to Saint Mark*. Fremont, Ohio: Chantry Music Press, 1962. Lengthy setting for choir and soloists, with simple accompaniment; chorales interspersed.

Byrd, William. *The Passion According to St. John*, ed. Paul Thomas. St. Louis: Concordia Publishing House, 1967. Brief setting for SAB choir with unaccompanied soloists.

Hillert, Richard. *The Passion According to St. John*. St. Louis: Concordia Publising House, 1974. Simple setting for choir and accompanied soloists.

Nelson, Ronald. *The Passion According to Saint Mark*. Minneapolis: Augsburg Publishing House, 1962. Setting of Biblical and other texts for choir, soloists, narrator, congregation, and instruments; chorales interspersed.

Schuetz, Heinrich. *The Passion According to Saint Matthew*, ed. Richard T.

Gore. St. Louis: Concordia Publishing House, 1955. Lengthy setting for unaccompanied choir and soloists.

Victoria, Tomás Luis de. *The Passion According to St. John*, ed. Austin Lovelace. St. Louis: Concordia Publishing House, 1974. Setting for choir and narrator (originally cantors).

Substitution of a musical setting of the Seven Last Words of Christ on the Cross for a complete Passion is possible, but because of its abbreviated text it is less satisfactory liturgically. Examples of settings of the Seven Words appropriate for church use are:

Nystedt, Knut. *The Seven Words from the Cross*. Minneapolis: Augsburg Publishing House, 1961. Setting for choir and soloist.

Schuetz, Heinrich. *The Seven Words of Christ on the Cross*, ed. Richard T. Gore. St. Louis: Concordia Publishing House, 1950. Setting for SSATB, soloists, organ, and strings (or organ alone).

Free Compositions

Compositions that are not written for any liturgical function and do not fit into any of the categories identified above probably form the largest segment of sacred choral music printed in America. Some of it is worthwhile as service music; most of it is not. The selection or rejection of such choir music for liturgical worship services will be made on the basis of the choir director's musical experience, liturgical competence, and willingness to become a leader in the worship life of the congregation. If so-called free compositions are rejected, it will probably be because so much excellent music is available to benefit the choir and the congregation, liturgically as well as musically, that little time remains for other music. If free choral pieces are chosen, it will probably be because some particular musical or emotional factor is dominant—perhaps the choir, director, or congregation simply "likes the music." If free pieces are chosen, they should, as far as is possible, relate closely to the theme of the day and be sung as Distribution music, as a choral Offertory, or perhaps after the Gradual-Alleluia.

Choral Rehearsal and Organization: A Checklist

The administration of the church choir partakes of many of the same goals and techniques as that of other choirs. Church choirs, however, differ in membership, philosophy, and performance practice from other choral groups, and the purpose of the following checklist is to identify the fundamentals of choir rehearsal and organization as they apply to the church choir. Many of the points briefly noted here are developed extensively in books devoted to choral conducting.

1. The purpose of the church choir rehearsal is to prepare the members thoroughly and efficiently to lead the congregation in worship and to sing appropriate service music.

2. The rehearsal environment should be pleasant: a well-lighted, well ventilated, acoustically lively room furnished with chairs that promote good singing posture.

3. Adult choirs can rehearse profitably for about 60 to 90 minutes; younger singers can rehearse for about 30 to 60 minutes. Breaks for rest are not generally needed if the rehearsal is conducted with good humor, efficiency, and various activities appropriate to the age of the singer.

4. Rehearsal seating should follow one of the generally accepted plans of voice distribution. Every few rehearsals another standard arrangement may be used for a few minutes or for an entire rehearsal before returning again to the first plan. A circle plan or a quartet (or "mixed-up") arrangement can occasionally be advantageous for promoting vocal blend and independence.

5. Rehearsals should begin promptly with a brief devotion relating the work of the choir to the worship of the church, the church year, and the needs of the parish and the choir members. Members can lead prayer, or they can offer petitions in the prayer of a leader. An opening hymn sung in parts or unison can be included. Rehearsals should also close with prayer and a blessing.

6. A very few minutes spent on vocal warm-ups at the beginning of the rehearsal provide the most efficient means of developing consciousness of essential vocal principles. The warm-up period may include brief instruction on melodic and rhythmic elements of score reading. In the course of a rehearsal the attention of the choir should be drawn to application of the elements identified at the beginning of the rehearsal.

7. The rehearsal itself should begin with the singing of the music for the coming Sunday; first the propers, then the settings of the Hymn of the Week and the special liturgical music. The remainder of the rehearsal may be devoted to music for the following Sundays, alternating difficult and easy works according to the requirements of the music and the choir.

8. The final moments in rehearsal should be spent reviewing music for the coming service, preferably in the church and with the accompaniment that will be used. The choir must be aware of the liturgical position in the service of each item to be sung, particularly when special introductions or modulations are necessary.

9. Choral performance in church must be preceded by a brief rehearsal just prior to the service. A one-minute vocal warm-up may be followed by the singing of significant or troublesome parts of the music to be performed. After brief final instructions and comments by the director, a short prayer is said, and the choir proceeds reverently into the church well before the beginning of the service.

10. An accompanist may be of great assistance to the director and the choir, provided that the keyboard is not played continually in rehearsal. Choral growth is achieved through independence from keyboard support, and it takes place only when the vocal sound is heard clearly.

11. Singers should have pencils in hand during rehearsal and develop a shorthand system of marking breathing places, errors, interpretation, or changes in text or music.

12. The choir should become sensitive to its function in worship, to its leadership role in the liturgy and hymns, and to the opportunities available in the service for personal and corporate devotional growth.

13. Choir members should be challenged to grow vocally and musically, developing their individual abilities, while expanding their knowledge and appreciation of the art of singing and the nature of music in general.

14. A systematic plan for incidental instruction in musical score-reading should be developed, using numbers, sol-fa syllables, or letter names in order to assist those who do not read music fluently. Some of this activity may be done during the initial warm-up; some may be completed outside of rehearsals.

15. The choir must continually be encouraged towards precise intonation and pitch accuracy. Occasional sectional rehearsals and unaccompanied singing by all will assist in the quest for good intonation. Choirs generally sing in tune after they have learned to listen carefully.

16. Choir members should be encouraged to execute rhythmic patterns with unity and precision. Singers should mentally conceive the rhythm of each area before singing. The mental division of the beat by the singer will help build accurate rhythmic performance.

17. Church choirs have a special obligation to strive for clear and natural projection of the text. An important part of the choral message will be lost if vowels are not well formed and if the consonants are not crisply and accurately placed.

18. The singers should be encouraged to assume responsibility for various aspects of the choir program: care of the choral library, room arrangements, devotions, care of robes, social gatherings, and attendance records.

19. The director, in consultation with the pastor and organist, should prepare the plan of liturgical participation by the choir far in advance of actual performance. Liturgical items to be emphasized or embellished should be systematically identified, and plans for informing or for securing the participation of the people should be projected.

20. The director must strive to master the basic techniques of conducting, such as the conventional beat patterns and independent use of the left hand. The most efficient conductor conveys maximum meaning with minimum motion.

21. The director must be aware of the liturgical significance and function of each work to be sung, and must communicate this awareness to the choir.

22. The director's preparation of all music scheduled for rehearsal must be thorough and complete. He should know all of the individual vocal parts well, isolate difficult passages, and mark breathing places in advance of the rehearsal so that he can anticipate musical problems and conduct an efficient rehearsal.

23. After each rehearsal the director is obliged to review and evaluate the work of the choir. Taping selected portions of the rehearsal will assist him in this task, which can be considered part of his preparation for the following rehearsal.

24. The director should try to instill in the choir members the attitude of joint participation in a noble task. Willing cooperation, helpfulness, Christian concern for others, humility, and enthusiasm all characterize the members of successful church choirs.

25. As a church musician, the choir director is obligated to read the professional literature—musical, liturgical, and theological—examine newly published choral music, and attend professional workshops and seminars.

26. Social gatherings of the choir promote a congenial spirit and general interest in the group.

27. The director should know each member well and show concern for each individual. This is Christian love in action. It is also a means of helping each person become a better choir member.

28. At least once each year the director should hold a private conversation with each member in order to express appreciation and to offer support and encouragement for continued participation and vocal growth. A brief individual vocal audition (vocalizing or singing a hymn) at this time will make it possible for the director to offer pertinent yet tactful observations about vocal development.

29. Liturgical function and historical precedent both suggest that the choir and its director be suitably robed, preferably in black cassock and white cotta, or perhaps in a simple alb with cincture.

30. Choir processions, particularly on festivals, are of value primarily if the choir sings from the front or chancel area of the church. If the choir sings from the rear of the church, it is difficult to rationalize the need for its involvement in processions. If processions are used, they should be accomplished without ostentation.

31. Choir music, robes, and supplies should be provided for in adequate measure from the general congregational treasury and not from funds contributed by choir members. The service of the choir is liturgical and musical, not financial.

> The Lord will save me,
> and we will sing to stringed instruments
> All the days of our life,
> at the house of the Lord.

(Is. 38:20)

See also the related articles in *Key Words in Church Music:* alternation practice; anthem; canonical hours; cantata; canticle; chant, Anglican; chant, Gregorian; choir, history; concertato style; de tempore hymn; Gospel motet; Leisen; mass; metrical psalmody; motet; office hymn; oratorio; Passion; polychoral style; psalmody, Gregorian; sequence; Service; Venetian school

CHAPTER V

The Music of Instruments

Herbert Gotsch and Edward W. Klammer

Herbert Gotsch

Historical Overview

The freedom with which the church today uses musical instruments in its worship is convincingly demonstrated even by a cursory examination of current publications. Examples abound not only of the use of such traditional instruments as organ, piano, flute, violin, oboe, trumpet, and trombone, but of glockenspiel, handbells, alto bells, recorder, guitar, finger cymbals, small drum, tambourine, triangle, electric bass, hand-clapping, harp, xylophone, snare drum, bongos, tom-tom, and woodblock as well. The catalogs of publishers of church music include frequent advertisements of many for these instruments.

The listing of such instruments, suggested for use in church, might surprise, if not shock, those whose musical tastes were established in the first half of this century when any instrument other than the organ (piano or reed organ for more impoverished parishes) was almost legalistically ruled out of the church's worship. Certain to be shocked by all of these instruments, even the keyboard instruments, would have been the stricter followers of some of the proscriptions of Zwingli and Calvin against all music but congregational (i.e., unaccompanied and unison) singing.

Also warning against the spiritually corrupting influence of instrumental music were the church fathers of the early centuries of the Christian era who saw some of the Gentile Christians using the commemoration days of saints to retain slightly disguised versions of popular pagan festivals of theater and circus that included licentious female musicians. Even St. Paul reflects the disparagement of instrumental music in worship when he equates the lack of love in speaking with the noisy gong and clanging cymbal used in various mystery rites and by the rival Sadducees in the temple worship. (1 Cor. 13)

In the formal worship of the Old Testament an entirely different attitude existed. Many instruments accompanied the singing when King David brought the Ark of the Covenant up to Jerusalem. As part of his organization preparatory for the worship in the temple which his son Solomon was to build, David had instruments made and certain families of the Levites designated and trained to play them. These preparations reached a climax at the great dedication of the temple when musicians with cymbals, harps, and lyres and 120 priests who were trumpeters raised the song in praise to the Lord as His glory filled the house of God. In later centuries when long periods of religious decline in Jerusalem were interrupted by the reforms under good kings like Jehoshaphat and Hezekiah, and when after the Babylonian captivity the walls of Jerusalem were rebuilt and dedicated, these instruments of David are specifically mentioned again, accompanying the singing to the Lord.

The existence of these two antithetic attitudes towards instrumental music in the church reflects two similar attitudes towards the use of anything but the Word in worship. The one view holds that when man takes the wood, the metals, the membranes of God's creation, forms them by his crafts into contrivances for producing sound, and uses these to accompany his worship, he is offering God a sacrifice of the work of his mind and body and returning to the Creator gifts from His creation. The other view notes the appeal, whether sensuous or sensual, of instrumental music to human nature and ascetically rejects an intrusion of the secular world into worship.[1]

The latter point of view was dominant in the early centuries of the Western church. Although the building of organs is referred to from about 900 A.D. on, and the existence of other instruments is know from medieval writings and illustrations in manuscripts, practically nothing is known about how, or even whether, they were used in church music. Not until the 12th or 13th century, after the beginnings of polyphony, can the use of instruments be assumed—first playing the long sustained notes of a cantus firmus, later doubling the voices in the other moving parts, and then possibly playing alone certain parts for which there is no text in the manuscripts. From 1300 on the use of instruments with voices was normal performance practice. Most of the music of the 16th century, which later periods often regarded as the ideal *a cappella* music, would have been originally performed with instrumental doubling of one or more voices. In the baroque era this role was greatly expanded by composers who wrote obbligato parts and independent ritornellos for the instruments in their church music; the cantatas of such 18th-century composers as J. S. Bach required an orchestra of 10 to 20 players.

When using instruments in worship, the musician must be concerned with the relationship of music and the Word. Vocal music in its many forms contributes greatly to the proclamation of the Word from God to man and in man's response to that Word. If they do not obscure the text, instruments used with vocal music may also contribute to that proclamation. For some, pure instrumental music has a questionable role in the service; Peter Brunner, for example suggests that he does "not consider it appropriate to present music which is detached from its association with the Word as a component of congregational worship."[2]

Organists and directors who have the freedom and desire to make use of instrumental resources available to them will do so with some care. Music that tends merely to demonstrate virtuosity of the performer rather than to contribute to the themes of the service will be avoided. The attitude and location of the musicians must give the impression that they are part of the worshiping community. Faced with the commendable trends introduced by the liturgical renewal movement regarding the church as a place for gathering the family of God around the altar for a communal celebration of Word and Sacrament, and with the unfortunate inflationary building costs of enclosing space, modern ecclesiastical architecture has yet to solve the problem of providing adequate facilities for the music of the service from the standpoint of worship, acoustics, and physical space. Where instrumentalists must be visible, special attention should be given to insure that their demeanor is appropriate for the circumstances.

The Organ

Character and Composition

Earliest references to an instrument with the principal characteristics of the organ—multiple pipes each providing a different pitch, the tone activated from a supply of wind produced by a hydraulic device or a bellows rather than the human lung, and a mechanism for selecting the pipes into which the air will be admitted—are found in pre-Christian eras and among the Romans of the first centuries. They suggest an instrument for secular, outdoor use, probably with considerable volume. There was some refinement of the organ by Byzantine craftsmen before its introduction into western Europe as gifts to royalty before the year 900. A Latin poem lauded an organ in the cathedral at Winchester in the 10th century: 26 bellows were "pumped by a crowd of 70 powerful men . . . all covered with much perspiration"; the listener would "soon cover his ears with his hands" as "through the entire town the pipes are singing and booming."

This reference also indicates a change in the location and function of the organ from a secular, festive, and possibly outdoor instrument to one closely associated with the church. Although small portative instruments continued to serve various secular functions, the development of the organ until well into the 19th century would be primarily the responsibility of the church. However, even here the organ was not limited to liturgical or ecclesiastical use. The church sometimes served as one of a city's concert halls. Frescobaldi is reported to have attracted an audience of 30,000 for his playing, and one of Sweelinck's responsibilities at his church was to play a daily organ recital for the businessmen of Amsterdam before the stock market opened.

The organ is unique in many ways. Even when the size is limited by modest means, it is the largest and mechanically most complex instrument. The range is not limited to the five octaves of its keyboards, but is extended at least three octaves by stops of octave and suboctave pitches. Its range and tonal complexity make it the most challenging instrument for audiophiles either to record or to demonstrate the fidelity of playback equipment. In a concert hall the same instrument may provide the delicate continuo realization for a solo aria and the massive sonorities required by the Saint-Saëns *Third Symphony*. But perhaps the most unique feature of the organ is the fact that the complete success of a given instrument is so heavily dependent on factors that are beyond control of the organ builder or player. If architects and building committees fail to consult with or follow the advice of recognized organ authorities on such matters as spatial requirements for the pipes, sufficient egress and proper distribution for the tone, and surfaces on the floor, walls, and ceiling that will enhance rather than absorb the reverberant energy so necessary for successful music from instruments, choirs, and congregations, there will be a handicap for which no skill or care in planning, building, and voicing can compensate.

Strictly speaking it is not correct to refer to an instrument of two or three manual divisions and a pedal as *an* organ; *each* of these is rather an organ that may be used independently or in combinations with the other "organs." The German term "Werk" has no satisfactory English equivalent, but it is a term less confusing than "organ" for the divisions of the instrument. A *Werk* is a grouping of pipes mounted on a windchest, frequently encased, but not necessarily enclosed, and controlled from one keyboard. The early organs consisted of a single *Werk* in which each key (actually a large lever) sounded a number of pipes of different pitches corresponding to those provided today by stops of 8′, 4′, 2⅔′, 2′, 1⅓′, etc. This large mixture, on which no variation or gradation of tone was possible, developed into the German *Hauptwerk*, the French *Grand Orgue*, the English Great Organ. Pedals were first used as an auxiliary to the lower manual keys, an idea probably borrowed from Dutch carillons, to sustain longer notes and to increase the range that could be played beyond the limits of the hands. At first, the pedals were connected by "pull-downs" to the manual keys, but later complete pedal organs were developed.

Because of the inflexibility of this organ, it was necessary to devise a way of varying the corpus of tone. The earliest way was to move a smaller, self-contained Positiv organ to the proximity of the main organ. When the organist wanted a different corpus of tone, he turned to play on the Positiv. Soon this Positiv was so located that its keyboard would be above or below the keyboard of the Great Organ. Because the pipes were located on the rail of the gallery that held the organ and behind the organist, the German prefix for "back" was incorporated into the name of the division—*Rueckpositiv*. An additional organ with its own keyboard was placed at the player's breast (*Brustwerk*) or later above the Great Organ (*Oberwerk*).

One of the most essential characteristics of the organ almost from its beginning was that the tone produced by a single key is the compound result of the tone of a number of individual pipes drawing wind from a common chest and generally of different pitches. With no knowledge of the contribution of harmonics or overtones to tone color as demonstrated by the physicist Helmholtz in the 19th century, early organ builders compensated for the comparatively colorless tone of a single flue pipe by having each key sound a series of pipes mathematically related so that each of the shorter pipes was a fractional length (½, ⅓, ¼, etc.) of the longest pipe. Instead of being designated by these fractions each of these ranks was named according to the length of the pipe producing the lowest note of the keyboard. Originally there was no way of selecting or separating out any of these ranks and there was no change of tone color possible on the single organ. When a means of stopping the wind to selected ranks of this large mixture was finally developed, builders were able to liberate individual ranks or registers or stops for use in smaller combinations or to add to the organ individual registers that had not been part of the mixture. This led to the beginning of registrations in which intensity and tone color could be varied in two ways: varying the combinations of pitch levels sounding at one time, and developing new ranks of pipes of contrasting timbres.

Registration

Registration is the art of selecting singly and in combination the organ registers appropriate for the music being played. Although composers and editors of organ music often supply registrations, these may or may not be well chosen; they may or may not be compatible with the instrument which an organist plays. Furthermore, much music does not include any registrations. For these reasons every organist must be able to prepare his own registrations. This ability requires:

1. A knowledge of a systematic classification of organ pipes.
2. An understanding of the function and contribution of each of the pitch levels at which ranks of pipes are found.
3. A knowledge of the different types of registration required by the various textures of organ music.

Classification of Organ Pipes[3]

According to the manner of tone production, organ pipes are of two types: *labial* or *flue*, in which the tone is produced by the impact of a stream of air upon a sharp liplike upper edge of the mouth; and *lingual* or *reed*, in which a metal reed is the sound-producing agent. Within each type the tone of different stops will vary according to such factors as the scale of the pipes (ratio of diameter to length); whether the shape of the pipe is cylindrical, conical, or tapered; whether the top of the pipe is open, covered, or partly covered; and the width and shape of the mouth.

Labial Pipes

Traditionally, labial pipes have been divided into two major classifications and a minor one: Class I or Principal, Class II or Gedackt-Flute, and the Strings.

The Principal pipes supply the most basic organ tone, the tone that forms the supporting backbone of the instrument. Principal tone is full, rich, and aggressive throughout the entire range. When the various pitches at which it is present are combined, the resulting ensemble has a blend and clarity that is ideal for contrapuntal music. This class of pipes is also known as "Diapason," although this term may imply the thicker and heavier type of tone found in organs from the earlier part of this century. The principal pipes also provide the normal scale, the standard against which other classes of pipes are described as either wide or narrow.

Principal stops will be represented at 16′, 8′, 4′, 2⅔′, and 2′ pitches as well as in the mixtures. According to design logic the lowest pitch at which this class is present in a division is given the name principal. The remaining stops receive names that describe their pitch relation to this principal: Octave, Quint, or Twelfth; Octavin, Super-Octave, or Fifteenth. This practice is not carried out consistently in the naming of stops on all instruments. English organs frequently designated the 4′ rank as Principal even when the class was represented at a lower pitch in that division. Modifications in the basic structure or scale of principal pipes are sometimes indicated by prefixes such as Italian-, Geigen-, Violin-, Harfen-, Spitz-, or Weit-.

Gedackt pipes of Class II are covered or stopped at the top. Because a stopped pipe produces a tone an octave lower than an open pipe of the same length, such pipes need be only half their stated pitch length. Hence, there is a saving in space and material when 16′ and 8′ stops are covered rather than open. The basic tonal characteristic of Gedackt pipes is a somewhat hollow sound due to the presence of only odd-numbered harmonics in a stopped pipe. This sound serves as an excellent foundation when combined with stops of higher pitches. Gedackts include Untersatz and Subbass 16′, Gedackt, Pommer, Bourdon, and Quintaton at 16′ and 8′ and occasionally at 4′, and Stopped Diapason 8′.

Related to the Gedackt pipes are the partly covered pipes, in which the cover or stopper of the pipe is pierced with a narrower open cylindrical tube or chimney extending upwards. Such registers, generally found at either 8′ or 4′, can be recognized by the prefix Rohr- or Chimney-: Rohrfloete, Rohrbourdon, Chimney Flute. Also belonging to the partly covered group would be two stops generally found at 4′, Spillfloete and Koppelfloete; the partial covering is achieved by having a cylindrical section of pipe topped by a section that tapers to a much smaller opening.

Flute pipes are open, full length, and generally have a fuller tone than the gedackts since all the harmonics are present. Included would be

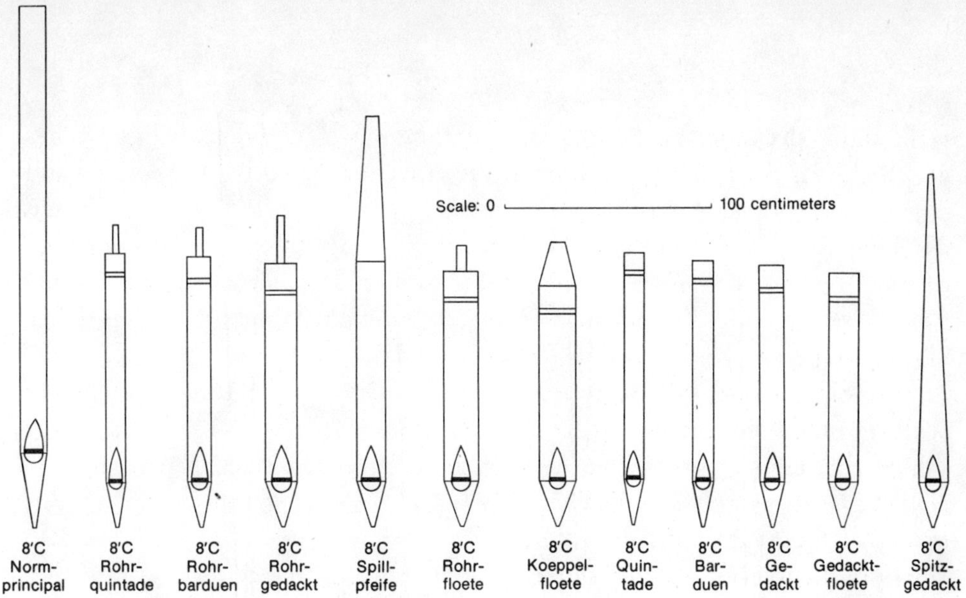
Scale: 0
100 centimeters
8'C Norm-principal
8'C Rohr-quintade
8'C Rohr-barduen
8'C Rohr-gedackt
8'C Spill-pfeife
8'C Rohr-floete
8'C Koeppel-floete
8'C Quin-tade
8'C Bar-duen
8'C Ge-dackt
8'C Gedackt-floete
8'C Spitz-gedackt

Fully and Partly Covered Pipes

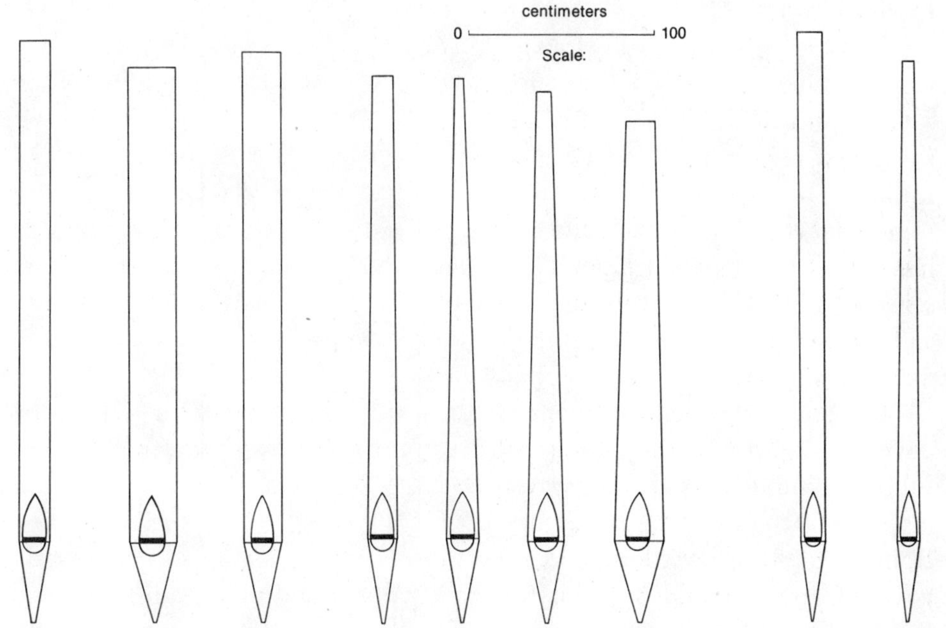
centimeters
0
100
Scale:
8'C Norm-principal
8'C Nacht-horn
8'C Hohl-floete
8'C Flach-floete
8'C Spitz-floete
8'C Gems-horn
8'C Block-floete
8'C Sali-cional
8'C Spitz-gambe

Open Cylindrical and Open Conical Pipes

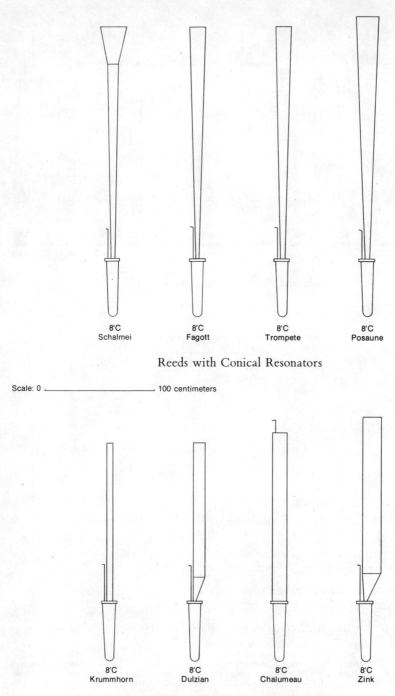

8'C
Schalmei

8'C
Fagott

8'C
Trompete

8'C
Posaune

Reeds with Conical Resonators

Scale: 0 ⌞_____⌟ 100 centimeters

8'C
Krummhorn

8'C
Dulzian

8'C
Chalumeau

8'C
Zink

Reeds with Cylindrical Resonators

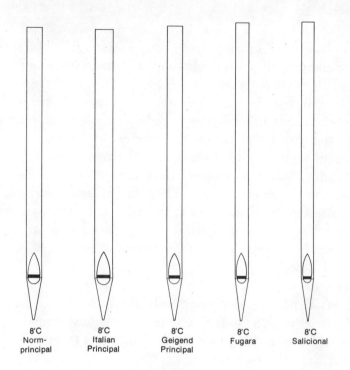

| 8'C | 8'C | 8'C | 8'C | 8'C |
| Norm-principal | Italian Principal | Geigend Principal | Fugara | Salicional |

cylindrical pipes at 4′ and 2′ such as Nachthorn and Hohlfloete, tapered pipes such as Spitzfloete and Gemshorn at 8′ and 4′, and the Blockfloete, Waldfloete, and Flachfloete at 4′ and 2′. Mutations at 2⅔′, 1³/₅′, and 1⅓′ are frequently of this type.

A special group of labial or flue pipes of lesser importance than the above two classes are the string stops. These have a narrower scale, a thinner and more cutting tone. Less suited to contrapuntal and rapid passages, they find their value in chordal passages where their peculiar sonority is a desired feature. They include Viola da Gamba, Salicional, Viola, Spitzgamba, and Dulciana. A special effect produced with string stops should also be noted. The term celeste refers to a second string stop which is tuned slightly higher or lower than the first one of this type; the resulting beats from the variation in tuning add an undulating effect to the ensemble that is pleasing in certain softer registrations. The celeste should never be used in contrapuntal passages nor in combination with more than a single 8′ or 4′ stop.

Reed Pipes

As a class, the reed stops have the greatest variety of tone color and brilliance and may, if desired, also have the greatest amount of weight and volume of all the registers on the organ. The length of the tone-producing agent, the thin metal reed, regulated by a tuning wire, is the principal influence on the pitch, while the shape and length of the resonator or pipe body has the greatest effect on the tone quality. Reeds are divided into three groups according to the shape of the resonators.

Pipes with conical resonators from this group include the reeds that are most commonly found on organs. They may be used both as solo stops and to add a capstone brilliance to the full ensemble. The basic stop is the 8′ Trumpet; when used at 4′ it is usually called Clarion; at 16′ Posaune or Bombarde. The Fagott is generally found at 16′ and 8′ pitches and the Oboe or Hautbois at 8′.

Pipes with cylindrical resonators have an effect similar to that of stopped labial pipes—reinforcing only the odd-number harmonics. The resulting tone is thin and also somewhat hollow sounding. The most common registers in this group are the Dulzian at 16′ or 8′, Krummhorn 8′, Clarinet 8′, and Rohrschalmei 8′ or 4′.

Pipes with fractional length resonators are of many different shapes leading to the greatest variety of tone color. Most commonly found are the Vox Humana, Rankett, and all kinds of Regals. German prefixes are often attached to the term regal; consultation with a dictionary will show that these are terms that describe the shape of the resonator: cone, knob, sphere, funnel, etc.

Pitch Levels of Stops

Since tone color is dependent on the presence and intensity of the harmonics or overtones, the different pitch levels of organ stops, equivalent to the harmonics, can be drawn in different combinations to produce different tone qualities. The organist is like a painter working with a palette of colors that he combines to obtain the tone colors he wants. Consider the number of possibilities that can be obtained from a set of just five pitches, 8′, 4′, 2⅔′, 2′, and 1³⁄₅′. It is possible to arrange 15 different combinations of two, three, four, or five stops. If a 1⅓′ stop would be added, at least 16 more registrations could be obtained. Not every combination tried will be equally pleasing, but each will have its own distinct quality. The organist must evaluate each combination and judge whether it can serve the music being played.

It will also help an organist to recognize just what each of the pitch levels contributes when used in combinations. The following is a brief summary of these contributions:

8' —Provides notated pitch line, rarely used alone, choice between different 8' stops made on basis of amount of fundamental weight desired rather than tone color.

16' —On manuals restricted to textures lying high in range and needing additional gravity; on pedal functions as normal pitch basis for lowest voice.

4' —Provides singing line that livens up the 8' pitch line; the most essential pitch for defining harmonic and melodic contours when accompanying voices.

2⅔' —Adds stimulating, lively color to tonal effect; 1⅓' has same effect especially when added to 4' tone.

2' —Adds brilliant, bright, clear, sharp outline to the tone.

1⅗' —Adds pungent "reediness," but should be used only in combination with 2⅔' (as Sesquialtera) or 1⅓' (as Tertian); normally restricted to single voice, solo registrations, except in certain French baroque works that specifically call for tierces or the Grand Cornet.

Mixture—Brightest color, serves as crown for the full organ tone.

When combining these different pitches in registrations, organists should recall what result a painter would get if he would combine all or most of the colors on his palette—a nondescript grey. The organist will also discover that the more pitches he uses at one time the less distinctive the tone color becomes.

Types of Registration

On the basis of the music that the organ plays both in services and recitals, there are four basic types of texture which affect registration: plenum, solo, background, duo-trio.

Plenum registration is frequently indicated in organ music, particularly by Bach, as "Pro organo pleno." Etymologically the phrase suggests the word "full." But organists must not understand this as implying the same concept as "full" in orchestration. It does not mean "Full organ" with every stop drawn. Plenum registration is derived from the old large "mixture" of principal class pipes of various unison and fifth sounding pitches. Its primary charactertistic is the presence of principal tone for at least the highest pitch in the combination.

Plenum registration is used in contrapuntal and harmonic textures in which all voices are equal. This would include the accompaniment of the congregation in hymns and liturgy, preludes and fugues from the baroque era, toccatas, and many organ chorales. Since plenum registration is required for most of the organ music in the service, the first requisite for an adequate organ in a church is its ability to provide good plenum registrations in varying levels of volume.

Although accompanimental textures are chiefly associated with background registrations, it is possible that an accompanimental registration because of the fullness of the solo registration or the choir must be of sufficient aggressiveness to require principal stops. Then a minimum plenum would be used.

The following chart may be of help in discussing plenum registrations.

Plenum Registration

	1	2	3	4	5	6	7	8	9	10	11	12	13
16' Quintaton									x				
8' Principal	x		x			x	x		x	x	x	x	
8' Rohrfloete		x		x	x			x					
4' Octave	x	x	x	x		x	x	x	x	x	x	x	x
4' Nachthorn					x								
2⅔' Quinte						x	x		x	x	x	x	(x)
2' Octave			x	x	x	x	x	x	x	x	x	x	(x)
Mixture							x	x	x	x	x	x	x
16' Dulzian										x		x	
8' Trompete											x	x	x

Registrations 1 and 2 are the minimum plenums. At least two pitches must be present. Registrations 3, 4, and 5 would represent the next level—three different pitches. Registrations 2, 4, 5, and 8 illustrate the role of gedackt-flute stops in plenum registrations. They may replace principal registers at the lower pitches; but principal tone must be retained at the highest pitch. This substitution of Class II registers is used on the Great of large organs to achieve a plenum with less weight and on subsidiary manuals or the Great of smaller organs because principal pipes of the inferior pitches are not included in the specifications. Registrations 9 and 10 introduce 16′ tone into the plenum (it is unlikely that both the labial Quintaton and the reed Dulzian would be included on one division, so either one or the other registration would be available); 16′ tone will add gravity to the ensemble, but will be more appropriate in chordal than in contrapuntal textures. Registrations 11 and 12 add the brilliance of the Trompete. Registration 13 demonstrates the substitution of a reed for an inferior principal stop; such a registration would be limited to monophonic or homophonic textures.

Although the chart is based on a large division, it may be used to illustrate plenum registrations for a small division by using only the stops available. Small organs or those designed without several plenum possibilities on each manual need intermanual couplers for some of the registrations.

Note that in the classical plenum registrations there is no duplication of pitches in the labial pipes. Two exceptions to this principle are found in French registrations. Various French authorities from the 17th and 18th centuries call for registrations which include both principal and gedackt-flute pipes of 8′ and 4′ pitch. Modern French registration beginning with the music of César Franck calls for an entirely different approach that is spelled out in detail in reliable editions of the music. The basic plenum will include all 8′ and 4′ principals, flutes, and gedackts in the Grande Orgue plus the coupling of similar stops from other divisions.

Solo registration is used when it is necessary for one of the voices to stand out clearly separated from the background of the others. The separation may be achieved in four ways:

a. By volume—this is the most obvious (and possibly the least musical) way. Select a stop that is louder and it will serve as a solo.

b. By color of individual ranks—the reeds stops are particularly suited to this use—Krummhorn, Fagott, Oboe, Regal.

c. By color achieved through combining ranks of gedackt-flute pipes of different pitches. While combinations of 8′ and 2′, or 8′ and 1′ may serve as solo registrations, this type is particularly dependent on the judicious combining of the nonoctave mutation ranks, Nasat 2 2/3 Tierce 1 3/5 ′, and Larigot 1 1/3 ′. These registers are frequently present in compound stops: Sesquiltera (2 2/3 ′ and 1 3/5 ′) and Terzian (1 3/5 ′ and 1 1/3 ′).

d. By combining the principles of b. and c. The tonal effect of various reed stops may be modified by the addition of upper pitches: Krummhorn and 1⅓′ Larigot; Oboe and 2⅔′ Nasat; Trumpet, 4′ Principal, and II Sesquialtera; etc.

The following chart will demonstrate some of the solo registrations possible, although it is unlikely that every stop given will be present on a given organ:

Solo Registrations

	1	2	3	4	5	6	7	8	9	10	11	12	13	14	15	16	17	18	19
8′ Gedackt	x	x	x	x	x	x	x	x	x	x	x	x	x	x	x				
4′ Spillfl.					x		x			x	x	x			x	x	x		
2⅔′ Nasat		x		x	x	x	x						x	x			x		
2′ Blockfl.	x					x	x			x									x
1⅗′ Terz				x	x	x	x	x											
1⅓′ Larigot			x					x	x	x	x				x	x			
16′ Rankett																	x	x	x
8′ Krummhorn												x	x	x	x				

Registrations 1, 2, and 3 are solo combinations using only 2 stops. Registration 7 includes the five ranks that made up the classical Cornet. Since the essential color pitches for the cornet are the 2⅔′ and 1⅗′ above the 8′ pitch line, registrations 4, 5, and 6 show how the fullness of the Cornet may be modified by the omission of either or both 4′ and 2′ pitches. Registration 8 is equivalent to the Tertian. Registrations 9, 10, and 11 use the 1⅓′ Larigot as the basic color producer. Registrations 12, 13, 14, and 15 show modifications of the reed tone by addition of other pitches. The remaining registrations do not include the 8′ Gedackt for the pitch line, but would be played with octave transposition, a way of increasing the versatility of a small instrument or division. Registration 16 would be played an octave lower and 17, 18, and 19 an octave higher to achieve the necessary 8′ pitch line.

Background registration is a nonprincipal ensemble registration just the opposite of plenum registration, yielding and recessive in character. It is needed when the organ is serving as accompaniment to other instruments, to solo voices or small ensembles, to a solo registration on another manual, and as a contrast to plenum registrations as in episodes of fugues or

186

antiphonal passages. Background registrations are composed of combinations of gedackts and flutes such as 8' and 4'; 8', 4', and 2'; 8', 4', 2⅔', and 2'. Particularly in accompanying voices it is better if the 4' is somewhat brighter in tone than the 8'. Strictly speaking, strings would not be included as components of background registrations; but in practice an 8' Viola da gamba or Salicional that blends well with the 4' flute in a division may occasionally be used. But if a principal rank would be introduced, it would no longer be a background, but a plenum registration.

Duo-trio registration is required in textures of either two or three voices in which each part is to be distinct. Considering duos and the manual voices of trios there are three ways in which contrast may be obtained.

a. Contrast by range—if the parts are spatially separated they stand clearly apart even if there is no contrast in color. Background registrations would be chosen for each part using two different manuals.

b. Contrast by color of individual ranks—chiefly reeds with cylindrical resonators and regals in contrast with stops from the flute-gedackt class. Particularly in small organs the contrast may be between Viola da gamba or other string stops and gedackts. This type of contrasting registration is more appropriate in slower tempos. The reed or string stop with its more incisive tone would be used for the lower of the voices. If only a single stop is to be used for the upper voice, a 4' flute played an octave lower may provide a clearer line than an 8' gedackt played at normal pitch.

c. Contrast by pitch level combinations used in each part—this is the type that on most organs provides the greatest variety. All stops would best be from the gedackt-flute class, although on a small organ it might be necessary to use a principal stop of 2' pitch. The following table gives some of the possibilities:

Left Hand	Right Hand
8', 4'	8', 2'; or 8', 2⅔'
8', 4'; or 8', 2'	8', 1⅓'
8', 4', 2⅔'	8', 2'; or 8', 4', 2'; or 8', 2', 1'
8', 4', 2'	8', 4', 1⅓'; or 8', 2', 1⅓'

Other combinations could be found, but two principles should be noted from these examples: Nonoctave ranks (2⅔', 1⅓') appear in only one of the two parts. The combination that includes the highest pitch is assigned to the upper voice or right hand.

Pedal registration follows the same principles as for the manuals. But there are some special considerations.

Plenum pedal registration is generally, but not always, based on 16' pitch. The pedal plenum will require upper pitches at least through the 4' for contrapuntal clarity. If mutations and mixtures are used on the manual they should also be present in the pedal combination. Because of the expense of open pipes for the 16' Principal, this pitch will usually be represented by stops of the gedackt class. On small organs the same may be true of the 8' pitch. But a 4' principal stop (frequently named Choralbass) will be able to provide the principal tone color when used above 16' and 8' gedackts. If there is a 16' Principal, its use should be restricted to supporting only the fullest of manual plenums. Unless it is unusually precise and clear in speech, it may tend to blur and thicken a contrapuntal bass.

Ideally the pedal should contain sufficient stops so that couplers are not needed in plenum registrations. If this is not the case, a judicious use of a coupler may compensate. Assuming that the manual parts are played on a great plenum without intermanual couplers, appropriate stops from one of the other manuals could be coupled to the pedal, thereby enlarging the number of stops available to it while still maintaining its independence from the other voices. Coupling the pedal to the manual used for the upper voices causes some loss of clarity and independence and should, if possible, be avoided.

Solo registrations on the pedal will be primarily by volume and by color of stops, especially reeds. Principal stops of 8' or 4' may also be useful. A cantus firmus line in the alto or tenor voice can frequently be treated as a solo by playing it, an octave lower than notated, on the pedal with a 4' principal-tone stop. A solo by combining ranks of different pitches is of more limited value on the pedal. Where mutations sounding the third or fifth are present in the pedal, their contribution will be to sharpen the 8' or 16' pitch line rather than to create various tone colors.

Although 16' tone is thought of as normal for the pedal, background and trio registrations may effectively be based on 8' stops, especially if the pedal shares melodic motives with the manual parts. Most useful at 16' and 8' are the various gedackt stops; tapered flutes such as Gemshorn and

Spitzfloete would be used at 8' and 4' pitches. A single 8' stop might be sufficient under a soft manual registration, but generally at least two pitches are needed. The addition of a 4' and a 2' stop to the 8' and 16' and 8' increases the clarity of the pedal line.

Use of the Organ in Worship

Rubrics in our hymnals and service books today do not include directions for the use of the organ. How the organ is used depends to a considerable extent on aural traditions. Students may be inclined to play according to the manner they heard as they grew up or they will imitate their teachers. Practices at churches in a given area may tend to reflect the usage at the mother church. Church colleges that have a large number of graduates serving as organists at churches of its denomination have a standardizing influence on the organ playing of that denomination. It should also be recognized that variances in the training and competencies of organists, the adequacy and versatility of the organs used, and the musical sophistication of congregations influence the role of the organ.

Everything that an organist does regularly in the service is included in one of the following sections. The order of the sections is intended to rank their importance in the worship of the congregation. The organ functions in worship:

1. *To lead the singing of the congregation in hymns and the ordinary of the liturgy.*

There is probably nothing in the service that places so modest a demand on the experienced organist's technique as the playing of hymns and liturgy. But it is here that he can have the greatest influence on the unity and spirit of the worshiping community; and if he or his predecessors have by their playing influenced the congregation to be a strong, effective singing body, it is here that his most joyful experiences in service playing will be. While the spiritual edification will be derived from an understanding of the texts of the hymns, there is a corporate inspiration and feeling of unity that is felt after a hymn has been sung well by the individuals in the assembly of Christians. But to achieve this, an unrehearsed and untrained group of individuals must express itself with some degree of accuracy in such musical elements as pitch and rhythm without the leadership of a conductor. It is the primary duty of the organist to be a servant of the congregation and supply this leadership. To carry out this duty he must give careful attention to significant elements of hymn playing.

189

The most important of these is rhythm. This term refers not just to the notation, reading, and sounding of the temporal organization of notes, but to what might be called the whole feeling of movement in music. Good hymn leadership by an organist requires good rhythmic playing, which includes all those factors that contribute to the achievement of a regular momentum or strong feeling of propulsion in the singing. And this leadership must come from an instrument that lacks the percussive attack of the consonants in singing, the tonguing of a wind instrument, and the action of a hammer on the piano strings.

Any organist whose first teacher used one of the better instruction books will recall the rules of performance for notes repeated in the same voice (break by half value the notes whose length is one beat or less, by a consistent rhythmic value or fraction of a beat for longer notes). These rules are necessary to achieve contrapuntal clarity of voice leading. But for hymn playing careful attention to breaking of repeated notes is necessary for rhythmic clarity. Play the passage in Ex. 1 on the organ, tying the repeated notes in the alto and tenor voices; then play it lifting the repeated notes just before they must be struck. Finally play it as notated in Ex. 2 which illustrates the proper breaking of the repeated notes. To assure rhythmic precision of the breaks, think of the rests as notes played upwards. Notice how much more incisive and precise the attack for each

Ex. 1

Ex. 2

chord is in the second example. It is the precision thus achieved that is necessary for good rhythmic leadership of a congregation. The extent to which repeated notes should be so observed in all voices in hymn playing will always be subject to some disagreement among experienced players and teachers. But several principles should be kept in mind:

a. The competent player has the technical ability in reading hymns to recognize and detach rhythmically all repeated notes in all voices. At times he will also modify his handling of repeated notes, but then it will be by intelligent choice, not by ignorance or lack of technical ability to observe them.

b. When the repeated notes occur between two chords in all four voices from a strong to a weaker beat, one or both of the inner voices would best be tied. But from a weaker to a strong beat, such as at the beginning of a phrase that starts with an upbeat, all voices will have to break if the proper accent is to be heard properly. Example 3 from the Sanctus of *TLH* illustrates both possibilities. If, however, this repetition of all voices of two chords occurs at the beginning of the tune, detaching for all voices serves to propel the congregation into the proper tempo, especially if the tune and text suggest more vigorous singing (e.g., *TLH* 36, 246, 262, *SBH* 131).

c. Particularly with a faster tempo, bass notes that repeat at the end of a phrase ending on a weak beat would better be tied. (*TLH* 226, *SBH* 126).

d. When a congregation has a very fine sense of rhythmic propulsion and does not depend as much on the organist for such leadership, he may choose to tie repeated notes from strong to weaker beats in any of the lower three voices without adverse effect; but the opposite case, repeated notes from weaker to stronger beats, always require rhythmic breaking.

Ex. 3

191

Another important factor contributing to the momentum of congregational singing is the regular pulse in most hymns which should be maintained both within and between stanzas. This pulse is the heartbeat of good congregational singing. Exept in some modern tunes with free meters, a few old chorales that retain the original hemiola rhythms (*TLH* 61, *SBH* 12), and most plainsong tunes, this regular pulse is based on the metrical accent and will be the half note in duple and quadruple meters and the dotted half note in triple and compound meters (assuming the quarter note as the unit beat; halve or double this if the unit is the eighth note or the half note).

Within the stanza, maintenance of this pulse is facilitated if the organist understands the relationship between the musical phrases of hymns and breathing. The organ is an instrument of unlimited breath, the human voice is not. Too many organists demonstrate the truth of the first half of that sentence rather than use intelligent phrasing at the organ to assist the congregation in taking the necessary breaths without losing the rhythmic pulse. This phrasing is accomplished by always observing a one beat rest exactly one beat before the beginning of the next phrase except in those melodies in which there is a continuous quarter note motion from one phrase into the other; in this latter case the phrase break would be equal to a half beat. If there are one beat rests notated no further adjustment is necessary. Where there are no rests the last note of the previous phrase must be shortened by the value needed for the rest. Where *TLH* uses half and heavy bar lines and the *SBH* the sign " ' " at phrase endings (confusing practices carried out inconsistently in both books), there should be no break in the rhythmic motion. Users of these books will have to make decisions reconciling maintenance of the rhythmic pulse with fermatas, longer rests between phrases, and tunes of four or more phrases with continuous movement and no longer notes at phrase ends from which time for a breath may be taken. Adjustments may include lengthening of note values and insertion or deletion of rests but should never cause a displacement of the accents of a phrase so that they do not coincide with the accents of the pulse.

A rhythmic connection must also be established between stanzas so that the pulse set up in one stanza need not be always reestablished in succeeding stanzas. Since it is advisable generally to extend the last chord of each stanza to allow for a deeper or extra breath, the organist will have to continue to feel this pulse while holding the chord and then break the chord for a one beat rest precisely one beat before the first chord of the next stanza. This one beat rest functions exactly like the preparatory beat in conducting. An organist who is consistent in making this rhythmic connection will find his congregation developing a kind of conditioned reflex, responding to this break as a choir responds to the preparatory beat, taking a breath, and attacking the tone on the next beat.

The question of the tempo at which hymns should be sung is one for which no single answer can be given except that it should be a steady one, give the impression of stability and poise on the part of the organist and congregation, promote vigorous and spirited singing, and be comfortable for the congregation. Many variables influence tempo. A large building with generous reverberation requires a slower tempo than a smaller one with comparatively dry acoustics. A congregation composed mainly of young families normally sings faster than one where the median age is older. The import of the text and the season of the church year influences the tempo. As a general rule German chorales from earlier than 1600, when used with the rhythmic subtleties of their original form, require a somewhat more modestly paced tempo than those of later centuries. Certain tunes like *St. Anne* and *Sine nomine* also require slower and more stately tempos. Triple meter hymns require a very disciplined tempo so that they do not sound rushed. Younger or inexperienced organists for whom hymn playing offers no reading or coordination difficulties must especially guard against erring on the fast side in choosing tempos.

Since the performance of most musical compositions anticipates the final cadence with some kind of ritard, the applicability of this practice to hymns is often considered. If restricted to the final stanza, an almost imperceptible broadening of the pulse may heighten the impression of finality, but if done too perceptibly this broadening of tempo may rob the close of the hymn of its vitality. Obviously, such ritards at the end of each stanza will completely destroy the rhythmic vitality of the singing.

When "Amen" is to be sung at the close of the hymn the congregation should know it will be sung, know when to sing it, and sing it in a manner which suggests that it is an affirmation to the text of the hymn. When it is impossible for a congregation to know from its hymnbook that an "Amen" will be sung at the end of a hymn, the organist may tie the soprano note from the final tonic chord of the hymn to that of the first chord of the "Amen" to let the congregation know that an "Amen" will follow, break the other three voices exactly one beat before this chord as a preliminary

193

beat, and maintain the rhythmic momentum without ritard so that both chords of the plagal cadence coincide with the strong pulse of the hymn.

The playing of the chants and responses in the ordinary of the liturgy generally follow the rhythmic principles for playing hymns, but with a few special considerations arising because the texts are prose. One of the problems is getting the congregation started together on its short responses. Regardless of whether the pastor chants or speaks, the accents of this versicle will set up a rhythmic pulse. The organist should time his attack so that the first accent of the response will coincide with this pulse. For the prose chants there is nothing the organist can do to influence the pace of the congregation on the reciting tone. But if a congregation tends to slacken its pace he can increase its vitality on the measured cadences by playing these with great rhythmic precision, sounding each chord not with, but almost imperceptibly ahead of the congregation.

Registration for hymns and liturgy should follow the principles of plenum registration. The volume should be sufficient to support and lead the singing, but not so much as to cover the voices. Two registration practices will contribute some variety to the singing. Do not always use 16′ tone on the pedal. A pleasing relief will be felt in some internal stanzas if the pedal is based on an 8′ pitch line. In services that have a smaller number of worshipers, the absence of 16′ tone from the bass voice on the pedal might be appropriate throughout. Climactic stanzas and doxologies may benefit from an increase in the tone of the organ.

2. *To provide intonations or introductions for the singing of the congregation or choir.*

Before a congregation sings the first stanza of a hymn the organist must play an introduction that will indicate what tune will be sung, set the tempo and rhythmic pulse, and establish the pitch and tonality. If the hymn follows some other action in the service involving the people, this introduction should be long enough to allow them to locate the hymn in their books. For many organists this will be merely a playing through of the hymn on a lighter registration with the same rhythmic considerations as when leading the congregation. Longer hymns, particularly if familiar to the congregation, may have a shorter introduction achieved by omitting repeated phrases or selecting only a limited number of phrases, not necessarily consecutive, that still make musical sense when played successively.

More interesting is the use of a chorale prelude to introduce the hymn.

This was a function of the organ in Lutheran churches from the 16th to the 18th centuries that resulted in major contributions to organ literature even before the organ was used to lead congregational singing. Short chorale preludes, such as those by Johann Christoph Bach, are found in several collections and instruction books. J. C. Bach's set of 44 such preludes suggests this use in its title: "Chorales that may be used for preludizing in the divine service." Organists auditioning for a position during this period were expected to demonstrate their ability to improvise such preludes. Short organ chorales from the literature can be used to intone the hymn, provided they clearly set forth the melody to be sung and a rhythmic connection can be established to the first stanza. Publishers of church organ music have issued any number of collections of organ intonations for various hymns. Study and analysis of the many available intonations will provide organists with models for writing or improvising such intonations on other tunes. The following suggestions, while by no means attempting to be exhaustive, direct the reader to simple and readily available organ intonations for the beginning organist.

Beck, Theodore. *Intonations for the Hymn-of-the-Week.* Concordia Publishing House.

_____ . *47 Hymn Intonations.* Concordia Publishing House.

_____ . *Intonations on Selected Hymns.* Concordia Publishing House.

McKinney, Howard D. *Preludes for Fifty-Five Well-Known Hymn Tunes.* J. Fischer.

The series from Augsburg Publishing House, *Free Organ Accompaniments* and *Free Hymn Accompaniments* also include intonations.

Although the registration for introducing a hymn should not be as full as for singing, it should be sufficient to suggest the spirit with which the hymn is to be sung.

3. *To serve as an ensemble participant providing accompaniment for vocal, choral, or solo music, or doubling voice parts in "a cappella" music when a choir needs such support.*

By its very nature the role of accompanist for solo and choral music is one that is often in the background and little appreciated by listeners. But this in no way decreases its importance or requirements. The organist or pianist who is fortunate enough to have gained considerable accompanying experience during student days will find that such experience has contributed to his skills as an ensemble player and in sight reading. The church organist will find himself faced with several different types of accompaniments.

The simplest type of accompaniment is one in which the organ merely doubles all or some of the voices in order to support singers who do not have sufficient confidence for successful a cappella singing or to fill out the tonal spectrum when there is an unbalanced distribution of singers among the voice parts. Such necessity for an accompaniment should not be thought of as an unfortunate situation; the use of instruments doubling voices was a standard performance practice for much Renaissance and baroque music that appears to be a cappella. Occasional organ or instrumental doubling of voice parts for a choir that could be independent of such support would be a desirable tone color contrast to a constant unaccompanied sound. For this type of accompaniment, registration should achieve a cohesive blend with the voices—background registrations of single 8′ and 4′ stops from pipes in close proximity to the choir. The accompaniment should be played as unobtrusively as possible, releases and phrasing coinciding precisely with the breathing of the choir; repeated notes in all voices should be tied so that the rhythmic propulsion will depend entirely on the choir.

A second type of accompaniment is the playing of a continuo part—the keyboard part of baroque solo, choral, and ensemble music; the left hand duplicated the notes played by the bass instruments while the unnotated right hand part was a harmonic filling or realization according to figures accompanying the bass. Since the playing of a continuo from the original figured score requires considerable improvisatory skill, the realization is normally included in the performing editions used today. Registration for a continuo part at the organ must respect its role of supplying a harmonic background supportive of the melodic parts—mild 8′ plus 4′ or even just 8′ for solos and duets, 8′ and 4′ principals at the most for choral parts. The majestic organ tone required in the concerted choral music of the 19th and 20th centuries is out of place in the music of Bach and Handel, their contemporaries and predecessors.

The organist must also consider the instruments that may or may not be playing along. If there is no violoncello or bassoon to play the bass part, the left hand should play this part on a separate manual, registered with a more incisive tone than the right hand. Since the contrabass or string bass sounding an octave lower than written would frequently have played in the tutti sections, the organist may need to use a 16′ stop (assuming presence on the manual of one with discrete and precise speech). Many vocal scores are published with the keyboard part a transcribed reduction of the full instrumental score. If the instruments called for in the score are being used in the performance and no separate continuo part is provided, the organist should not duplicate what these instruments are playing. He should rather reduce his part to the bass plus the harmonic framework. This may necessitate some editing on the basis of study of the full score.

There are a few vocal solos and a fair number of anthems that have idiomatic organ accompaniments. These range from early English anthem composers like Orlando Gibbons, who often prepared two versions of accompaniments, one for strings and the other for organ, to such modern composers as Leo Sowerby, S. Drummond Wolff, Eric Thiman, Healey Willan, and many others. The organist will approach such music as he would any organ music contemporary to it as far as registration and other details of performance are concerned. Special care should be taken to note when the accompaniment is subservient to the voices and when certain parts are structurally more important, rather than play with a constant monochromatic tone.

The greatest problem for organists arises from those accompaniments that are conceived in terms idiomatic to the piano, but are generally unplayable on the organ as written. These may include commendable music in which the original orchestral accompaniment is reduced to a piano score as in numbers from the works of Bach and Handel, but more often they are vocal solos with dubious musical and artistic qualities. Organists whose positions given them minimal control over the selection of such music have little choice but to attempt somehow to negotiate their way through the part. Henry Coleman (*The Church Organist*, Oxford University Press, 1968) has aptly described this task:

> The player's object will be to reproduce the musical content of a piece with as few notes as are necessary, arranged in such a way as to lie easily under the hands and feet. . . . The skill in "arranging" consists in knowing what notes to retain and (which is more important) what notes to reject. ...He should endeavour to reproduce the essential points of the music while omitting all that is unnecessary.

Characteristics of these accompaniments that are not compatible with the organ include:

a. Harmony supplied by arpeggios, either within a single octave or spread over several, whose effect depends on the sostenuto pedal of the piano.

b. Harmony supplied by repeated or afterbeat chords.

c. Use of extreme registers for tonal contrast, greater brilliance, or fuller tone in the bass.

d. Much octave doubling of notes and chords for greater sonority.

Several suggestions may assist the organist in making the necessary adaptations:

—Practice the accompaniment at the piano to become familiar with the essential points of the music that must be reproduced at the organ.

—Both arpeggios and repeated chords are compensations for the piano's inability to sustain harmonies at a constant dynamic level. The organist should reduce the arpeggios to the essential harmonic framework and sustain these chords. If there is a need for some rhythmic motion, the position of a chord may be shifted on the principal beats or some kind of arpeggiated motion supplied with a single voice on another manual against the sustained chords.

—The use of a 16′ stop for the bass and 4′ and 2′ stops on the manuals provides fullness and brilliance so that the octaves and full chords from piano accompaniments may be simplified.

—Manual changes and contrasting registrations will supply tonal contrast. Extreme bass or treble ranges should be modified by octave transposition.

—Use solo and background registrations to make the structure of the music clearer rather than restricting the playing to a single setting of stops.

4. *To provide music incidental to certain major actions in the service—the gathering and exiting of the congregation, the processing and recessing of officiants or special participants in the service, the gathering and presentation of the offerings, and the communing of the people.*

A large part of solo literature for the organ was written for use in services. In spite of its long historical association with worship as a solo instrument, there is a danger that the organ may be used in the service in ways incompatible with worship ideals. This danger is not something recent. KOO of 16th-century Lutheran churches give quite detailed instructions on the use of the organ in the services, but also include many warnings to organists not to play dances and secular, voluptuous, popular, boisterous, or disgraceful songs in the service. It would not be too difficult to add to these proscriptions in terms of the 20th century. But rather than approach the problem from the negative side, it would be better to examine how the music of the instrument can function by making a positive contribution to worship.

The greatest contribution to the worship of a congregation from organ literature is the large body of settings of chorale and hymn tunes that are still a part of the church's repertoire. Insofar as the worshipers can recall and associate the words or general idea of the text with the music being played, the organ can here assist and posssibly intensify the message of proclamation or response in the hymns.

A smaller amount of music of a much more utilitarian nature is written to precede motets and chants by the choir or officiant. These pieces, usually not too long, establish the tonality and give the pitch for the vocal music that follows. Generally titled praeludium or toccata and written in the various modes, these pieces came from composers throughout Europe—the Venetian Gabrielis, the Roman Frescobaldi, the Spanish Tomás de Sancta Maria, the Polish Johannes of Lublin, the south German Kindermann, the north German Scheidemann, and many others.

A much larger body of music finds an appropriate place in certain parts of the service because music without a text still has the ability to communicate. Such communication is not in the form of precise verbalization. The meaning of such "abstract" music will differ from one hearer to another. But used primarily at the introduction and conclusion of the service, such music may make a relevant appeal to the human mind and emotions, reflecting, reinforcing, or perhaps even setting a certain mood, spirit, or emotional quality which is compatible with the message suggested by the texts of the service.

Intelligent choices from literature of music that will best contribute to the effectiveness of the service requires examination of the items of the service assigned to the solo organ.

The Prelude. Regardless of whether or not the formal title prelude is used, practically all services begin with some kind of organ music. The value of this opening music can be interpreted in various ways. Together with the postlude, it serves as a frame to the service, setting the temporal bounds for the worship. It also establishes a desirable atmosphere among the worshipers. The people are a heterogeneous group, have entered the church after all kinds of activities—teaching a restless Sunday school class, rushing hectically to get the family to church on time, searching for a parking place, exchanging social or business communications in the narthex. The music at this point makes an aural appeal to the senses and minds to leave the varied backgrounds behind and to unite together on the rites and ceremonies that are to follow; in one sense, it brings order out of disorder. Certain acts may also properly occur during this music, such as the lighting of the altar or chancel candles and the processing of officiants and choir.

The ideal prelude is based on a hymn of the service, preferably the first, whose thoughts are relevant for that service. Unless the hymn melody is quite evident in the texture of the prelude, it would be well if it were identified by title in the service folder or bulletin so that the congregation can understand its function. Among the many collections of organ music based on hymns and chorales, several of the standard collections that are especially useful for the organist of modest ability include:

The Parish Organist. 12 volumes, Various editors. Concordia Publishing House.

Keller, Herman (ed.). 80 Chorale Preludes. C. F. Peters.

Lang, C. S. Twenty Hymn-Tune Preludes. Two sets. Oxford University Press.

Wyton, Alec. A Little Christian Year. Carl Fischer.

Because of limitations in his library or repertoire or because many of the tunes in common use have not interested composers to write worthwhile settings, an organist will often have to choose a "free" prelude, one not based on a cantus firmus. This will be taken from such pieces as fantasies, toccatas, and especially preludes and fugues. When exercising this greater freedom of choice, an organist must discipline himself to be sure that what he plays is compatible with the thought of the service and not just a demonstration of his technical and musical prowess. Especially useful, among the many such collections of free organ music, for organists of modest ability is

Thomas, Paul (ed.). The Church Organist. Four volumes. Concordia Publishing House.

For many organists and parishes a single short prelude is long enough. But if the organist has sufficient skill and repertoire there is no reason why the prelude need be confined to a single piece. The music could start some minutes before the service and continue until officiants and choir are in place for the first hymn. This would allow the organist to play several settings of the first hymn or longer works from the literature. But such longer preludial music should still be in the character of the service. It should not become a recital. Neither should it be the pallid, innocuous soft background music piped into many commercial establishments. The music should not lull the congregation to inactivity, but should arouse and prepare them for their work as people of God—the liturgy.

The Voluntary. Unless a hymn is sung while the offerings are received, the organ will usually play during this action. Because this follows the proclamation of the Word in the lessons and sermon, the music played should not attract attention to itself, but rather should reflect the message just heard. This would suggest at best a limitation to organ settings of hymns used in the service or other related hymns. In fact, a strong case could be made for the thesis that if the organist cannot provide music related to the hymns at this point of the service, he should keep still and allow the offerings to be received in silence. This is an extreme point of view and most congregations are probably not ready for that much silence, but it is one organists should keep in mind if they must choose other music to play here.

Because the duration of the action of receiving the offerings and presenting them at the altar is variable according to the attendance from service to service, the organist, the pastor, and the ushers should cooperate by some kind of prearranged signal so that a satisfactory ending for the voluntary will be coordinated with the actions and movement in the chancel. Unless an organist is a skillful improviser and can musically extend or abbreviate the chosen voluntary, he might better choose music which will be somewhat shorter than needed and have a second short setting of the same tune or the hymnal harmonization of the tune ready to play if additional music is needed.

Music during communion. During the communing of the people it is appropriate according to the Lutheran tradition to have communion or de tempore hymns sung by the congregation, or motets and hymns sung by the choir. If the organ also plays, its music should be restricted to settings of the hymns being sung or other hymns for communion or proper to the day.

Postlude. As the prelude introduces the worship of the day by anticipating the hymns and general spirit of the service, so the postlude sends the people on their way with one more reminder of some of these principal ideas of the service. Since the Eucharist ends with thanksgiving the postlude could also reflect the joy that the Christian takes from celebrating the Sacrament and carries out with him to his daily life. It would again be preferable if the hymns of the service could provide the themes for the postlude.

5. *To provide music that serves as a transition from one musical part of the service to another.*

There was a time when the organ was expected to provide a soft series of chords whenever there was nothing being said or sung. This might be termed "Music to do things by," "Music to rise by," "Music to kneel by," "Music to walk from the altar to the lectern by," "Music to seat late-comers by." Constant background music smacks of those radio stations which must always be transmitting some kind of audible signal lest during

Ex. 4

Modulation from G to D with intonation of *Nunc Dimittis* ("The Order of Holy Communion," TLH)

a break in the sound for a few seconds some potential customer spinning his tuning dial might miss the station. The meaninglessness of such a practice in worship is obvious.

But there are places within the services where an organist can draw on skills as an improviser to lead from one musical part to another if they are

Ex. 5

Modulation from *Te Deum* to *Kyrie* using soprano motive and rhythm from *Kyrie* ("The Order of Matins," TLH)

Ex. 6

Modulation from *Venite* to the hymn "Praise to the Lord, the Almighty" ("The Order of Matins," TLH)

in different keys. But a word of caution is in order about modulations. The music theory necessary for modulating is best demonstrated as a succession of simple four-part chords. If the modulations within the service consist merely of these exercises of chords, they belong with the background music criticized above. In this case it should be remembered that five seconds of silence may sometimes be the best modulation. The chords should serve merely as the harmonic framework that supports a melodic connection between the sections.

Several examples that might occur in playing services from *TLH* will illustrate the technique. Notice that the modulation may also serve as an intonation by quoting material from the hymn or chant following in both the old and new keys. (Ex. 4, 5, & 6.)

6. *To enrich the experience of singing hymns through the use of varied harmonizations or accompaniments and solo organ verses.*

There are devices by which organists can introduce some variety into the singing of hymns. But such devices, like spices, are most effective if used with moderation.

Two of these devices, varied harmonizations and varied accompaniments are not always clearly distinguished. A varied harmonization will keep the tune in the soprano voice; the variety may come through a different chord choice than that in the hymnal, the omission of the pedal based on 16′, or the use of a harmonization in three voices rather than the traditional setting in four voices. A varied accompaniment could also be referred to as an organ descant in which not only the harmony is enriched, but a new upper voice will introduce a melodic line that serves as a counterpoint to the original tune.

In some parishes it is enough to expect the organist to accompany all the stanzas of the hymn according to the standard hymnal. But when stanza after stanza appears with precisely the same harmony, there is a certain monotony it might be well to avoid. Alternate harmonizations with more variety in chord choice may assist in relieving this monotony. The organist may have the skill to prepare his own reharmonizations of the tunes. The organist's book for *WS*, for example, supplies two harmonizations for each tune; these may be used alternately. Other examples or models are found in some of the chorale books from Germany that include a standard four-voiced chordal harmonization and a more contrapuntal three-voiced setting for each tune.

Descant accompaniments will be used more sparingly. The presence of melodic material other than the tune in the soprano may confuse the singing of all but musically sophisticated congregations. Use of such accompaniments should be restricted to organists who have sufficient technique to handle them with ease, to very well-known tunes for which the congregation does not depend as much on the melodic leadership of the organ, to those services in which the choir is present to lead the singing, and to single climactic stanzas. Some more recent examples of varied harmonizations and varied accompaniments for organ which are useful for the organist of modest ability include:

Bender, Jan. *The Hymn of the Week*. *Organ Settings*. Concordia Publishing House.

————. *New Organ Settings for Hymns and Chorales*. Two volumes. Concordia Publishing House.

Bunjes, Paul. *New Organ Accompaniments for Hymns*. Concordia Publishing House. (Includes melody and descant parts for instruments.)

Free Organ Accompaniments to Festival Hymns. Vol. 1. Augsburg Publishing House.

Free Organ Accompaniments to Hymns. Vol. 2. Augsburg Publishing House.

Johnson, David. *Free Hymn Accompaniments for Manuals*. Two volumes. Augsburg Publishing House.

In churches that have the practice of occasionally performing the principal hymn of the service alternately stanza by stanza between choir and congregation, the organ may also participate as a solo instrument by playing a short setting from the literature based on the tune being sung. This is a practice that has its roots in 16th-century Lutheranism, when the intonation and the playing of alternate stanzas was the only way the organist participated in the hymns.

Other Accompanimental Instruments in Worship

Because of spatial, financial, or other reasons some churches must get by in their worship with substitutes for an organ. These include the reed organ or harmonium, the piano, and electronic instruments. Many of the principles of service playing remain the same, but there are some adaptations a player must make to compensate for the instrument.

Where a *piano* or *reed organ* must be used to accompany groups of singers of such a size that more tone is needed, a player may get a fuller texture by playing the bass voice in octaves and the upper three voices with the right hand. When the written tenor is more than an octave from the soprano it should be transposed an octave higher and played between the soprano and alto. While careful use of the damper pedal of the piano will help to achieve legato, the reed organ will require careful finger substitution to avoid choppy playing.

A surprising amount of organ literature is playable on these instruments. Since most 17th- and 18th-century organ music from regions of Europe other than north and central Germany was written for instruments with no or minimal pedal divisions, there is much good *manualiter* music available. Especially serviceable are the large number of English verses and voluntaries by such composers as Purcell, Blow, Walond, and Stanley that have recently been made available in authoritative editions. Many organ chorales were also written for manuals alone; examples would be the chorale partitas of Boehm, Pachelbel, and J. S. Bach, and the chorale fughettas of the latter. Especially useful collections for manuals are:

Trevor, C. H. (ed.). *Old English Organ Music*. Oxford University Press.
Phillips, G. and others. *Tallis to Wesley: A New Series of Original Organ Music*. Hinrichsen. Over 30 volumes of music mostly on two staves. Much of the music in *The Parish Organist* and *The Church Organist* (see above) is also on two staves and does not require pedal.

The introduction of *electronic instruments* some four decades ago and especially the recent technological advances in the industry have made the substitution of such an instrument an option considered by many churches when planning for an organ. American organists with any kind of job mobility will undoubtedly be confronted more or less frequently with electronic keyboard instruments. While much of the popularity of these instruments, especially in churches that make decisions with minimal professional consultation, may reflect the dollar sign rather than an understanding of church music, it is also true that "knee-jerk" reflex actions keep many organists from honestly evaluating more recent developments by those parts of the industry that are trying to operate within the traditions of the liturgical organ.

Most of these recent developments are attempts to compensate for what have been musical defects in the electronic instruments: the artificial

206

sound of a tone produced by electronic means, the inability to generate a satisfactory imitation of the principal class of stops, and the limitation of the sound source to a few speakers. In evaluating the capability of the electronic instruments serving the church, attention should be given not so much to how many different kinds of flute, string, and reed tone are available, but to how satisfactory the different possibilities for plenum registration are. And the standard for comparison should not be an instrument that shows many of the faults of those built in early part of this century, but one that represents the current state of the art of reputable builders.

One of the more unsolvable problems with the electronics occurs when an organist in a church is confronted with an instrument more suitable for recreational music in the home—especially those using 12 or 13 levers instead of a pedal clavier, insufficient registrational possibilities even if the pedal clavier has more keys, incomplete manuals intended only for solo-accompaniment effects. The only possible solution is to try to get the same registration approximating a plenum on both manuals and playing manuals only in the same manner as a reed organ. Above all with electronic instruments: avoid the tremolo and coloristic effects intended for popular music.

An instrument still more recently accepted into many churches, at least for services that feature the religious "pop" hymns, is the *guitar*. The guitar is an ideal instrument for solo or less formal small group presentations of "folktype" music; some composers have also used it creatively in their choral music. But some problems should be recognized. Unamplified, the guitar is obviously limited to accompanying smaller groups in rooms of limited size. Amplified to provide sufficient volume for a larger number of singers, the instrument may lose its inherent charm to that high-decibel tone that overwhelms rather than accompanies.

Other observations to remember about the guitar: it is not an instrument to provide melodic leadership. A group struggling to learn a new melody will not receive the help from the guitar that it would from a piano or organ.

As a recreational instrument the guitar is "widely played badly." For small informal fellowship groups such novice playing may be unobjectionable. But corporate worshipers may very well be less than edified by a performance in which inadequacies of technique, unmusicality, or inexperience are evident.

Edward W. Klammer

Orchestral Instruments

The great increase in programs of instrumental instruction and ensemble playing in the elementary and secondary schools has presented churches with the resources for expanding the role of instruments in the service. While church publishers will provide some of the materials needed, church musicians will be able to make more effective use of the instrumentalists they have if they can also do some of the arranging according to their resources.

Instruments and Congregational Singing

In churches where musical instruments (other than the organ) have never been used, the easiest and safest way to introduce them is in connection with congregational singing, especially at a festival service. Most church members will accept the use of instruments in a service enthusiastically; however, there will always be some who will object until the practice is firmly established. A soprano instrument (or instruments) may play the melody at the same pitch level or an octave higher on selected stanzas of a hymn. Trumpets, violins, flutes, oboes, recorders, or clarinets may be used for this purpose. By such simple means young, inexperienced players will also have an opportunity to develop confidence for the playing of more difficult music at some future time. Instrumental descants may also be played. They are especially effective on doxological stanzas.

A somewhat more elaborate form of hymn embellishment is made possible by the use of a chorale concertato. A chorale concertato is a composition for congregation, choir, organ, and one or more instruments, based on a well-known hymn. Each stanza of the hymn is treated differently. In the last stanza, organ, choir (with descant), congregation, and instruments join for a grand climax. The settings of chorales by Johann Crueger (1598—c. 1662) and Johann Ebeling (1637—76) for mixed choir, organ, and two descanting instruments may also be used for this purpose. Whenever instruments are used in connection with a choral composition in the church service, whether a single instrument or an ensemble—brass, woodwind, or string—they should also be used to accompany appropriate stanzas of hymns.

Some suggested resources for instruments to be used with congregational singing are:

Instrumental Descants for Hymns

Mudde, Wilhelm. *Organ and Trumpet Accompaniments to Festival Hymns*. Augsburg Publishing House.

Schalk, Carl. *Festival Settings for the Small Parish—The Easter Season*. Simple settings of hymns and chorales with trumpet descants. Concordia Publishing House.

Wood, Dale. *New Settings of Twenty Well-Known Hymn Tunes*. Varied organ accompaniment with optional descants for voices and/or instruments. Augsburg Publishing House.

Chorale Concertatos

Bunjes, Paul. *All Glory, Laud, and Honor*. Choir, congregation, trumpet, and organ. Concordia Publishing House.

————. *All Praise to God Who Reigns Above*. Choir, congregation, trumpet, and organ. Concordia Publishing House.

————. *God of the Prophets*. Choir, congregation, trumpet, and organ. Concordia Publishing House.

————. *How Can I Thank Thee, Lord?* Choir, congregation, trumpet, and organ. Concordia Publishing House.

————. *I Know that My Redeemer Lives*. Choir, congregation, trumpet, and organ. Concordia Publishing House.

————. *Praise to the Lord, the Almighty*. Choir, congregation, trumpet, and organ. Concordia Publishing House.

————. *A Mighty Fortress Is Our God*. Choir, congregation, three trumpets, organ. Concordia Publishing House.

Pelz, Walter. *Crown Him with Many Crowns*. Choir, congregation, organ, trumpet. Augsburg Publishing House.

————. *Holy God, We Praise Thy Name*. Choir, congregation, trumpet, and organ. Augsburg Publishing House.

————. *Jesus Christ Is Risen Today*. Choir, congregation, trumpet, and organ. Augsburg Publishing House.

Wolff, S. Drummond. *Jesus Christ Is Risen Today*. For mixed choir, two trumpets, congregation, and organ. Concordia Publishing House.

Children's Choir Music with Instrumental Accompaniment

There is a great abundance of choral music with instrumental accompaniment for all types of choirs, from simple unison anthems for junior choirs and a single instrument to elaborate compositions for large mixed choirs with full orchestra.

Many anthems intended for children contain descants that may be played and sung, or played only on a flute, recorder, violin, clarinet, or some other instrument.

In compositions containing a canon, one part of the canon may be played on an instrument, or both parts may be reinforced by instruments.

The following listing includes several collections and cantatas for junior choirs that use various instruments:

Unison Pieces

> Bach, J. S. "Lord Jesus Christ, Thou Prince of Peace," from *A Second Morning Star Choir Book*. For unison or two-part and violin. The vocal parts are easy. The instrumental part requires a competent violinist. Concordia Publishing House.

> Hammerschmidt, Andreas. *Let the People Praise Thee, O God*. For unison voices, two violins (flutes, recorders, oboes, clarinets), and continuo. Concordia Publishing House.

> Neumark, George. "If Thou But Suffer God to Guide Thee," from *A Second Morning Star Choir Book*. For unison voices (or two-part), two melody instruments, and continuo. Concordia Publishing House.

> Schalk, Carl. "Ye Sons and Daughters of the King," from *The Star Carol Book*. For unison voices, keyboard instrument, triangle, and tambourine. Concordia Publishing House.

Collections for Junior Choirs

> Distler, Hugo. *Selections from Der Jahrkreis*. Twenty selections in which instruments may double the vocal parts (*colla parte*). Instrumental ritornellos are included for two of the compositions. Concordia Publishing House.

> Drischner, Max. *Make a Joyful Noise*. Twenty-five hymns and carols for unison voices, treble instrument (violin, flute, recorder, clarinet, oboe, trumpet) and organ, harpsichord, or piano. Concordia Publishing House.

> *Settings of Chorales for Treble Voices*. Various composers. Twenty-eight hymns and chorales for unison, two- and three-part children's choir, with one to eight instruments; recorders (or other C instruments), xylophone, glockenspiel, and various percussion instruments. Augsburg Publishing House.

Cantatas

> Beck, Theodore. *A Little Christmas Concert Based on "From Heaven Above."* For

unison, two- or three-part choir, three recorders, and keyboard instrument. Concordia Publishing House.

Bender, Jan. *From Heaven High I Come to Earth*. For two-part choir, soloists, congregation, oboe, violin, and organ. Concordia Publishing House.

Hillert, Richard. *The Christmas Story According to St. Luke*. For unison and two-part choir (or soloists), flute, oboe, two violins, cello, and organ. Concordia Publishing House.

Luebeck, Vincent. *Welcome, Thou King of Glory*. For SA choir, male voices ad lib., two violins (flutes, oboes, recorders), and continuo. Concordia Publishing House.

Zipp, Friedrich. *Come, Hasten, Ye Shepherds*. Unison voices and three recorders (or flutes), triangle, and bells, ad lib. Concordia Publishing House.

Mixed Choir Music and Instruments

Mixed choirs are fortunate today in having hundreds of excellent compositions from all periods at their disposal. Much of this music was originally conceived with instrumental accompaniment. Almost all of the "a cappella" literature from the Renaissance and baroque eras was originally performed with instruments doubling the voice parts. Heinrich Schuetz in his introduction to the *Geistliche Chormusik*, 1648, suggests various methods of performing these works:

1. All of the compositions may be sung, that is, without accompaniment of any kind.
2. All the voices of the motet may be played on instruments.
3. All of the voices may be sung and played, that is, the instruments double the voice parts *colla parte*. (Both Schuetz and Michael Praetorius state that the purpose of such combined singing and playing is threefold: to support the singers, to give variety, and to lend grandeur to the composition.)
4. Some voices may be sung while the remaining voices are played on instruments.
5. All voices of a motet may be sung by soloists.
6. Various sections of a motet may be divided between soloists and the tutti choir.
7. The organ may also play along, preferably all the parts rather than just a continuo style chordal accompaniment.

Michael Praetorius and other composers suggested similar performance practice in the introductions to their various works. Armed with such instructions from the composers themselves, the present day choral director is in a position to perform works from the Renaissance and baroque periods according to the instrumental forces he has at his disposal.

Double-chorus works that, because of the number of voices required, are usually beyond the forces available in most small choirs can easily be performed by such groups if one choir is assigned to a quartet of instruments. Many such works are available with brass quartet parts for the second choir. Where printed parts for such double-chorus works are not available, the choir director will have to prepare instrumental parts for a string, woodwind, or brass quartet. As another alternative, the second choir part may also be played on the organ.

Many of the baroque composers wrote cantatas with accompaniment for two melody instruments and continuo. It was customary in the baroque era to substitute instruments freely. Therefore, if a cantata was written for two violins and continuo and two violins are not available, flutes, oboes, or recorders may be substituted, or a combination of instruments may be used. If a continuo instrument is not available, the part may be played on the organ pedal with a 16' and 8' combination.

Bach chorales are often performed with accompaniment. There is no denying their beauty when sung a cappella; however, originally they were accompanied by organ and instruments. If instruments are available, they should be played *colla parte*. For example, if three stanzas of a chorale are sung to the same Bach harmonization, it would be good to accompany stanzas 1 and 3 with organ and whatever instruments are available and to sing the middle stanza unaccompanied.

Many anthems for mixed choir, organ, and brass instruments are also readily available.

Some suggested resources for instruments used with mixed choir include:

Bunjes, Paul. *Comfort, Comfort Ye My People*. SATB, strings, organ. Concordia Publishing House.

Handel, G. F. *Jesus, Sun of Life, My Splendor*. SATB, strings organ. Concordia Publishing House.

Purcell, Henry. *Rejoice in the Lord Alway*. SATB, A, T, B soloists, strings, organ. Concordia Publishing House.

Choir and Brass

Bender, Jan. *God the Father, Be Our Stay*. SATB, brass quartet, organ. Concordia Publishing House.

Praetorius, Michael. *In dulci jubilo*. SATB, brass quartet, organ. Robert King Music Co.

Choir and Miscellaneous Instruments

Buxtehude, Dietrich. *Jesus, Joy and Pleasure*. For SAB choir, two violins (flutes, recorders, oboes), and continuo. Chantry Music Press.

Hammerschmidt, Andreas. *Holy Is the Lord*. For mixed choir (SSATB), two instruments (trumpets, flutes, oboes, recorders, violins), and continuo. Concordia Publishing House.

Petzold, Johannes. *The Christmas Story*. For SAB choir, organ, and a single instrument—flute, recorder, violin, or oboe. Concordia Publishing House.

Schalk, Carl. "The King Shall Come when Morning Dawns," from *A Second Crown Choir Book*. For two mixed voices with guitar or autoharp accompaniment. Concordia Publishing House.

Music for Organ and Instruments

The flute and violin sonatas of Bach and Handel and similar music of other composers provide excellent material for service preludes and voluntaries. The slow movements are particularly fine for use as voluntaries while the offerings are gathered. The same applies to trio sonatas by Corelli, Buxtehude, Vivaldi (available in several editions), and many other composers.

Many organ chorale preludes may be performed on the organ with the chorale melody played by a solo instrument instead of a solo voice on the organ. In addition, Johann Krebs and Georg Kauffmann, both pupils of Bach, wrote chorale preludes specifically for oboe and organ. Some suggested resources using the organ and various instruments are:

Organ and a Single Instrument

Kauffmann, Georg. *Six Chorales from "Harmonische Seelenlust"*. For organ and oboe (or clarinet or trumpet). Concordia Publishing House.

Krebs, John. Lud. *Ausgewaehlte Orgelwerke*. Chorale preludes for organ and oboe (or trumpet or clarinet). Kistner and Siegel.

Purcell, Henry. *Sonata for Trumpet and Organ*. Concordia Publishing House.

———. *Ceremonial Music for Organ with Optional Trumpets*. Some with one trumpet, some with two. Mercury Music Corp.

Rohlig, Harald. *A Little Shepherd Music.* For flute or recorder and organ. Concordia Publishing House.

_____ . *Eight Intradas and Chorales for Organ and Trumpet.* Concordia Publishing House.

_____ . *Christmas Music for Flute and Organ.* Variations on "Es kommt ein Schiff geladen." Concordia Publishing House.

Schalk, Carl. *Chorales for Lent.* One or two equal instruments with and without organ. Augsburg Publishing House.

Wolff, S. Drummond (ed.) *Baroque Composers of the "Chapels Royal."* Concordia Publishing House.

_____ . *Baroque Suite for Organ.* Concordia Publishing House. Both of the above for organ and one or two trumpets.

Organ and Several Instruments

Bach-Biggs. *Three Wedding Chorales.* Organ and two trumpets. Associated Music Publishers.

_____ . *Two Christmas Chorales and Doxology.* Organ and two trumpets. Associated Music Publishers.

_____ . *Two Fanfares and Chorale.* Organ, three trumpets, and timpani. Associated Music Publishers.

Music for Instruments Alone

Besides church music for choir and instruments, and organ and instruments, there is also music for ensembles of various kinds, and orchestra. Almost all of the sinfonias, preludes, and overtures to cantatas and oratorios are suitable for use in church services and concerts. Some material of this type is included in the following listing.

Two Like Instruments

Ehmann, Wilhelm (ed.). *Geistliche Zwiegesaenge.* Sacred Duets based on chorales. For two brass or woodwind instruments. Baerenreiter-Verlag.

Kettering, Eunice Lea. *Fifteen Carols Arranged for Two Instruments.* Originally intended for two recorders, but playable on almost any combination of soprano instruments. Concordia Publishing House.

Strings

Charpentier, Marc-Antoine. *French Noel "Laissez Paitre Vos Betes."* For strings, two flutes, and continuo. Concordia Publishing House.

Schiassi, Gaetano M. *Christmas Symphony.* For strings and continuo. C. F. Peters.

Willan, Healey. *Prelude on "Puer nobis nascitur."* Concordia Publishing House.
Brass
  Hillert, Richard. *Three Christmas Carols for Brass.* Concordia Publishing House.

Handbells

Whether just a few bells used in a simple accompaniment to vocal music or elaborate ensembles requiring 10 or 12 ringers, handbells have brought a new and appealing sonority into churches. Handbell choirs also provide another opportunity for ensemble participation by those willing to accept the discipline and responsibility required. Since each ringer is assigned certain pitches that he must play at the precise time, irregular attendance is impossible to tolerate in a handbell choir.

Because sets of bells are a relatively expensive investment, church musicians should be sure that they understand the techniques and organization required before undertaking a program. Besides the study of books on the subject, this preparation would best also include observation of successful groups in other parishes.

Practical Problems

Some of the problems connected with instrumental music for the church are similar to those faced by the choir director. One of the main problems is to find suitable instrumental music to fit specific needs. There is no simple answer to this problem. The church musician must constantly be on the lookout for material he can use either immediately or in the future. He must build a library of music to which he can turn when the occasion arises. The church musician should study the catalogs of music publishers who specialize in instrumental music and be acquainted with church music publishers who publish and carry music of this kind. Listings of such music, from simple junior choir anthems using a single instrument to large choral works with orchestral accompaniment, are available from most publishers.

Instrumentalists are not always readily available. Often, however, there are teenagers or elementary school children who have progressed sufficiently on a band or orchestral instrument to be useful for some of the suggestions outlined in this article. Look about for them and help them develop their talents. For certain works it is imperative that professionals or first-class amateur players be engaged. In such cases it will be necessary to pay the instrumentalists a fee. If your music budget does not contain an amount for musicians, try obtaining the needed monies from individuals in the congregation.

Using instrumentalists in church music means more work for the director. Besides conducting special rehearsals with the instrumentalists, he will have to purchase the music, check the parts against the score, see to it that measures are numbered, sometimes prepare instrumental parts, transpose parts if tranposing instruments are used, and take care of other details.

Instrumentalists usually enjoy playing more than a single composition in a service. Therefore, if a cantata is being performed that calls for two violins (or other instruments) and cello, the instrumentalists might well also be used for the prelude, the voluntary, and perhaps even the postlude. The three movements (usually fast-slow-fast) of the typical trio sonata will be very useful for this purpose.

The use of instruments in parish worship can bring a dimension to congregational praise that can be obtained in no other way. As the use of instruments serves to enrich and deepen Christian worship, it is a valuable tool or resource that the church musician cannot afford to overlook.

See also the related articles in *Key Words in Church Music*: alternation practice; chorale; church modes; church music history, Renaissance—the Reformation tradition; church music history, baroque; de tempore hymn; all articles on hymnody; notation; organ, history; organ, literature; organ, use in mass and offices; organ chorale; performance practice; tablature; thoroughbass; voluntary

CHAPTER VI

The Pastor and the Church Musician

Adalbert Raphael Kretzmann

When the congregation of Jesus Christ recognized the loss of the Old Testament cultus, they had to find something in music as rich and as glorious as that which the old temple had brought. They realized that the praise of God remained the joyous privilege of the children of God. The song of everlasting praise was to remain, and human beings would have to be entrusted with the "new" song.

How does a pastor show understanding and true devotion also in this department of the church's work? How can he truly become the consecrator, hallower, and sponsor of all the good gifts that come to him in a fine, devoted church musician? First of all, he must be very conscious of the fact that his office of Word and Sacrament is the same office that the church musician has in a special way. If both the church musician and the pastor are conscious of the basic principles that are involved in the New Testament worship of the Godhead, they find the gates wide open to real joy and great faith.

In the church of Jesus Christ there is only one sacrifice after the one-time sacrifice on the cross, and that is the thankoffering of the people of God. It is more than just saying thanks to God. It is the overwhelming conviction that everything good comes to us in and through God. This thanksgiving to God must manifest itself in attitudes of the highest quality. We cannot read what the apostles say about the new church in Ephesians and Colossians without feeling the richness of the relationship that brings proclamation and adoration together.

As Christians we have drawn the entire love and work of Jesus together in the Gospel, the "glad tidings," the joyous proclamation of the life and death and resurrection of our Lord. It expresses very simply for all of us the assurance that God has drawn near to man and that in that light everything must work itself out as a blessing to the people of God. It is a joyous message retold in glorious music and in thankful hymns.

Together in Dialog and Understanding

The pastor needs the poetic aids of hymns as well as the exaltation of music to make the "message" come alive with splendor. The hallelujahs sound best when they are set to music and have an added dimension which the pastor himself could never give in any words. This understanding of the power of music to add a new dimension to the proclamation of the Word ought to draw pastor and church musician together in dialog and understanding as nothing else can. The beautiful emotions evoked by the great music of Christmas, the Passiontide, and the Resurrection can scarcely be logically defined or explained, but certainly any bringer of glad tidings should recognize that he has one of the ablest allies in an understanding, good church musician. The *whole* man is redeemed by Jesus Christ and the *whole* man responds to the message. The two media, preaching and music, are thus not only culturally and aesthetically involved, but they have a proclaiming and theological dimension that can hardly be estimated unless we have fallen prey to the popular but erroneous feeling that the "spoken" Word is *the* thing. This causes not only the neglect of the Sacrament but brings about a blankness for the great musical and visual arts that comes close to a rejection of the outreach of God through their media.

The injunction of the apostle in Col. 3:17 should be remembered: "Whatever you do, in word or deed, do everything in the name of the Lord Jesus, giving thanks to God the Father through Him."

In 1530, when Luther was spending his time in Coburg while his colleagues were presenting the new confession to the emperor at Augsburg, he noted down five points which all pastors and church musicians should remember:

> Music is a gift of God.
> Music rejoices the soul.
> Music turns away Satan.
> Music arouses innocent joys (with music anger, greed,
> lust, pride, etc. must fade away).
> Music is a peaceful art form (contrasted with the training
> and drilling for war, etc.).

We all observe at once that these cannot be applied theologically to all music as a criterion, but it is of great interest that Luther preserved this great gift of God as a special heritage of the church, whereas Zwingli and Calvin rejected it with the claim that there was too much opportunity for abuse. They knew and felt, as all of us do, that Satan moves in with music that is not exactly of the right kind. They seemed to forget that Luther separated church music from music in general. (This may give direction or thoughtful reevaluation to some of the things perpetrated under the name "music" in the church today.) The church musician has his original guide in Gennadius of Marseille (†492): *Vide ut quod ore cantas, corde credas et quod corde credis operibus probes* ("Take heed that what you sing with your mouth you also believe with your heart, and that what you believe with your heart you prove by your works").

Together in Proclamation

The words can be applied to all of us, but when you want to draw a tight ring around "proclamation" in the church, then pastor and church musician are bound together in this great thing. Surely the office of the church musician must center primarily around the worship services of the congregation, and there it is inescapable that the finest kind of understanding be developed between the pastor and the musician. The church musician must know, as soon as possible, the exact character and feeling of every single service throughout the year. As the pastor's sermon thought and themes are reflected in the hymns which he chooses, so he must give the church musician time to prepare music that makes the worship service a unit and not a series of disjointed and sometimes utterly unrelated (good) parts. This requires study and preparation on the part of the pastor, a complete openness and willingness to regard the importance of the work and service of music as being the important, single, ingredient of the service alongside of Word and Sacrament. Both of the latter only come alive when this preparation and cooperation are manifest in all the work and worship of the church. This may mean preparation that goes into quarterly or even annual selection of texts, themes, and hymns far in advance, so that the conscientious church musician may have opportunity to select and bring to the worship the very best compositions (or even well prepared improvisations) as preludes, voluntaries, postludes, choir selections, etc. There is no reason to try to expand the great distance between the pulpit and the organ into a great impassable gulf. Each worship service should begin with the assurance that both in the pulpit and in the music there has been preparation, consideration, understanding, true love of the Gospel, and true cooperation.

Search for a reason if you find great differences between the pastor and the church musician. Who has forgotten the Gospel, and why has it happened? Can you explain moods and temperaments in the light of the cross? Has the congregation come to expect tensions born of pride? Why should there be pride when the only interest is the glory of God? Is not the service of music as important a function of the ministry as any other part of it when souls are involved? Study will be needed, and good discussions, long and deep, will have to prepare for worship sometimes or arise out of the participation at either end of the church at other times. Honesty is required of us, and love and faith can give us good answers and better music and finer and more thoughtful offerings of praise.

The details in which both pastor and church musician share are, of course, found in the base plan of the worship services. It may even be that the daily offices are involved with music of some kind, or, in a larger congregation, Matins and Vespers. There is a definite plan to the services of marriage and burial in which both ends of the church are deeply and evangelically involved. The understanding about correctness is subordinated to the desire of having the Gospel message come through for love and consolation and ultimate redemption. Where there are regular schools, children's choirs or larger choirs will become a real challenge and bring an almost indelible character to the life and faith of the young members of the congregation. Confirmation classes will give an opportunity for interpretive work in the hymn book and the liturgy. Time must be set aside for rehearsal with instrumentalists. In the day school (if any) as well as the Sunday school, attention must be given to the joyous outpouring of faith for and with the children.

Out of the discussion and planning, the missionary and cultural thrust also come through. Plans for organ recitals, visiting choirs, etc., must be organized on a regular schedule so that both pastor and the church musician can see clearly the emphasis for each particular presentation in order to keep spontaneity, variety, and originality alive and avoid a patterned sameness that is so often the death of good church music.

To establish a sense of significance it is necessary to make reference to services, recitals, concerts, etc., both *before* and *after* the event so that the public may be helped to understanding enjoyment and spiritual involvement. It is often hard for a church musician to be his own publicity agent, and he will need the encouragement and the help of the pastor in the articulation of his ideals and hopes. Good laymen trained in public relations and publicity can also be very helpful on the music committee.

Encouragement to do "big" things is a vital necessity. The narrowness of thinking that the church has only a mission to preach, without discerning the mission to the *whole* man, has been a blight for years and years. The fear of overemphasizing things that are not of the essence of Christianity has held many good Christian performers back and has lost forever the opportunity to open a new way to the heart of man and make him more ready to receive the message of the cross.

Proper allowances must be arranged for the church musician so that he is free to buy music for experimentation as well as performance. The great volume of literature in the field of music will necessitate a constant search for what is best and most impressive so that the liturgy will shine through, give variety to the choral and to the organ music, and prepare the way for constant growth in all things spiritual. The liturgical piety of a good organist and choirmaster is often the key to exemplary behavior on the part of the choir and participation by the singers in the full functions of the worship service. If the church musician has once recognized the potential of a great singing congregation, he will be very careful but also very insistent on moving the congregation ahead to new experiences in worshipful singing. In planning the organ music, proper concern must be exercised so that it fulfills its function as the leading musical instrument in worship services as well as the accompaniment for choir and congregational singing. Other instruments must also be taken into consideration, and the versatility of the church musician should be acknowledged regularly and graciously by proper support.

Together in Ministry

As Paul Manz so aptly put it, "The church musician is one who is also called to *minister* to people, but in a unique way. To be sure, he does preach and he does teach. Yes, he also comforts the bereaved, and he helps to sustain the weak. Often he counsels the troubled and distressed, and he always assists at the distribution of the Sacraments. He does all this, but *never* from the altar, lectern, pulpit, or font, but from the choir loft and organ bench. Furthermore, he does this all in a nonverbal manner in spite of the fact that we have been led to believe that *all* theological and liturgical communication is verbal. Certainly it is not, as both music and art so ably demonstrate.

"We expect a great deal of our professional church workers and rightly so. A church musician must be able to analyze the musical forms of the hymns and liturgical chants. He must know basic harmony and how to employ it effectively. He must be able to transpose and to sight-read. Furthermore, he is expected to know, understand, and appreciate the chosen instrument of the church. While at times this is difficult to accomplish, it is, nonetheless, a reasonable expectation on the part of the parish. Whatever the chosen instrument of the parish—pipe organ, piano, or electronic—it is his servant, and it is his springboard to creativity. It may never be his master; it must be an extension of himself, and through it he must lead, communicate, and *minister* in a simple, persuasive, yet forceful manner born out of his theological convictions.

"His theological conviction is perhaps the most important ingredient. It transposes a church musician into a minister. When he uses musical language and ideas to illustrate and illuminate theological concepts, he becomes a minister in the very finest sense.

"We have been created by God, the Father, redeemed by Jesus Christ, his Son, and called, gathered, and enlightened by the Holy Spirit for one purpose only, namely to worship, praise, and adore God forever. Worship has but one theme: to praise God. David puts it well when he says, 'Let everything that hath breath praise the Lord! Praise ye the Lord!' While it has only one theme, it has many variations. Each service, each Sunday, each season, each festival, and each occasion for worship deals with praise and doxology but with differing and varying degrees of colors and intensities, nuances, and tempi. Worship with praise and doxology is a great *Te Deum*; worship without praise or doxology is nothing more than a *tedium*, an intellectual experience at best, a mere exercise, a bore. Hopefully, a sensitive church musician can recognize the theological vibrations of prayer and exhortation, adoration and doxology, and transpose these concepts into an exciting worship experience. In this process he is not only a musician but a ministering church musician." (*Church Music Memo*, Spring 1977)

Together in a Growing Understanding of Liturgy

The church musician, by virtue of his position, is a person of more than passing importance, for on him is largely dependent the proper expression of public worship, and in him is vested an educational power that is wielded not only over a few individuals but over the entire congregation. It is true that in case of necessity we may be forced to ignore him, yet we all feel, under normal conditions, the value of his presence and services. He rules, for weal or woe, over the most subtle influence that is brought to bear upon the people. While in all else listlessness may be in control, yet music may permeate quietly and unobtrusively into the soul with the gentle touch of revivifying power. *Gladness* ought to be expressed, and from the organ comes the jubilant invitation to rejoice. *Penitence* is to take possession, and by the plaintive sighings of the organ our emotions are led in the proper way. So, to all intervening states music adapts itself, and readily lends its power and influence to obtain the desired results. Unless deafness is our portion we can scarcely escape its influence, for where it is heard, there it takes quiet possession. How essential is it then, that this power should be properly and judiciously exercised; that its influence should be understandingly used and made most effective. *In the church* such understanding is of vital necessity to its proper use. Hence the value of continued growth in an understanding of worship for pastors and church musicians alike.

The value of such study is plainly evident to all who are interested in any way in the proper comprehension of the subject under consideration, and of these none should be more interested than church musicians. They, by their very position, *are constrained to follow such lines of study.* They are continually confronted by liturgical questions, theoretical and practical, and should be in a position to properly deal with them. This necessitates study, and study which is not of the superficial type, for here as in other relations

> "A little learning is a dangerous thing;
> Drink deep, or taste not the Pierian spring."

To do this, church musicians must step backward into past ages, even beyond the dawn of the Christian cultus, for in the Jewish ritual we find the first established form of worship to the only true God. And as the prophecies preceded the Sun of Righteousness and found in Him their fullest expression, so has the ancient Jewish ritual yielded to the spirit of Christian worship. This ancient worship of the Jews however, was not entirely destroyed but only superseded, and we find it in many ways coloring the more enlightened worship of the new era. This condition we note in the transfer of the Psalter bodily to the new form of worship, in the merging of the Passover into the Festival of Easter, of the Festival of Harvest or Pentecost into the Christian Pentecost or Whitsunday. Thus is seen the inception of the new cults of worship, meagre in point of details, yet carrying over the holy songs of the temple worship and infusing them with renewed life. Man realizes with pleasure that Christ Himself sang thus with His disciples at their last Passover. And from the heathen Pliny in his letter to the Roman Emperor, we learn that the early Christians were wont to come together to sing their "psalms, and hymns, and spiritual songs." Soon certain great truths came into clearer light and about them were clustered forms of expression. These integral parts readily found points of contact and thus the liturgy was gradually woven into one harmonious whole.

The attention of the church musician finds an abundant field of operations in tracing the growth of the liturgy until it became overweighted and was returned in the Reformation among the Swiss Reformers to a bald, bare type of worship, and among the Germans to a conservative mean. In tracing the growth of the liturgy the church musician, if he is thorough, will be led into a consideration of the ramifications of that growth as they group themselves into families, e.g. the Eastern and Western Church; and as these are again subdivided in the East into the Greek, Armenian, Nestorian, etc.; and in the West into Roman, Gallican, Ambrosian, Mozarabic and others. By thus approaching the subject in its broadest and most general aspects, the ground plan is laid according to an ample measure and of substantial material, so that the superstructure will not be endangered by the weakness of the foundation.

In this way is gained not simply knowledge, but a glimpse is also obtained of the animating spirit of liturgics generally, and of its different manifestations. Liturgics is simply engaged with the proper setting forth of the worship of God. It aims to put that worship in the most chaste form, to beautify it, as the Psalmist has said to "worship the Lord in the beauty of holiness," to invest every act with fullest significance, to impress the great truths of Christianity, to declare to man in many ways that he worships, that he is in the presence of the Most High. The spirit of liturgics is essentially the spirit of worship. With church musicians, in a greater degree than with most men, should this spirit be present, that God may be worshiped in spirit and truth, and that all things may be done decently and in order. This spirit goes much further than simply to follow rubrical directions, but is a spirit moving on the face of the waters bringing order out of chaos. It is a guardian angel protecting us from excrescences, from mutilations and extraneous matters. It guides and directs where there are no written laws and at all times and under all conditions it exerts its powerful, even if silent, influence.

It will not be long before the church musician will find that the liturgy is not simply a form of worship but is essentially a confession of faith. We see this in the differences between the Greek and Roman Church, and find it especially marked in the Nestorian liturgy where its parts are adapted to meet the archerror of Nestorianism, namely, its Christological doctrine. The Reformers found abundant error in the Roman liturgy and among their early tasks was the necessity of purging and purifying the liturgy, that it might give proper expression of the true faith. This confessional character of the liturgy must be ever kept in mind, so that we may not only possess the spirit of worship but also the spirit of *true* worship.

A general knowledge of liturgics, however, is not sufficient, for, as we intimated above, there are many digressions and many animating spirits. This should lead church musicians to more specific lines of study, that they may learn to know the animating spirit of each church body, the significance of their forms of worship, and the general trend of their teachings and practice. This will be especially valuable in the consideration of such church bodies as are immediately about the organist or even those of the same country. Each body will have distinctive characteristics and will disseminate its particular influences in a narrow sphere by its practices and in a broader sphere by means of its publications. Church musicians should know them well in order that they may avoid their extravagances, profit by their shortcomings, escape their weaknesses and not be led astray by the passingly beautiful. Rather be strong enough to influence them or they will surely influence you. This means that of all churches you must be best acquainted with your own. Information that is general should be reinforced by that which is specifically to your purpose. Here there enters that study of the church of the Reformation with her conservative tendencies, yet strongly contending for the truth; the central position she gives to the Word at the same time not neglecting the place and power of the Holy Sacraments; the retention of much that was proper, lawful, beautiful, and not contrary to Scripture. Her animating spirit should be thoroughly imbibed if we would comprehend her liturgy.

The spirit of liturgics being the spirit of worship we can readily imagine that the best results will only be obtained by those who approach the subject with true Christian understanding. The mysteries of the Christian faith as expressed in the liturgy should be received into sympathetic minds and hearts, or else we will have nothing more than senseless lip-worship.

As the church musican proceeds in his study, he will learn that the liturgy does not stand alone, an isolated, forsaken creature, but is intimately bound up with many phases of church activity, and has continually exercised its influence over them. The position of the altar, the stained glass windows, and other symbolical creations have sprung largely from this same consideration. But, what is more to the point of our subject, is the influence exerted by the liturgy over church music. If we step back again into the temple at Jerusalem we will find that the music is principally vocal, sustained and accompanied by instruments such as the harp, psaltery, horn, trumpet and cornet. Undoubtedly, King David, in providing for the courses of priests to take charge of the temple worship, made ample provision for the musical portion of that worship, music that would be adapted especially for the services of the temple to set forth the glory and honor of God. In the number of instruments, in the multitude of singers we see the indications of this elaborate musical arrangement. When we enter the Christian era we do not have this elaborate ritual, but it would be most natural for us to think of the Christians as appropriating some of the temple music. And, in that age of purity we would expect the thought of their hymns and spiritual songs to influence and modify their musical settings. A large repertoire of music they undoubtedly did not have, but what they did have we would expect to be marked by chasteness and simplicity. In the quickly succeeding centuries we have seen the growth of the liturgy and it is reasonable to suppose that its musical accompaniment did not lag far behind. As we grow in historical understanding, we learn that music had become a very necessary part of worship and special efforts were made to properly render it by establishing schools for singers whose spheres of activity were within the church. At about the same time, and perhaps resulting from the special interest awakened in the subject, the church modes were established. These modes, ascribed partly to Gregory the Great and partly to Ambrose, Bishop of Milan, are the links uniting ancient and modern music. The modes were, without doubt, influenced by the liturgy. Their use was to render vocal and more impressive the subject matter of the liturgy. From this we readily infer that music was not the dominating power but rather the liturgy, and the music was the obedient servant of a most worthy mistress, seeking to save her to the best of its ability.

This truth we see again exemplified in the productions of the classic period of figurated church music. When music had sunk so low as to give cause for serious consideration of its abandonment in connection with the liturgy, Palestrina arose, imbued with the spirit of the liturgy, which threw its influence about him to such an extent as to thoroughly permeate his works by its devotion. "This was the commencement of a revolution in sacred music, which by his influence became simple, thoughtful, aspiring, sincere and noble, but destitute of passion and tenderness. The most spiritual of all arts it raised the heart into immediate communion with the Infinite . . . it found opportunity to express and to elevate by its various combinations of sounds every kind of Christian feeling." Hence a proper understanding of the liturgy is essential to the proper and full understanding of church music.

Such liturgical knowledge proves its value when church musicians seek to express the liturgy in the best way possible. Music, be it remembered, is the most acceptable and effective means by which to obtain this end. For "a fervent spirit of devotion instinctively seeks to express itself in song. On the strains of poetry," or prose, "joined with music it finds an easy and natural utterance of its elevated emotions." This leads us to the thought of the purpose of music in the church. In the liturgy we render the sacrifices of prayer, praise, and thanksgiving and receive the ministrations of the Word and Sacraments. The music of the liturgy should be expressive of the same emotions that are expressed in the liturgy itself. Such music should be able to express devotion—a devotion that reaches the heart of the believer and stirs it with the thought of God. It should be expressive of praise that arouses the soul to honor God. Its ministrations should deepen the impression of prayer. And in thanksgiving it should find no difficulty in rendering vocal the outpourings of the appreciative heart.

Whatever the liturgy demands, that is the province of church music to express. If the piercing sorrows of Good Friday encompass us, to this the music is to adapt its cry; but if the joys of Easter strive for expression, then the music breaks forth in joyful tones. Church music must first of all express the varying changes of the liturgy and in such a way that the thought of the liturgy is exalted and not the music alone as such. Such music must fill the requirements of devotion for its very purpose is to enhance, not to detract from the spirit of worship. In this connection we are reminded of Augustine's definition of a hymn. "Know ye what a hymn is? It is a song with praise of God. If thou praisest not God, thou utterest no hymn; if thou praisest aught else which pertaineth not to the praise of God, although thou singest and praisest, thou utterest no hymn. An hymn, then, containeth these three things, song, and praise, and that of God." (On Ps. 148.) And thus does the proper expression of the liturgy contain these three things, song, and praise, and that of God.

Upon the proper rendition of even the best music depends largely its effect. We recall the story related of the world renowned Miserere as sung in the Sistine Chapel at Rome. A copy of this famous music was at one time sent to a specially favored church, but the attempt to render it was so disastrous that accusations were made that the copy was not an authentic one. The cause, however, of its failure was finally located in the manner of rendition. So the entire musical part of public worship depends very much on the *manner* of rendition for its proper effect and for this the church musician is held responsible. Here again appears the value of his liturgical study coupled with his musical knowledge in properly adjusting the forces of the organ and choir to meet the requirements of the situation. If he is wise, he will try to inspire his choir with the same liturgical spirit in order that they may cooperate with and not unknowingly oppose him.

A further value of consistent and constant study is that it gives to the church musician a proper appreciation of the dignity and power vested in his position. Not that the individual is to become puffed up in his own conceit—rather that his attitude should be one of humility. He is a leader of the congregation's musical and liturgical life and may, in large degree, form the spirit of its worship. But he first of all should be a devout worshiper; otherwise he cannot properly form the worship of others. "Can the blind lead the blind? Shall they not both fall into the ditch?" Having understood the responsibility of his position, the church musician should earnestly seek the knowledge necessary to the proper discharge of his duties. This will give him a correct spirit of worship and will give him the power to properly express the same: a spirit of worship, however, which is not that of the individual but the *Geist* of the church body, whose animating spirit he seeks to express. His ministration will not then be ruled by caprice, but a masterful hand will rest upon the helm to guide the ship into the peaceful waters of devotion. Study will give him the necessary command of resources that will enable him the better to meet the obligations of his position.

For the church, one of the greatest reasons for thankfulness will be the homogeneity of the service as a result of continued liturgical study among both pastors and church musicians. No longer will the church musician be going in one direction, the pastor in another, and the congregation, perhaps, in still another, but there will be unity of aim and purpose. The opening part of the service will be a gradual unfolding of spiritual worship until it reaches the climax and then gradually until it comes to rest on the word of peace. The sermon will reach the hearts of people who have been prepared to receive it, and its effect will not be nullified by a church musician who is unable to rise to the dignity of his position.

The advantage to the congregation can not help but be noted where served by such a consistent combination of forces. It will be as a strong lever lifting the devotion of the people. The heart of man seeks to be elevated to the proper plane of divine worship, and the higher that plane is, so is the greatness of his spiritual enjoyment. All matters, not leading to that end or distracting the attention, are out of place. Man's sense of worship should be increased not diminished, and that sense should not be simply sentiment but a true relation to God, truly expressed in a true spirit of worship. The result will be a positive, beautiful, uplifting sense of the spirit and privilege of worship, which is communion with God as becomes the sons of God.

Together in Planning

The relationship of the church musician to all the others in the congregational hierarchy—pastors, assistant pastors, teachers, choir leaders, instrumentalists, vicars, etc., is most vital. All are engaged in the one work—the Gospel. The service that the Gospel demands for the "outside" must first be gained "inside." All of us who do the works of mercy need the singing heart and music to share with dreary, dried-up lives. All are members of the church, the body of Christ. All have basically one and the same function, to make Him known. This ties down to specific emphases but also brings out the theme of redeeming love in everything we do and say and sing. In all these things, however, the church musician, with his gifts, becomes a solo voice for the congregation. He is a leader in joy and peace for all who sing with him. His relationship to the pastor as minister of the Gospel should be abundantly clear to everyone who has contact with either one of them. He is the primary cooperator with the preacher so that the Word becomes more palatable and the hearer becomes more ready to listen. Music, in this sense, is to inspire and open up the way of the Holy Spirit. This is almost impossible if the preaching schedule is not known and remains a mystery until Friday or Saturday night before the service. Planning, hard planning, careful planning, insistent planning, time-consuming planning, but happy planning makes the whole thing work and makes the faith sing.

The pastor can be the one who makes the church musician, but the church musician can also be a great help in making the pastor. The inspiration that comes to the preacher from music may be the difference between dull sermons and sermons that are bright with the love of Christ and the beauty of holiness. While the pastor deals with the means of grace directly in Word and Sacrament, the church musician moves right in alongside to see to it that the response of joyous praise or proper penitence is not bypassed in the rest of the worship service. Surely all singing and all church music lives on the *viva vox evangelii* ("the living voice of the Gospel"), and therefore the pastor must see to it that he brings the message of the Gospel in a live way in order to inspire a live response.

A Constant Doxology

Doxology is the name of the game—we give God praise and glory. The Triune God cannot be worshiped in mere earthbound words. Only as His praise is sung and the best in music is written to support that praise, will the heavy heart find relief from its burdens and be able to go out to lift the burdens and bring the help and offer the assurance that is the Gospel out where it is needed most.

None of us, thank God, is self-made. Always and at every critical point in life, especially in our profession, God sends us the right people to support us, inspire us, revive us. Each one of us, as he thinks back over his years of service, remembers how, at each critical point, his ministry was saved and his career rebuilt by the fine touch of a great co-worker who would not let the music of the Gospel fade but revived it again and again until you could not but go singing on your way with new courage, new hope, and a renewed faith. Great figures from the organ bench and choir loft often overshadow the pulpit. You come with hesitation to the last prayer on the lowest step of the pulpit and suddenly the music was what you had prayed it would be—uplifting, certain, sure, strong, and filled with all the outpouring of the Spirit of God. The congregation sometimes wonders about the grateful look directed to the organ bench. They would hardly understand if you insisted on telling them "that was exactly what I needed in order to bring you what we all need." Forty-three years of service in the same church and in the same pulpit under the strain of the conditions in the modern city would simply have been a nightmare and a beastly confusion if it had not been for the sustaining power that came from great music and great musicians in order to make the service a genuine thankoffering to God.

As the pastor needs his quiet time in order to let the Spirit take over, so the church musician must have a built-in time for quiet preparation. Even while most organists would insist that theirs is the most joyful and happy office in the world because they are constantly involved with singing and making music to the Lord, we must also acknowledge that the making of music, even under the happiest circumstances, is a serious business. The finely tuned ear of the congregation, brought up on the perfection of musical performances on radio and television cannot bear the wrong note or the imperfections that grow out of no work, no practice, no love, no understanding for worship.

If we are to rise to the heights of a constant doxology, we must rise together. The pastor as well as the church musician dare not shave percentages—it must be perfection by a wide margin. The world whom we strive to reach will not grant us grace to be *almost* right with the Gospel and its music. It must be perfect. For that it will have to reflect all the love and strength and beauty that is the Gospel and our Lord Jesus Christ. Whatever dares to be less must face failures and realize shortcomings and repent to the sound of the unworthy and the unfit moving in on the sacred precincts of the thankoffering of faithful Christians.

See also the related articles in *Key Words in Church Music*: cantor; all articles on theology of church music

CHAPTER VII

Music in the Church Today: An Appraisal

Richard Hillert

Church music is still in the process of making history. It continues to function in its role as a vehicle uniquely suited for the people of God in corporate worship, and it continues to be central to artistic concerns in the church, as shown by the constant and lively search for a useful and meaningful repertory.

We remind ourselves of these simple facts because they provide something of an essential perspective. There are times when church music as an art and as a practice seems to struggle for survival, when even its reason for existence is brought into question. But there are also moments of glory, those times in the life of worship when music becomes a true and fulfilling vehicle of grace, signifying the very presence of God.

Church Music During the 20th Century

In its long and venerable history church music has been one of the shining lights of Western civilization, although it has not been central to the development of the whole art of music for at least two centuries now. But neither is its history a closed book. The 20th century has some notable and eventful chapters of its own to add to the annals of worship and its music.

A definitive history of 20th-century church music will be written someday when the varieties of shapes and manifestations of recent change are more clearly discernible. But it is already quite evident that music used in the service of worship today is in most places quite radically different from what it was at the beginning of this century.

Our century has required of church music an exceptional adaptability and a creativeness that recall the challenges of the 16th-century Reformation era. And, as so often in the history of the arts, there has been the challenge of an almost perpetual tug-of-war between tradition and innovation.

The church itself has been challenged, not only in the area of its music but in all its ways of worship, to reexamine and reevaluate long accepted and comfortable traditions. In most places the confrontation between tradition and innovation has had an invigorating and renewing effect. And this renewal is the most important thing that has happened to church music during the 20th century. Renewal has been the byword in many quarters and has had countless implications, not the least consequential of which is that church music is still around during this last quarter of our century and still continues to flourish among us.

Church music renewal emanated from several places already during the very early years of this century. One of the significant movements was within the Evangelical churches in Germany. The German experience was later to be duplicated in many other Protestant places and eventually even in reaches beyond Western Christianity. In Germany, as elsewhere, the renewal of church music had its corollary in the new awareness and appreciation of the role of liturgy as the central core of the life of the church. And this was complemented by new and profound preoccupations with theological and sociological concerns.

Symbolical of the urgent sense of renewal was the "back to Bach" movement with its new identification with the forms of pre-19th-century polyphony, described by Oskar Soehngen as a "determined detachment" from the art of late romanticism. Music was assigned again the dignity of its liturgical role in proclaiming the Gospel and singing the praise of God. This brought a startling contrast to the 19th-century attitude by which music in the church served as an agent for experiencing religious emotions or for expressing pious sentiments or "beautifying" the service.

A most important outgrowth and a sign of the vigor of German church music renewal was that it fostered a new school of composers. Johan Nepomuk David, Ernst Pepping, and Hugo Distler were among those who produced a new repertory that reflected both traditional procedures in composition as well as 20th-century stylistic innovation. Their choral and organ works paralleled the "new objectivity" of composers such as Stravinsky, Bartok, and Hindemith. For a significant period of time in Germany between the two world wars, new music in the secular world and new music in the church shared common roots, both aesthetic and stylistic.

The reform in organ building was another aspect of renewal that had signiciant beginnings in Germany. This movement signified a return to honesty and craftsmanship, clarity and balance, and an informed reverence for the best, preromantic traditions in organ design and building. These concerns, first proclaimed by Albert Schweitzer as early as 1906, were later taken up by organ designers in French, American, and English cultures and indeed in many places not traditionally identified with Western civilization. The organ movement has gone through several phases that have affected the course of church music in our time, its repertory, composition for the church, and the quality of sound that in many places has come to be associated with the church. The enthusiasms for real organ sound are not universally shared. But, while the real organ may be regarded as the ideal, the electronic invasion has mounted some important and disturbing challenges of practicality in matters of space, versatility, and economy. In any case these concerns are a measure of the aliveness of music in the church today.

The tensions between tradition and innovation took on slightly different forms in the English churches. From the beginning of this century English music began to be preoccupied with higher standards of professionalism in church musicianship and with a better quality of congregational and choral music than that which characterized much of Victorian music making.

It is in the area of congregational song that the English have most influenced the course of 20th-century church music. *The Yattendon Hymnal* (1899) and *The English Hymnal* (1906) were the first in a series of innovative hymnals that established hymnic standards, in both text and music, by which practically every English-language hymnal since then has been measured for its quality. They established the most challenging guidelines to be followed in the making of a hymnal or in selecting a hymn repertory: to draw upon the best musical material from many origins, confined to no particular historical period, or denominational, ethnic, or stylistic source. The scholarly and practical exemplification of this guideline, together with the application of equally high criteria in supplying hymnic-poetic words of the highest quality, has immeasurably enriched all of 20th-century hymnody.

Church music in the Roman Catholic cultures of western Europe reacted more slowly to the cultural and sociological changes of the turn of the century. But music continued to play a central role in corporate worship, upholding some of the oldest traditions in church music. The motu proprio *Tra le sollecitudini* of Pius X (1903) tried to redefine the role of music in corporate worship. It urged use of the choral repertory of classical polyphony alongside the traditional plainchant, the latter as it has been "authenticated" by the Benedictines of Solesmes, and it discouraged the use of musical styles associated with the opera. Over 50 years later, Pius XII, notably in his encyclical *Mediator Dei* (1947), reaffirmed these ideals and in addition encouraged the use of appropriate "modern" music, both instrumental and vocal. This opened the door of Roman Catholic church music to the contemporary composer.

French organists from Vierne to Messiaen, in their improvisations and compositions, had all along used advanced techniques in 20th-century composition. This was significant in a century in which "modern" music seemed to be regarded in many places as inappropriate for the service of worship. It was not until 1950 that church music began slowly to accept the advanced idioms that had long characterized 20th-century music in general.

The church music scene became once more enlivened by the social and cultural changes that developed after 1950. These created both new incentives for renewal as well as some unfortunate retreating into pessimistic reactionism. The latter turned up among the younger church composers in Germany, those who had followed in the wake of Distler but felt compelled to keep up with the most avant-garde trends in composition. Composers such as Helmut Bornefeld and Wolfgang Fortner turned from the writing of church music for worship to the writing of church music for the church concert—situations that need not tolerate the limitations imposed by the context of liturgical and congregational song.

In other places church music after 1950 retreated to the opposite end of the musical spectrum. Popular and folk idioms were introduced as musical vehicles for congregational song. It was thought that employment of vernacular musical idioms would provide a quick and easy method for evangelizing and attracting the young to the church. Among the first and well-publicized of these examples was Geoffrey Beaumont's *20th Century Folk Mass*, which employed what he described as the "normal every day popular type of music" as a vehicle to carry, in English, the ritualistic text of the Communion liturgy. There followed a long succession of pop-folk and, eventually, rock masses and hymns—an explosion of neo-Gospel hymnody that presented conventional church music with its liveliest challenge of the century.

The challenge to the church in its ways of worship as well as its music was felt most strongly in the Roman Catholic church. The Second Vatican Council was assembled at the instigation of Pope John XXIII to address itself with urgency to the newest conflicts between tradition and innovation, to "get in step with the needs of the times."

The promulgation of *The Constitution on the Sacred Liturgy* (1963) had wide-ranging effect on the course of worship and church music practice as few other events of our time. This document spelled out the new concerns in liturgical music and emphasized the use of the vernacular in the text of the mass, the participation of the congregation in the sung parts of the liturgy, and at the same time the preservation and careful fostering of the treasury of sacred music from the great heritage of the past.

The first reaction on the part of many worship leaders was to see the pronouncements of Vatican II as a conflict between the use of the people's song and the artful music of the plainchant and polyphonic choral traditions. These problems presented a startling parallel to those confronted by the 16th-century Protestant reformers. The uncertainty and tentativeness that resulted as well as the sheer creativity by which the church has sought for solutions has constituted, largely, the most recent history of music in the church.

All of these developments, the conflicts between tradition and innovation, the raising of artistic and musicl standards, and the reevaluation of ritualistic ways of worship as a response to social and cultural changes, became an integral part of the scene in American churches as well. Since 1950, developments in American church music have become increasingly important, if not central to the action. The emergence of an autonomous American music, that of Ives and Copland, of Thomson and Cage, represented a factor of very real importance to the state of music in American churches in this century.

American church music has learned much by its contact with developments in Europe. These influences have been reflected in varying degrees, depending upon national, ethnic, and denominational differences. The Lutheran churches, for example, have identified more closely with developments in Germany and Scandinavia, while other American Protestants more directly parallel what has transpired in England. And the liturgically oriented communions, Lutheran and Episcopal, have reacted more sensitively to changes in Roman Catholic thought and practice. It is inevitable that such interaction should be on the increase, not only between European and American churches, but in an ecumenical sense. No matter how we may wish to look at it, this is a fact of contemporary coexistence, and its effect on the conduct of church music has been profound.

The ecumenical interaction, in America as elsewhere, is integral to church music renewal. Where centuries-old traditions have prevailed, the renewal movement has tried to retain what is good and useful. Where unprecedented social and cultural changes have predominated, tradition has been questioned and new, innovative musical solutions have been sought. That is the creative process of history. While church music continues to serve in its unique role as a vehicle for corporate worship, this brief recounting of 20th-century developments points to some basic changes in the function of that role.

The Changing Role of Music in Worship

The changing role of music in worship is most evident in liturgical churches. Worship, with the liturgy at its center, becomes again the object of musical expression. Music for its own sake, whether hymnic, choral, or instrumental, is misplaced when it is used merely as a program filler. In liturgical worship the varieties of traditional and innovative liturgical forms determine the text, the structure, and the function of the music. Often what may seem to be "innovative" is simply a renewal, a creative rejuvenation of earlier, but unfamiliar liturgical forms or practices. It is in that sense that renewal embraces both tradition and innovation.

In liturgical churches the church year calendar, with its annual cycle of days and season, is the central framework supporting worship in all its forms, determining its dynamic character with the changing days and seasons. The renewed emphasis on the primacy of the church year and the appreciation of its potentialities in worship continues to have a major influence on the newer developments in church music.

Similarly, the renewed appreciation for and observances of the Holy Communion as the chief service every Sunday and festival day has affected the practice of church music in its repertory and in its function. This is at the core of both liturgical and musical renewal. The nature of church music and the philosophy undergirding its practice has changed in the 20th century and will continue to change in accord with the importance given to the Holy Communion by the clergy, by church musicians, and by the worshipers whom they lead.

The renewed appreciation for the forms of liturgy in the daily prayer of the church continues to affect the course of church music as well. These forms, traditionally Matins and Vespers among Lutherans, are extremely flexible and thus easily adaptable to great varieties of musical response, from the simple congregational office hymn to the most elaborate choral service. The true realization of the potentialities of these services lies in the future and is in no way yet an accomplished fact.

All this concern for renewal with its emphasis on the traditions of Holy Communion, the daily prayer of the church, and the church year may easily be regarded as esoteric exercise. And indeed that has been the case all too frequently. But a central premise of the renewal of liturgy and music has been to return the words and acts of corporate worship to the people. That includes the sung parts of the liturgy. This has been a congregational ideal from medieval times, and a specifically Lutheran ideal from the beginning of the Reformation, but it has not always been successfully implemented. Through the history of Lutheranism and in the process of transplantation in America this ideal has become gradually diluted and absorbed by American Protestant practices in which the versified hymn, rather than the prose text of the liturgy, serves as vehicle for the congregation's primary musical expression. Attempts in the liturgical churches to involve the congregation in singing the main parts of the liturgy are developments of recent origin that have been introduced quite gradually during the last century.

The liturgy as the people's song was a subject of primary concern in the pronouncements of Vatican II. The "active participation of the people" and the "skillful fostering" of "religious singing by the people . . . also during liturgical services" so that "the voices of the faithful may ring out according to the norms and requirements of the rubrics" are phrases used in *The Constitution on the Sacred Liturgy*. To provide a songful and simple liturgical music for the people, expressive and dignified enough for frequent repetition—that is the difficult challenge laid down, not only to Roman Catholic church musicians, but wherever the liturgy has received new emphasis. The people's song in the liturgy was at the center of the pop-folk cult in church music during the 1960s and '70s. It remained and will continue to be the subject of foremost creative attention.

With worship the focal point and liturgical forms providing the structure for musical expression, the congregation's more conventional role in the singing of hymns is brought into new perspective. Hymnody is returned again to a liturgical context. That has been, historically, the origin of the best of Western hymnody—the office hymns that came out of the medieval daily prayer, the versified and paraphrased psalms and canticles and Eucharistic hymns that were freshly created or developed out of traditional sources into the corpus of the Reformation and post-Reformation chorale and French and English psalmody, and the body of hymns that provide congregational responses to the appointed lessons of the liturgical year. There must still be a place for the "old favorites," but increasingly the hymns included in corporate worship are appointed with careful concern for the way they reflect the predominant liturgical theme and take their place within the liturgical structure of worship.

The congregation as the basic medium for hymnic expression poses few problems of musical practicality. And for a congregation to sing the canticles and responses that are essential to the Holy Communion there are also few problems, so long as it is not expected to sing at sight a succession of unfamiliar settings. When, by competent and responsible pastoral and musical leadership, a congregation becomes comfortable with a given musical setting of the Communion or the daily prayer services, there are few problems with the liturgy as the people's song.

When the people's song in the liturgy is logically extended to include congregational involvement in the psalmody, problems of practicality in learning and performing become quite real. Since the appointed psalms for the day are "proper," variable from day to day, they require for their singing or chanting numerous and variable musical settings. The same is true of the proper canticles and offertories. Whether these may be performed with musical formulary systems or with through-composed settings, they constitute musical and practical problems for the congregation. It is doubtful that these have yet been or will soon be easily solved. The problems of devising truly congregational musical settings of the psalms and propers in English may not be impossible to solve, but could well occupy the attention of a whole generation of worship leadership. An impeccable scholarship will be required and a thoroughly informed appreciation of tradition, together with an understanding of the potentialities and limitations of congregational worship in its contemporary context.

The Repertory of Music in Worship

Along with the changing role of music in its association with corporate worship has emerged a renewed concern for a useful and meaningful repertory. It is this concern that maintains the viability of church music.

Organists, choir directors, choir members, composers, publishers, and worship leaders of all kinds, not to mention lay members themselves, are all concerned in one way or another with the selection of pieces. And there is indeed much to be concerned about, from the heritage, from the "old favorites," from the contemporary repertory, and the "new favorites." There is more, in fact, than at any other time in history.

The repertory of church music is, first of all, a prime concern of the composers who write for the church. They want to know as much as they can about all the music that has been written, that vast and sometimes mysterious body of material out of music history, as well as the forbidding plethora of current publishers' outpourings of "contemporary" church music. Composers are especially interested in knowing what is in the practical repertory of church music, what is being used. And they want to know where are the gaps that need to be filled with new music. In order to fill these "gaps" with meaningful music the composer needs to bring to his task more than a facile pen. He needs also an understanding of worship and the liturgy in all their historic as well as contemporary aspects. He needs to understand and empathize with the potentialities and limitations of a congregation and the small parish choir, unless he purposely chooses to remain out of touch with that part of the reality of church life today.

The repertory is also, of course, a matter of constant concern to all who serve as leaders in a church music program. Really active and imaginative directors and organists whose activities are mainly oriented toward music for the worship service, can go through about as many pieces of music in 52 weeks as any other performing musician, save those engaged in the business of popular entertainment. A thorough awareness of the available repertory of church music is essential to their profession.

And that repertory is today, by sheer volume, historically un-precedented. Musical scholarship of the last 100 years has made it possible for us to become aware of and to possess a more accurate knowledge of an immensely greater part of the corpus of our musical heritage in a way that would have been impossible in any generation before. We laud all endeavors at musicological reconstruction and continue to be amazed at the wealth of new-old musical treasures from early Christian chant through the beginnings of polyphony and the consummations of the Renaissance and baroque eras. This phenomenon is a major musical wonder of our era and constitutes a fact of life that requires careful consideration in evaluating the state of church music in our time.

The fruits of musical scholarship and the vastness of the repertory it has yielded confront us with the urgent challenge of how we shall use the historic traditions of church music in the 20th century. And how shall we maintain a balance between the church's historic musical heritage and the simultaneous need to develop and maintain a vital relationship with those contemporary worshipers who look to us for leadership?

As much as any other cultural musical enterprise in our society, with the possible exception of the operatic and symphony orchestra establishments, the church has habitually derived the greater part of its musical repertory from its historic past. This is understandable, although not necessarily justified, when we consider the richness of that past and historic character of the liturgy itself. The overarching form of the historic Eucharist, together with its varied substructures, and the even more flexible layouts for the offices such as Matins and Vespers, are saturated with traditional associations. These quite naturally invite traditional music, psalmody set to Gregorian or other formulary chant, 16th- to 19th-century hymnody, organ music from the baroque era, and polyphonic choral music from Dunstable to Bach.

There is little doubt about it, the working repertory of church music in our time is taken predominantly from cultural sources that predate the 20th century. And for the most part these sources represent musical expressions of high artistic order and exemplary craftsmanship. They are readily available from the publishers' counters and will become increasingly so. They are, furthermore, custom-made to complement the traditional liturgical forms and, because they are musically strong, they can easily be adapted to nontraditional liturgical contexts. And they are, for performance, unproblematic as to musical idiom.

The renewed appreciation for the repertory of the church's musical heritage was initiated not only by the movement for renewal in worship, but in a practical way by the work of 19th- and early 20th-century musicologists. Their discipline has been indispensable to church music renewal. It has introduced the elements of honesty and genuiness—a concern for authenticity in the musical score, especially in that of pre-19th-century origin. Instead of dealing with adulterated and over-ambitiously edited scores of older music, the aware musician has become concerned for correctness in editions of baroque organ music, for example, for the truly idiomatic realization of figured bass accompaniments to vocal music, for the "original" version of polyphonic choral selections, and for the pristine version of chorale or hymn tune.

For practicing church musicians some of these concerns may seem to be entirely too theoretical. Those concerned for aesthetic quality in their working repertory are wholly dependent upon publishers' performing editions. It is to the credit of editors and publishers of church music that their practical editions of older music are, in many cases, increasingly reliable as to musical scholarship.

The reach for authenticity has been extended to other areas as well, to a concern for historic authenticity in the sound of vocal and instrumental music, as witnessed most obviously in the organ movement. The authentic score and the authentic sonority demand also authenticity in performance practice. All these elements of church music renewal are affected by and in turn are reflective of the available repertory.

The church musician today has available more choral music from the past and present than he can possibly use in a given situation, no matter how many services per Sunday and weekday, no matter how many choral groups he has to lead. And the same bewildering availability of really practical music confronts the church organist.

But the problem of the repertory is not that it is so large. The problem, strangely, is that it is too small. The vastness of the repertory is a problem only in that it forces the church musician to be very selective. This may become a time-consuming prospect, creating the temptation to settle upon a routine and comfortable repertory of pieces that "work well" and are used year after year.

The real problem of repertory is that it does not fully reflect contemporary worship needs. That is, in part, because of recent developments in liturgical and church music renewal: the inauguration and adoption of a new series of lessons for the church year, adopted by a large segment of the contemporary Christian church, and the revised orders of service in the Holy Communion and the daily prayer of the church.

Where the new lectionary, with its three-year pericopal series, has been adopted, the standard readings of several centuries' standing have fallen into disuse, and along with them a good part of the inherited music closely associated with texts and central thoughts of the traditional readings. But, regardless of the prevailing pericopal structure, the full realization of the varieties and potentialities of musical response to the appointed lessons of the day has fallen short of the ideal. Composers, publishers, educators, and leaders of music in worship can all be held accountable for this neglect.

Where the new liturgical forms for the Holy Communion and the daily prayer of the church (Matins, Vespers, and Compline in the Lutheran rites) have been adopted, new attendant vocal and instrumental music is required. There exist now a great number of newly devised texts for which no traditional music has existed and for which new settings are imperative. These include those parts of the liturgy that cannot be done by the congregation without benefit of rehearsal or for which no congregational settings have been supplied. Among these, in addition to the psalmody in new translation, are the appointed alleluia verses and tracts, the appointed offertories, and the alternate canticles provided for The Communion and daily prayer. New polyphonic or unison/accompanied Old Testament, Epistle, and Gospel motets based on readings from the new lectionary are needed. The same is true for new polyphonic or unison/accompanied settings of hymn stanzas for use in the alternation practice with congregation. Many of these hymns now appear in new text versions and are in need of ever more imaginative and skillful new settings.

In addition, choral settings of the ordinary of the Holy Communion (the Gloria, for example—but probably not the Sanctus) and the daily prayer of the church (the Benedictus, the Te Deum, Joyous Light of Glory, Psalm 141, and the Magnificat, for example) should be made available for occasional choral use. These might be used in alternation or as embellishments or extensions of the congregational song. The possibilities for variation and elaboration are almost endless, and demand only unlimited imagination and creativity.

In the selection of choral repertory and preparation for its use in liturgical worship, there is always the need for imagination and creativity. The potentialities for using the choir as an integral part of congregational worship, in the liturgy, the psalmody, and in the hymnody, are rarely attained. This concern for using the choir liturgically in congregational worship rather than as a vehicle for showy anthems, is more competently discussed elsewhere in this handbook. It is an issue most relevant to an appreciation for the state of music in the church today and demands the attention of an informed and understanding musical and liturgical leadership.

So also, the liturgically integrated use of the organ and other instruments demands the full attention of creative and imaginative musicians. The repertory of organ service music is a flourishing and varied one, and is often employed fancifully and with skill and real sensitivity to the liturgical moment. As for instrumental music in the church, the field is wide for exploration by composers, publishers, directors, and performers. The sounds of orchestral instruments, strings, winds, and especially percussion in all sizes and shapes of ensemble are now widely acceptable in the context of worship. This should, however, imply more than just an occasional "festival" use of brass and timpani with choral descants. It should mean also that, in the hands of trained and sensitive church musicians, musical sounds from whatever "exotic" source can potentially be employed as intrinsic vehicles for corporate worship. The psalmist's injunction to "make melody to our God upon the lyre" must imply that not every piece of music must have a direct association with a liturgical or hymnic text. Like the integrated choral song, the instrumental song is an issue that needs creative attention in today's church music.

The people's song in worship, in the sung or chanted parts of the liturgy and in the hymnody, is the ultimate and central concern in the practice of church music. A thoughtfully considered selection of hymns, giving perspective to the liturgical songs of the ordinary and integrated with the theme of the propers for the day, should be a primary concern of pastoral and musical leadership in worship. The congregational hymnic repertory needs constant and evangelical nurturing, for variety and relevance and for balance between what is traditional and what is innovative (for the church historically, and for the congregation parochially). Beyond that, music for the congregation is so important that it should never be regarded in a routine manner, as is the case in so many services in which the congregational hymn serves only to fill in the places between the spoken or read parts of the liturgy, or is subordinated only to enhance the pastor's sermon. The practice of liturgical worship encompasses the whole body of worshipers in hymnic exultation, the congregation, the pastor, the organist and instrumentalists, and the choir: a corporate expression employing hymns and liturgical songs in all the various forms of alternation and musical dialogue, "concertatos," and "celebrations," in an integrated service of worship. Ideally, this should become the prevailing and basically acceptable pattern for congregational song. It is a wholly viable practice, in parishes great and small and wherever music is an integral part of worship.

The contemporary ideal is that where music is used in worship, it functions as an integral part of the liturgical action. The choice of music is determined by the theme and lessons of the day or festival, and the whole assembly of worshipers, the congregation, the pastor, the soloists, choirs, and instrumentalists are all involved in a united corporate expression.

The State of Church Music Today

The ideal relationship between music and worship is, under the best of circumstances, not easily realized. But the situation in the church today is in many ways increasingly favorable to such a vital and creative relationship. An abundance of material and human resources is readily available to the church.

First among these resources are church buildings themselves, many of them well-designed for the sounds and functions of music in worship. The best of them accomodate the action of the liturgy as central to their architectural purpose. Aesthetically and functionally they complement the basic ideals of church music renewal.

There is also a growing number of new organs, designed with artistic integrity and with an understanding of their essential role in music and worship, and reflecting the principles of the organ renewal movement. At the same time more parishes are now able to provide for their worship the use of instruments, orchestral instruments and percussion instruments of the educational music variety, playable by amateurs as well as professionals. Resources such as these, together with the easy accessibility of published music and an array of other worship materials and aids, represent part of a superstructure that appears to be advantageous to music in the church.

In terms of human resources, it is the countless musicians involved in church music that is most important of all. That the practice of church music continues to command their respect and devotion is a marvel in itself. No matter whether they are from the ranks of enthusiastic and dedicated amateurs or whether they are highly skilled and equally dedicated professionals, they should all be saluted and cherished. All are indispensable to the art. Their devotion and selflessness are exemplary in a time when these qualities are to be found only with increasing rarity. And all of them share in a profound concern for the meaning and vitality of music in the contemporary worship life of the church.

The standards of professionalism among these musicians must naturally be quite varied, but the general trend has followed an upward course. The church musician's awareness of the significance of music in its liturgical role must be counted among the criteria by which to measure professionalism and competence. But competence in musical performance, whether as organist, choir director, or choir member, instrumentalist, or cantor, is a quality that should be compromised as little as possible.

One of the most vital and creative of human resources is the composer who writes for the church. As in the educational and concert fields, there are more composers now than ever before who are professionally equipped to meet the practical needs of contemporary music. The level of skillfulness and craftsmanship among composers for the church is, at its best, second to none, and on the whole, in this country, superior to that of a generation ago. The professional product, judging from recent publications, ranges from the most routine to the highest levels of creative achievement. Unfortunately there is a great deal more of the former than the latter. The composer's responsibility in the whole perspective of church music and especially in relation to the practical level of parish music is habitually underrated. This responsibility is, regrettably, sometimes evaded by composers and "arrangers" whose imitative works are so often little more than notated improvisations or unimaginative and routine settings, lacking the perspective of music's role in the liturgy. Publishers, too, not infrequently bypass the best of standards in their concern for commercial value rather than musical excellence. But on the whole the quality level of musical composition for the church today is high in terms of practical competence, while not infrequently undistinguished in artist merit. There are exceptions, and it is to be hoped there will continue to be more.

Among the human resources, there is also an impressive number of amateurs who continue to bring their talents and time into the service of music for worship. Many of these are members of an established choral or instrumental group. Others serve as organists and choir directors. They are to be nurtured for they are the most numerous among church musicians. These semiprofessionals and amateurs have a special need to be alert to the concerns for music in the parish. Their responsibility is, like that of the professional church musician, to assert musical leadership for the whole congregation throughout the church year.

For those in positions of music leadership there are opportunities for professional and avocational growth, offered by schools, publishers, and various auspices of the institutional church. Workshops, symposia, and conferences for church musicians and worship leaders are a fair reflection of the current state, but are effective only when the quality of their instruction is high and when their offerings are vital and relevant enough to inspire growth and creativity at the parish level.

Of all the arts associated with the church, music gets the most attention from the layman. It is a fact that cannot be overlooked. The chief beneficiary has been the art of church music itself. Perhaps music gets all this attention because it is both a personal and a collective art. In church more frequently than elsewhere both the personal and collective qualities of music are drawn upon for deep personal expression within the context of a collective social structure—a community of believers, the congregation—with which an individual can identify. Even people who claim to know nothing at all about music will assert that they "know what they like." It is a reality of significance in the church today.

Secular-vernacular tastes that have been formed by an all-pervasive media can be truly influential when they are carried over into the church. Those who "know what they like" may sometimes express strong vocal preferences for selections that fall short of the highest of musical and liturgical standards. Surveys conducted in preparation for the publication of the *Lutheran Book of Worship* clearly indicate that the level of quality in the hymn repertory of most parishes is considerably less than desirable. But the people feel strongly about inclusion or exclusion of their "old favorites." It should be observed that a vigorous faith is well able to survive any ephemeral crisis in the hymnic repertory. But this is yet another reminder of the need for informed, assertive, competent, and pastoral leadership in worship and music.

That kind of leadership is perhaps more in evidence than it was a generation ago. Surely there is in American churches, generally, a growing awareness of the riches of the musico-liturgical heritage of the past and an increasing sense of its relevance for the present. There is also, among enlightened leadership, a continuing need to participate and share in that heritage of the whole church with contemporary Christians everywhere.

The best of church music practices in America today display a fine resourcefulness in applying the musical heritage to the contemporary needs of our time and place. While there are equally significant developments in worship and music in other countries, Americans no longer look to European sources for their models and guidance in all things. There is

247

rather a mutual participation in the search for creative solutions to problems of worship and music.

Another sign of a new maturity in American church music is the growing realization that church music has its own vocation. While it is but a part of the whole musical scene, church music has its unique reason for being, its own traditions, its special purpose in worship that sets it apart from music for the theater or the concert hall, or music-for-education or entertainment or football games or political rallies. Surely the era is past now when sounds from the choir and organ loft should imitate the conventions of concert for seated audience or the cheap grandiosity of the musical production number. Church music is freer than that—it is free to be itself.

But not all about the state of music in the church today presents an agreeable and positive picture. There are some unpleasantries that need to be unveiled in the way of constructive and objective self-criticism.

To begin with, it is certain that church music will never fare better than the church itself. Worship above all is a direct reflection of the inner state of the church's health. With all its elaborate superstructure, the church buildings, the wealth of instrumental resources, publications of music and worship materials, educational facilities, and professional and scholarly competence, the practice of music in worship at the parish level is still, in many places, quite a dismal affair.

There are still too many parishes in which worship is treated as a perfunctory part of the ministry. The Holy Communion is observed exceptionally rather than every Sunday and festival day. Far from being central to an integrated worship, the liturgy is routinized, disarrayed, truncated, mutilated, or merely improvised, either because of local custom or pastoral whimsy or for other extraneous reasons. The kind of church music program we have been describing cannot possibly exist under such circumstances.

In many parishes the sermon is still the centerpiece of worship, symptomizing how strong has been the influence of American evangelical Protestantism, even among Lutherans who continue to claim for themselves a unique liturgical heritage. The quality of church music suffers when the hymnic repertory is so impoverished by its subservience to the vagaries of a succession of improvised worship "themes," and when the true significance of the thematic structure of the church year—that cyclic representation of the life of Christ central to the liturgical heritage—is either overlooked or misunderstood or regarded with a distracted indifference.

Where the church has thus lost sight of its liturgical heritage it is not to be wondered that its music has reached outside the church to determine and establish its ideals. Nothing better can be expected than the kind of traditionless music for traditionless worship that has characterized some of the church's music making. Apathy and lack of identity with a clearly understood liturgical heritage and musical tradition invite the kind of indiscriminate influences from secular sources that are sometimes introduced in the name of innovation. Contemporary church music is in need of the element of innovation, but not of the wrong kind. Innovation has no value for its own sake but is significant and meaningful only when it is rooted directly in a real tradition—and in a profound understanding of and appreciation for that tradition. Without tradition there is nothing to be innovative about.

When a balanced relationship between tradition and innovation is clearly perceived within the framework of the liturgy, there is nothing to bar any kind of music from the service of worship. That includes music from all times and places—folk, pop, and rock, Indian raga and American ragtime, electronic and avant-garde, any music that is useful to a congregation in the integrated action of *liturgical* worship.

It is only realistic to recognize that "substandard" practices in worship and music are much too common among our parishes. The entire worship and music leadership of the church, wherever and whoever that may be, should be in some measure held accountable. Most surely the situation is much improved over the past generations, but with the best of efforts and intentions, that leadership has failed to communicate adequately.

Perhaps the worship and music programs at our seminaries and colleges need to be improved. How adequately are our pastors instructed in matters of liturgical worship? A thorough understanding of the church year and the manner in which it finds expression in the liturgy is absolutely essential for a parish pastor who would provide leadership in the kind of worship program described here. Such an understanding is more basic and more essential than learning to chant the liturgy, as desirable as that may be. And surely more than just a passing acquaintance with the church's musical heritage, quite aside from a bit of instruction in hymnody, should be included in a pastor's education, so that he might approach with understanding the integration of music and liturgy in corporate worship.

Until our parish pastors as worship leaders have acquired that kind of understanding, our church music will always fall short of the ideal.

How adequately are our church musicians educated at the professional level? There are today more colleges and university church music programs than ever before. That should be strong evidence that church music is alive and well. But where an orientation in a vigorous and unique heritage in church music and liturgy, repertory and practice, is desirable, the nondenominational curriculums encountered most usually are inadequate. In many of our Lutheran colleges and universities the undergraduate church music curriculums are being crowded out by demands of other educational requirements.

Where such church music programs exist there is good instruction in organ and other instruments, in conducting, in composition, in choral participation, and in the academic areas. The challenge here is to provide a curriculum that is thoroughly professional but does not lose sight of the parish realities that will confront a student upon graduation.

It is frequently the choral program at the college level that needs careful attention. Often these choirs are concert oriented, and where there may be several choirs in a cocurricular program, it will be the concert touring choir that is the most prestigious and the one intended to attract the most talented students. Many of these choirs indeed have the highest choral standards and on their tours get rave reviews for their virtuosity in tone blending, attacks and releases, and flexibility of dynamic range. Their repertory is naturally selected to display the choir in the most stunning manner.

The college concert choir, with its predominantly SATB texture and *a cappella* sonority, is a uniquely American institution and has every right to be what it is. It should, however, in a church music program, be maintained in perspective. Its repertory, designed for concert, and its level and manner of performance can mislead a student by holding before him a model that could not possibly be imitated at the parish level. Setting the highest of standards is always desirable but false standards should be recognized for what they are. The more appropriate standards for choral music in the parish are set by smaller choirs with liturgically oriented repertory.

Just because parish music may, by its very nature, have "limited" resources does not mean there should be a lowering of professional standards. The most valuable part of a student's education is to learn to use the resources that are there. To develop a parish music program at the highest level of creativity and resourcefulness—that is the application of the highest professional standards. How to be creative and resourceful should be the basic practical objective both for a college program in parish music and for the worship leader and musician in the parish.

Problems and Projections

The cultural scene in which parish church music finds itself today is more complex than it has ever been. The protective walls of the church no longer shield out the influences of secularism and in most places today the simplicity and mutuality of a homogeneous ethnical society no longer exist. These are facts of life that place today's worshipers in a world quite different from even a generation ago. If the practice of church music has any relevance or meaning it will be affected by such a changing society. Yet, we insist on the value of certain traditions if for no other reason than to remind today's worshipers there are some values that can be counted on not to change.

But even the traditional practices of church music have not gone unaffected by the maze of contradictions of today's society—a society that is a mixture of high and low culture, of old and new traditions, and of constant and bewildering change. And, as Johannes Riedel has suggested, even church music is itself a diversity of cultures, meaning one thing to those whose worship orientation centers around the standard hymnal, yet other things to those whose music for worship is comprised of one or another of the varieties of spiritual song, and meaning yet something quite different to the scholar who relates church music to its historic or musicological origins. And to the musician in the parish it means a daily or at least weekly confrontation with the problems of music in worship and all that is implied in the practical application of elements of tradition and innovation.

For the parish musician tradition means more than simply an antiquarian preoccupation with the past. The basic concern is to make tradition, any musical tradition, meaningful in the context of worship. Where traditional music means exclusively familiar music, it stands in danger of becoming too comfortable to have any meaning at all. A preoccupation with any one style, of traditional hymn or organ or choral or concerted music, whether baroque or English anthem, or *a cappella* motet, can inflict a passiveness into worship, relegating the art to the level of the wall-to-wall music that nobody listens to.

Tradition is most meaningful when it is allowed to manifest itself in ever-renewing creative expression—when it is carefully balanced with innovation. Like tradition, innovation can take many forms. Using traditional, and familiar, music in a new worship context can be innovative. But like tradition, innovation can be used to excess. When a congregation is always confronted with new hymnody, new worship materials, unfamiliar liturgical forms, and when it is constantly assaulted with strange new musical idioms, the virtue of newness wears thin and is reduced to the level of meaningless novelty.

The use of the elements of tradition and innovation in worship and music requires a sensitive and delicate balancing. The one should be a challenge to the other, as for example in recent years traditional hymnody and liturgical music were challenged by the innovations of folk-pop-rock. The challenge addressed to the church was: "Please don't impose musical boredome on the worshiper." It confronted the institutional church with an opportunity to reexamine its musical habits and to seek for ways to develop a healthy renewal.

It is by such constant renewal that parish music comes alive and stays in touch with the worshiper. Not a preoccupation with either tradition or innovation, but a creative and imaginative drawing from both, and a resourceful application of the available repertory to an ever more meaningful liturgical action. That is the ultimate challenge in parish music today.

It is easy to over-simplify contemporary problems in church music. And it is indeed precarious to pretend to be able to discern and evaluate all that constitutes the present state of it. Whatever can be said may be wholly expendable and irrelevant in a few years. A bit of reflection about recent history will confirm this not only as a possibility, but as an inevitability.

Even more impossible is it to tell what the state of music in the church will be in the future. But, as one who is a composer of music for the church, I am deeply concerned about that future.

The church is likely to continue to be what Carl Halter has described as "a cultural vestige" surrounded completely by a secular society. And its main problems will continue to center on questions of Christian faith. Church music will always be no more and no less than the church itself. When our practices of music and the liturgy are deeply rooted in that faith,

252

we can be free to accept what is useful in all of our tradition, but, like Luther before us, we will not be afraid to alter it or to add to it.

The renewal of music and liturgy in corporate worship as it has been described here, and the creative application of its fundamental principles, is a reaffirmation of the faith. It is evidence of a continued concern for music's viability and expressibility as an art in the service of worship in praise of the Creator of all, and, with all its challenges, offers to church music in our time the most productive course for a creative future.

See also related articles in *Key Words in Church Music*: Catholic pronouncements and decrees on church music; choir, history; church music history, 20th century; notation; organ, history; theology of church music, 20th century

Resources for the Church Musician

Carlos R. Messerli

The range of subjects covered by the articles in this handbook reflects the broad knowledge and skills appropriate for the church musician today. Each article suggests that competence in one area of church music can be enhanced by understanding (if not mastery) of related fields. The following list of books and articles for reading and reference—limited to writings in English—is provided to further that suggestion and to extend the presentation begun by each author.

While every bibliography is a personal projection of the compiler's view, many works recommend themselves because of their wide acceptance, or because of the penetrating analysis, clear organization, or excellent scholarship of the author. When books of equal quality were available, preference was given to those suggesting to the reader additional resources in notes or bibliographies.

References

Music Dictionaries and Encyclopedias

Apel, Willi. *Harvard Dictionary of Music*, 2d ed. Cambridge, Mass., 1969.
The standard one-volume English-language reference for musical terms; includes some long articles; good coverage of church music.

Apel, Willi and Ralph T. Daniel. *Harvard Brief Dictionary of Music*. New York, 1961.
Brief definitions; some areas of church music receive longer treatment; pronunciation guide.

Baker, Theodore, ed. *Pronouncing Pocket-Manual of Musical Terms*. [1905] 1947.
Contains over 3,000 terms; useful in spite of its age.

Blom, Eric, ed. *Grove's Dictionary of Music and Musicians*, 5th ed., 10 vols. New York, 1954—61.
The standard musical encyclopedia in English.

Scholes, Percy A. and John O. Ward, eds. *The Concise Oxford Dictionary of Music*, 2d ed. London, 1975.
>An excellent small reference of terms, names, and titles of works.

Slonimsky, Nicolas, ed. *Baker's Biographical Dictionary of Musicians*, 5th rev. ed., with Supplement. New York, 1971.
>The most reliable, complete, and informative one-volume work of its kind in English.

Westrup, Jack A. and Frank L. Harrison, eds. *The New College Encyclopedia of Music*, rev. ed. New York, 1976.
>Terms and proper names; good coverage of church music.

Religious Encyclopedias

Bodensieck, Julius H., ed. *Encyclopedia of the Lutheran Church*, 3 vols. Minneapolis, 1965.
>Unusually full treatment of many aspects of Lutheran Church music.

Cross, Frank L. and E. A. Livingstone, eds. *The Oxford Dictionary of the Christian Church*, 2d ed. London, 1974.
>Includes a large number of ecclesiastical and liturgical terms, especially those of the Anglican community.

Lueker, Erwin L., ed. *Lutheran Cyclopedia*, rev. ed. St. Louis, Mo., 1975.
>One-volume reference; many entries.

New Catholic Encyclopedia, 16 vols., ed., staff of Catholic University of America; Vol. 16 ed., David Eggenberger. New York, 1967—74.
>Includes a lengthy treatment of many items related to Roman Catholic liturgy and music.

Church Music Dictionaries

Davidson, James R. *A Dictionary of Protestant Church Music*. Metuchen, N. J., 1975.
>Over 300 entries, some quite lengthy; liturgical and nonliturgical terms defined; entries list books for further reading.

Schalk, Carl, ed. *Key Words in Church Music*. St. Louis, 1978.
>A dictionary of longer articles; especially strong in areas of liturgical and traditional worship music.

Liturgical Dictionaries

Davies, J. G., ed. *A Dictionary of Liturgy and Worship*. New York, 1972.
>361 articles by 64 leading liturgiolists covering major world religious bodies; much information in a small book.

Davies, J. G. *A Select Liturgical Lexicon (Ecumenical Studies in Worship*, No. 14). Richmond, Va., 1965.
>800 liturgical terms from various branches of Catholicism and Protestantism.

Hughes, Anselm. *Liturgical Terms for Music Students.* Boston, 1940.

Brief definitions of over 200 terms common to Roman usage.

Histories in One Volume

Grout, Donald J. *A History of Western Music*, rev. ed. New York, 1973.

The most popular and reliable one-volume general history of music in English.

Woerner, Karl H. *History of Music; A Book for Study and Reference*, trans. and supplemented by Willis Wager from 5th ed. of *Geschichte der Musik*. New York, 1973.

A mass of carefully organized detail; no musical examples, pictures, or drawings.

Histories in Series

New Oxford History of Music. London, 1954—

The most comprehensive series available in English; coordinated recorded musical examples, music, and notes available.

Vol. I: *Ancient and Oriental Music.* Ed., Egon Wellesz. 1957.

Vol. II: *Early Medieval Music up to 1300.*, rev. ed. Ed. Anselm Hughes. 1955.

Vol. III: *Ars Nova and the Renaissance.* Ed., Anselm Hughes and Gerald Abraham. 1960.

Vol. IV: *The Age of Humanism, 1540—1630.* Ed., Gerald Abraham. 1968.

Vol. V: *Opera and Church Music, 1630—1750.* Ed., Anthony Lewis and Nigel Fortune. 1975.

Vol. VI: *The Growth of Instrumental Music, 1630—1750.* In preparation.

Vol. VII: *The Age of Enlightenment, 1745—1790.* Ed. Egon Wellesz and Frederick Sternfeld. 1973.

Vol. VIII: *The Age of Beethoven, 1790—1830.* In preparation.

Vol. IX: *Romanticism, 1830—1890.* In preparation.

Vol. X: *The Modern Age, 1890—1960.* Ed. Martin Cooper. 1974.

Vol. XI: *Chronological Tables, Bibliographies, and Index.* In preparation.

Norton History of Music Series. 6 vols. to date. New York, 1940—. Although not a formal series, the several volumes cover distinct and related periods; Reese's *Music in the Renaissance* is a particularly noteworthy component.

The Rise of Music in the Ancient World, East and West. Curt Sachs. 1943.

Music in the Middle Ages with an Introduction on the Music of Ancient Times. Gustave Reese. 1940.

Music in the Renaissance, rev. ed. Gustave Reese. 1959.

Music in the Baroque Era from Monteverdi to Bach. Manfred F. Bukofzer. 1947.

Music in the Romantic Era. Alfred Einstein. New York, 1947.

Music in the 20th Century from Debussy through Stravinsky. William W. Austin. 1966.

Prentice Hall History of Music Series. Englewood Cliffs, N. J., 1968—76.
A series that reflects reliable scholarship and readability throughout; available in paperback.
Music in the Medieval World, 2d ed. Albert Seay. 1975.
Music in the Renaissance. Howard Mayer Brown. 1976.
Baroque Music. Claude V. Palisca. 1968.
Music in the Classic Period, 2d ed. Reinhard G. Pauly. 1973.
Nineteenth-Century Romanticism in Music, 2d ed. Rey M. Longyear. 1973.
Twentieth-Century Music: An Introduction, 2d ed. Eric Salzman. 1974.
Music in the United States: A Historical Introduction. H. Wiley Hitchcock. 1974.
Folk and Traditional Music of the Western Continents, 2d ed. Bruno Nettl. 1973.

Periodicals

Choristers Guild Letters. Dallas, Tex.
Monthly; organizational and musical advice for leaders of children's choirs.
Church Music. St. Louis, Mo.
Semiannual; scholarly and practical journal; Lutheran orientation; reviews.
Diapason. Chicago, Ill.
Monthly; articles on organ, harpsichord, and church music; notices of activities.
Journal of Church Music. Philadelphia, Pa.
Monthly; practical articles on church music; suggested choral literature; Lutheran.
Liturgy. Washington, D. C.
Monthly; journal of the Roman Catholic Liturgical Conference; covers arts, dance, and worship planning. Supplemented by *Living Worship*; monthly planning guide for worship committees.
Music, The AGO-RCCO Magazine. New York, N. Y.
Monthly; published by American Guild of Organists; news of organ design, concerts, and guild activities; reviews.
Overtones. Bartlesville, Okla.
Six times a year; news of activities of the American Guild of English Handbell Ringers.
Reformed Liturgy and Music. New York, N. Y.
Quarterly; United Presbyterian; worship planning guide for hymns and choral music with the three-year lectionary.
Response. Valparaiso, Ind.
Three times a year; journal of the Lutheran Society for Worship, Music,

and the Arts; scholarly. Supplemented by *Accent*, five times a year; newsletter style; periodical article index.

Sacred Music. St. Paul, Minn.

Quarterly; published by Church Music Association of America; Roman Catholic; articles on music of the liturgy.

Worship. Collegeville, Minn.

Monthly; published by Benedictines of St. John's Abbey; theological journal with frequent articles on music.

Worship and Liturgy

Liturgical Theology

Brunner, Peter. *Worship in the Name of Jesus*. Trans. Martin H. Bertram. St. Louis, 1968.

A definitive work on Christian worship in the congregation.

Davies, J. G. *Worship and Mission*. New York, 1967.

Explores the healthy and dynamic tension of the aspects of mission and worship in the life of the Church.

Hoyer, George W. "The Child in Christian Worship," in *The Child in Christian Worship, Sixteenth Yearbook of the Lutheran Education Association*, ed. Roland H. A. Seboldt. River Forest, Ill., 1959.

A stimulating guide to the full, rich, joyous potential of liturgical worship for children (and for adults).

Comparative Liturgies and Sources

Baumstark, Anton. *Comparative Liturgy*, rev., Bernard Botte, trans. F. L. Cross. London, 1958.

Comprehensive study of comparative Christian liturgies of Europe, southwest Asia, and northwest Africa.

Deiss, Lucien, ed. *Early Sources of the Liturgy*, trans. Benet Weatherhead. Staten Island, N. Y., 1967.

Text and discussion of 10 early liturgies.

Thompson, Bard, ed. *Liturgies of the Western Church*. Cleveland, Ohio, 1961.

A collection of 13 liturgies that have had a profound influence on subsequent worship practice.

Underhill, Evelyn. *Worship*. New York, [1936] 1957.

A perceptive overview of worship practices in various Christian denominations.

Liturgical Year

Horn, Edward T., III. *The Christian Year*. Philadelphia, 1957. Brief but authoritative. Describes the nature and defends the value of Christian church year for Protestants.

Kleinhans, Theodore J. *The Year of the Lord; The Church Year: Its Customs, Growth, and Ceremonies.* St. Louis, 1967.

Less detailed and more lively than the foregoing.

Jewish Worship

Herbert, Arthur S. *Worship in Ancient Israel (Ecumenical Studies in Worship,* No. 5). Richmond, Va., 1959.

Treats basis, vocabulary, media, and aim of Jewish worship.

Idelsohn, Abraham. *Jewish Liturgy and Its Development.* New York, [1932] 1967.

A standard reference work.

Kraus, Hans-Joachim. *Worship in Israel; A Cultic History of the Old Testament,* trans. Geoffrey Buswell. Richmond, Va., 1966.

A detailed, scholarly study.

Patristic Worship

Cullmann, Oscar. *Early Christian Worship,* trans. A. Stewart Todd and James B. Torrance (*Studies in Biblical Theology,* No. 10). London, 1953.

A study of New Testament worship practice as revealed by incidents in St. John's Gospel.

Daniélou, Jean. *The Bible and the Liturgy.* Notre Dame, Ind., [1951] 1966.

A scholarly study of Scriptural and patristic foundations of the liturgy.

Hahn, Ferdinand. *The Worship of the Early Church,* tr. David E. Green, ed., John Reumann. Philadelphia, 1973.

A concise and stimulating study of early Christian worship.

Martin, Ralph P. *Worship in the Early Church,* rev. ed. Grand Rapids, Mich., 1964.

Many Biblical and other references mark the investigation of early worship.

Moulé, C. F. D. *Worship in the New Testament (Ecumenical Studies in Worship,* No. 9). Richmond, Va., 1961.

Reveals the importance of worship concepts and practice to the earliest Christians.

Schweizer, Eduard. *The Lord's Supper According to the New Testament,* tr. James M. Davis (*Facet Books Biblical Series,* No. 18). Philadelphia, [1956] 1967.

A modern critical study of the Biblical background and accounts of the Lord's Supper; thoroughly documented.

Roman Catholic Traditional Practice

Dix, Gregory. *The Shape of the Liturgy.* London, [1945] 1960.

A significant, detailed, historical study of the mass by an Anglo-Catholic; follows Protestant developments after the Reformation.

Jungmann, Joseph A. *The Mass of the Roman Rite: Its Origins and Development,* tr. Francis A. Brunner, rev. ed., Charles K. Riepe. New York, 1961.

A standard historical study of the Roman Catholic mass.

Roman Catholic Contemporary Practice

Deiss, Lucien. *The Spirit and Song of the New Liturgy*. Cincinnati, 1976.
Considers the accommodation of new styles of worship after Vatican II.

Koenker, Ernest B. *The Liturgical Renaissance in the Roman Catholic Church*, 2d ed. St. Louis, [1954] 1966.
A perceptive, even prophetic presentation; includes notes and a large bibliography.

McNaspy, Clement J. *Our Changing Liturgy*. New York, 1967.
A moderately "progressive" Catholic position on the liturgy since Vatican II; includes the official text of the "Constitution on the Sacred Liturgy."

O'Neill, Colman E. "The Theological Meaning of *Actuosa Participatio* in the Liturgy," in *Sacred Music and Liturgy Reform after Vatican II*. St. Paul, Minn., 1969, pp. 89—108.
Supports the retention of traditional artistic sacred music, while incorporating congregational participation in the mass.

Schuler, Richard J. "How Can You Have a Latin Mass?" *Sacred Music* 103:1 (Spring, 1976), 26—31.
Speaks positively about the use of Latin and traditional Roman Catholic art music in the liturgy of the post-Vatican II era.

Eastern

Verghese, Paul. *The Joy of Freedom: Eastern Worship and Modern Man* (*Ecumenical Studies in Worship*, No. 17). Richmond, Va., 1967.
The author attempts "to set Eastern worship in the context of the present world."

Anglican

Shepherd, Massey H., Jr. *The Worship of the Church* (*The Church's Teaching*, Vol. 4). Greenwich, Conn., 1952.
Analysis of the principles of Christian worship and the liturgies of *The Book of Common Prayer*.

Lutheran

Brand, Eugene. *The Rite Thing*. Minneapolis, 1970.
An inspiring monograph which seeks to arouse the consciousness of the worshiper.

Brown, Edgar S. *Living the Liturgy*. Philadelphia, 1961.
One of the best small commentaries on the traditional common service.

Kalb, Friedrich. *Theology of Worship in 17th-Century Lutheranism*, trans. Henry P. A. Hamann. St. Louis, Mo., 1965.
Examines the metamorphosis of Lutheran Orthodoxy in the 17th century.

Reed, Luther D. *The Lutheran Liturgy*, rev. ed. Philadelphia, 1961.
The most thorough historical and practical treatment of Lutheran liturgies in English.

Vajta, Vilmos. *Luther on Worship, An Interpretation*, trans. and condensed, Ulrich S. Leupold. Philadelphia, 1958.
> Examination of Luther's theology of worship.

Von Schenk, Berthold. *The Little Service Book*. New York, 1954.
> An introduction to the liturgy; a jewel intended for children or adults.

Free Church

Abba, Raymond. *Principles of Christian Worship with Special Reference to the Free Churches*. New York, 1957.
> Clear and concise presentation of the foundation of worship of Baptist, Congregational, Methodist, and Presbyterian churches.

Contemporary Thought

Horn, Henry E. *Worship in Crisis*. Philadelphia, 1972.
> A courageous discussion which raises more questions than it answers.

Shepherd, Massey H., Jr., ed. *The Liturgical Renewal of the Church*. New York, 1960.
> A collection of six essays presented to the Liturgical Conference, Madison, Wis., in 1958.

Psalms

Psalms: History and Interpretation

Dahood, Mitchell J. *Psalms*, introd., trans., and notes (*The Anchor Bible*, Vols. 16, 17, 17a). Garden City, N. J., 1966—70.
> A classic study utilizing latest scholarship.

Green, Lowell C. "The Use of the Psalms in the Liturgical Hours," *Church Music*, 76·1, 28—36.
> An excellent historical study with obvious contemporary application.

Lamb, John Alexander. *The Psalms in Christian Worship*. London, 1962.
> The use of the Psalms in the early church and in six major segments of the church in subsequent years.

Mowinckel, Sigmund. *The Psalms in Israel's Worship,* tr. D. R. Ap-Thomas. Oxford, 1962.
> An influential study; emphasizes the cultic background of the Psalms.

Shepherd, Massey H., Jr. *The Psalms in Christian Worship: A Practical Guide*. Minneapolis, 1976.
> A well-written introduction to the history and use of the Psalms.

Psalms: Translation

Shepherd, Massey H., Jr., ed. *A Liturgical Psalter for the Christian Year*. Minneapolis and Collegeville, Minn., 1976.
> A selection of 60 psalms in fresh translation with suggested antiphons and notes on liturgical use.

The Psalms: *A New Translation from the Hebrew and Arranged for Singing to the Psalmody of Joseph Gelineau* (The Grail). Philadelphia, 1963.

A translation that tries to maintain characteristics of the Hebrew poetry; widely used.

The Psalms of the Jerusalem Bible. Garden City, N. Y., 1970.

A largely successful attempt to remain faithful to the original poetry; explanatory notes.

Church Music

General

Routley, Eric. *Music Leadership in the Church: A Conversation Chiefly with My American Friends.* Nashville, Tenn., 1967.

Nine essays on significant aspects of church music and theology.

Church Music History

Harrison, Frank. "Music and Cult: The Functions of Music in Social and Religious Systems," in *Perspectives in Musicology,* ed. Barry S. Brook, Edward O. D. Downs, and Sherman Van Solkema. New York, 1972.

A scholarly study of the use of music in Western liturgical traditions; thoroughly documented.

Hutchings, Arthur. *Church Music in the Nineteenth Century* (*Studies in Church Music*). New York, 1967.

An overview of one of the weaker periods of church music activity.

Routley, Erik. *The Church and Music: An Inquiry into the History, the Nature, and the Scope of Christian Judgment on Music,* rev. ed. London, 1967.

A historical survey of the attitude of the church towards music for worship.

Jewish

Idelsohn, Abraham Z. *Jewish Music in Its Historical Development.* New York, [1929] 1967.

Extensive survey of Jewish music from Biblical to modern times.

Sendrey, Alfred, and Mildred Norton. *David's Harp: The Story of Music in Biblical Times.* New York, 1964.

A popular treatment of the music of the Jews.

Werner, Eric. *The Sacred Bridge; The Interdependence of Liturgy and Music in Synogogue and Church during the First Millenium.* New York, 1959.

Clearly organized, well documented, thorough.

Roman Catholic

Apel, Willi. *Gregorian Chant.* Bloomington, Ind., 1958.

A fundamental work of admirable scholarship.

The Constitution on the Sacred Liturgy of the Second Vatican Council and The "Motu

Proprio" of Pope Paul VI, with a Commentary, Gerard S. Sloyan. Glen Rock, N. J., 1964.

The documents of Vatican II that relate to liturgy and music; an adult study guide.

Crisis in Church Music? Proceedings of a Meeting on Church Music Conducted by the Liturgical Conference and The Church Music Association of America. Washington, D. C., 1967.

Twelve articles address the post-Vatican II Roman Catholic problems from conservative and liberal points of view; perceptive article by Carl Schalk summarizes Lutheran church music practice.

Fellerer, Karl G. *The History of Catholic Church Music,* tr. Francis A. Brunner, Baltimore, Md., 1961.

Valuable survey of music of Catholic composers, but little information on liturgical performance.

Anglican

Dearnley, Christopher. *English Church Music, 1650-1750 in Royal Chapel, Cathedral, and Parish Church.* London, 1970.

Douglas, Winfred. *Church Music in History and Practice; Studies in the Praise of God,* rev., Leonard Ellinwood. New York, 1962.

The history of church music with an Anglican emphasis.

Fellowes, Edmund H. *English Cathedral Music,* rev. ed. Jack A. Westrup. London, 1973.

A historical review by a persuasive partisan.

Le Huray, Peter. *Music and the Reformation in England, 1549—1660 (Studies in Church Music).* London, 1967.

A thorough study of a glorious period of English church music.

Long, Kenneth R. *The Music of the English Church.* New York, 1971.

A splendid, readable survey covering music from the Reformation to the present day.

Rhys, Stephen, and King Palmer. *A B C of Church Music.* Boston, 1967.

Miscellaneous practical and historical information from an Anglican point of view.

Stevens, Denis. *Tudor Church Music,* rev. ed. New York, 1966.

A slender volume, rich in information and insight concerning Anglican polyphony from 1485 to the early 17th century.

Lutheran

Blume, Friedrich, with Ludwig Finscher, Georg Feder, Adam Adrio, Walter Blankenburg, Torben Schousboe, Robert Stevenson, and Watkins Shaw. *Protestant Church Music, A History.* New York, 1974.

The single most important historical work for serious students of

Protestant church music; largely Lutheran in orientation; Scandinavian, Anglican, and American practices treated; detailed and reliable.

Buszin, Walter E. *Luther on Music (Lutheran Society for Worship, Music, and the Arts, Pamphlet Series* No. 3). St. Paul, 1958.
Examines Luther's references to music.

Horn, Henry E. *O Sing Unto the Lord; Music in the Lutheran Church.* rev. ed. Philadelphia, 1966.
A layperson's guide; emphasis on the Common Service.

Halter, Carl. *The Practice of Sacred Music.* St. Louis, Mo., 1955.
A practical manual based on sound theological, liturgical, and artistic foundations.

American Practice

Ellinwood, Leonard. *The History of American Church Music,* rev. ed. (*Da Capo Press Music Reprint Series*). New York, 1970.
A helpful overview.

Stevenson, Robert. *Protestant Church Music in America; A Short Survey of Men and Movements from 1564 to the Present.* New York, 1966.
A wealth of information; good bibliography.

Congregational Song

Brand, Eugene L. "Congregational Song: The Popular Music of the Church," *Church Music* 68·1, 1-10.

Contemporary Practice

Hillert, Richard. "Sources and Sounds of the New Music," *Church Music* 72·1, 1—11.
Survey of major trends in composition since World War II.

Miller, William Robert. *The Christian Encounters the World of Pop Music and Jazz.* St. Louis, Mo., 1965.
A plea for the Christian to approach music of the pop culture with patience and understanding.

Peyser, Joan. *The New Music; The Sense Behind the Sound.* New York, 1971.
Lucid writing coupled with ample quotations from composers provide rare illumination of the 20th-century scene.

Routley, Erik. *Twentieth Century Church Music (Studies in Church Music).* New York, 1966.
The author states that he presents "the beginning of a conversion, not the record of a complete historical phase."

———— *Words, Music, and the Church.* Nashville, 1968.
A lively challenge to the contemporary leaders of church music.

Schwartz, Elliott, and Barney Childs, eds. *Contemporary Composers on Contemporary Music.* New York, 1967.

An unusually revealing sampling of opinions of leading 20th-century composers.

Church Choir Leadership

Decker, Harold A., and Julius Herford. *Choral Conducting, A Symposium*. New York, 1973.

Important articles by Howard Swan, Lloyd Pfautsch, Walter S. Collins, Daniel Moe, and Julius Herford; a basic choral reference work.

Ehmann, Wilhelm. *Choral Directing,* tr. George D. Wiebe, Minneapolis, [1949] 1968.

An outstanding resource written by a respected musicologist, choral director, and educator.

Ehret, Walter. *The Choral Conductor's Handbook*. New York, 1959.

A multitude of well-organized, brief suggestions.

Finn, William J. *The Art of the Choral Conductor*. Evanston, Ill., [1939] 1960.

A classic in the field of choral leadership.

Garretson, Robert L. *Conducting Choral Music*, 4th ed. Boston, 1975.

A standard textbook.

Green, Elizabeth A. H. *The Modern Conductor; A College Text on Conducting Based on the Principles of Nicolai Malko as Set Forth in His "The Conductor and His Baton,"* 2d ed. Englewood Cliffs, N. J., 1975.

A popular, comprehensive text.

Halter, Carl. *The Christian Choir Member*. St. Louis, 1961.

An inspiring booklet that briefly outlines the unique requirements and rewards of church choir membership.

Marshall, Madeleine. *The Singer's Manual of English Diction*. New York, 1953.

The classic work in its field.

Moe, Daniel. *Problems in Conducting*. Minneapolis, 1968.

A booklet of musical examples with commentary designed to develop skills in conducting, particularly those needed for contemporary music.

Nordin, Dayton W. *How to Organize and Direct the Church Choir*. West Nyack, N. J.

A good source book of practical suggestions for church choir work; weak on liturgy, hymns, and organ.

Pooler, Frank, and Brent Pierce. *New Choral Notation; A Handbook*. New York, 1971.

A dictionary of most common types of nontraditional choral notation; many musical examples.

Suñol, Gregory. *Text Book of Gregorian Chant According to the Solesmes Method*, tr. G. M. Durnford. Tournai, 1930.

A handbook presenting generally accepted principles and their application.

Church Choir Literature

Nardone, Thomas R., James H. Nye, and Mark Resnick, eds. *Choral Music in Print*, Vol. I, *Sacred Choral Music*, Philadelphia, 1974.

Nardone, Thomas R., ed. *Choral Music in Print: 1976 Supplement.*
Monumental lists of music in print.

Smallman, Basil. *The Background of Passion Music; J. S. Bach and Predecessors*, 2d ed. New York, 1970.
A small but distinguished manual.

Ulrich, Homer. *A Survey of Choral Music; (The Harbrace History of Musical Forms)*. New York, 1973.
A reliable guide.

Wienandt, Elwyn A. *Choral Music of the Church*. New York, 1965.
A detailed examination of the music and its performance in church.

Wienandt, Elwyn A., and Robert H. Young. *The Anthem in England and America*. New York, 1970.
Informative overview of a genre of immense size.

Young, Percy M. *The Choral Tradition; An Historical and Analytical Survey from the Sixteenth Century to the Present Day*. New York, 1962.

Children's Choirs in Church

Jacobs, Ruth Krehbiel. *The Children's Choir*, Vol. I. Philadelphia, 1958.

Tufts, Nancy Poore. *The Children's Choir*, Vol. II. Philadelphia, 1965.
Practical information gathered from material published by the Chorister's Guild.

Jacobs, Ruth Krehbiel. *The Successful Children's Choir*. Chicago, 1948.
Practical help on musical and nonmusical matters.

Kemp, Helen. *Helen Kemp on Junior Choirs*. Dayton, Ohio, 1962.
Excellent booklet; inspirational!

Lundstrom, Linden J. *The Choir School, A Leadership Manual*, rev. ed. Minneapolis, 1963.
Describes the history, goals, and organization of choir schools as related to the modern church.

Church Soloists

Schalk, Carl. "Solo Literature for the Liturgical Service," *Church Music* 71·2, 5—11.
Delineates the function of the church soloist; valuable list of solos for each day of the traditional church year.

Instruments in Church

Klammer, Edward W. "Using Instruments in Parish Worship," *Church Music* 70·1, 8—13.
A practical guide that sets goals and provides resources.

Ode, James A. *Brass Instruments in Church Services*. Minneapolis, 1970.

Presents history, performance procedures, and repertoire.

Pirner, Reuben. "Instruments in Christian Worship, A Historical-Theological Perspective," *Church Music* 70:1, 1—7.

Spelman, Leslie P. *Organ Plus: A Catalogue of Ensemble Music for Organ and Instruments*. New York, 1975.

A slender pamphlet listing a variety of repertoire possibilities.

Organ Design

Andersen, Paul-Gerhard. *Organ Building and Design*, tr. Joanne Curnutt. New York, 1969.

Detailed and thorough discussion.

Bunjes, Paul. "Great Foundational Works on the Art of the Organ," *Church Music* 67·1, 49—52.

Review of seven major publications from Schlick to Audsley.

Gehring, Philip and Donald Ingram. *The Church Organ, A Guide to Its Selection*, 2d ed. Valparaiso, Ind., 1973.

Twelve pages of essential information; bibliography.

Phelps, Lawrence L. "A Short History of the Organ Revival," *Church Music* 67·1, 13—30.

A most significant article covering developments in Europe and America.

Sumner, William L. *The Organ; Its Evolution, Principles of Construction, and Use*, 4th ed., rev. and enl. London, 1973.

A classic in the field.

Organ and Its Literature

Apel, Willi. *The History of Keyboard Music to 1700*, trans. and rev., Hans Tischler. Bloomington, Ind., 1972.

A rare work, both thorough in coverage and broad in scope.

Arnold, Corliss R. *Organ Literature: A Comprehensive Survey*. Metuchen, N. J., 1973.

A historical survey of organ literature and a bibliographic catalog; valuable!

Edson, Jean S. *Organ Preludes: An Index to Compositions on Hymn Tunes, Chorales, Plainsong Melodies, Gregorian Tunes, and Carols*. Metuchen, N. J., 1970.

2 volumes that index thousands of hymn preludes by composer and tune name.

Organ Preludes: Supplement [to above] Metuchen, 1974.

Expands coverage in area of Scandinavian hymns and French Noels.

Gotsch, Herbert. "The Organ in the Lutheran Service of the 16th Century," *Church Music* 67·1, 7—12.

A significant contribution that sheds light on contemporary practice.

Nardone, Thomas R., ed. *Organ Music in Print*. Philadelphia, 1975.
A comprehensive list.

Kirby, F. E. *A Short History of Keyboard Music*. New York, 1966.
A scholarly and comprehensive survey.

Klotz, Hans. *The Organ Handbook*, tr. Gerhard Krapf. St. Louis, 1969.
A unique source which treats organ design, history, literature, and service playing; bibliography.

Organ Improvisation

Bender, Jan. *Organ Improvisation for Beginners; A Book of Self-Instruction for Church Musicians*. St. Louis, 1975.
A systematic textbook designed for diligent and ambitious students.

Gehrke, Hugo. "Ornamentation in Organ Playing: A Descriptive Review of Some Standard Sources," *Church Music* 67·2, 52—53.
Review of eight important works.

Krapf, Gerhard. *Organ Improvisation: A Practical Approach to Chorale Elaboration for the Service*. Minneapolis, 1967.
A challenging method book; well-chosen musical examples.

Performance Practice

Donington, Robert. *The Interpretation of Early Music*, new version. London, 1974.
Contemporary sources are cited to suggest performance practices for early music, largely that of the baroque era; excellent bibliography.

Donington, Robert. *A Performer's Guide to Baroque Music*. New York, 1973.
Numerous baroque references reveal suggested solutions to performance problems; shorter than the foregoing work.

Ferguson, Howard. *Keyboard Interpretation from the 14th to the 19th Century; An Introduction*. New York, 1975.
An excellent, scholarly presentation of practical solutions to problems of performance practice; bibliography.

Jenne, Natalie R. "An Introduction to Baroque Performance Practice and Sources," *Church Music*, 70·1, 46—53.
Surveys notation, ornamentation, dance rhythms, thorough bass, and ensemble performance.

Dart, Thurston. *The Interpretation of Music*. New York, [1954] 1963.
Examines major stylistic periods and problems with insight and imagination.

Hymnody: History and Practice

Ameln, Konrad. *The Roots of German Hymnody of the Reformation Era (Church Music Pamphlet Series: Hymnology,* Number One). St. Louis, Mo., 1964.
A brief and reliable study of the chorale.

Benson, Louis F. *The English Hymn; Its Development and Use in Worship.* New York, 1915.
A valuable historical handbook.

Bodensieck, Julius, ed. *The Development of Lutheran Hymnody in America.* Minneapolis, 1967.
Articles reprinted from the *Encyclopedia of the Lutheran Church,* ed. Julius Bodensieck.

Gehrke, Ralph. *Planning the Service; A Workbook for Pastors, Organists, and Choirmasters.* St. Louis, Mo., 1961.
Valuable guide for selection of choral and organ music, and especially hymns for Lutheran worship; features traditional Hymn-of-the-Week plan.

Julian, John. *Dictionary of Hymnology, Setting forth the Origin and History of Christian Hymns of all Ages and Nations.* New York, [1907] 1957.
Scholarly, comprehensive; emphasizes hymn texts.

Reynolds, William J. *A Survey of Christian Hymnody.* New York, 1963.
Music and text of 160 hymns illustrate the survey; rhythmic chorale ignored.

Riedel, Johannes. *The Lutheran Chorale; Its Basic Traditions.* Minneapolis, 1967.

Schalk, Carl F. *The Roots of Hymnody in The Lutheran Church—Missouri Synod; The Story of Congregational Song—the Hymnals and the Chorale Books from the Saxon Immigration to the Present (Church Music Pamphlet Series: Hymnology, Number Two).* St. Louis, 1965.
Traces the preservation of the rhythmic chorale by the Synod.

Hymnal Handbooks

The Hymnal 1940 Companion, 3d rev. ed. Prepared by the Joint Commission on the Revision of the Hymnal of the Protestant Episcopal Church in the U.S.A. New York, 1956.
Primarily textual study; includes indexes and list of organ compositions based on melodies of *The Hymnal 1940.*

Dearmer, Percy and Archibald Jacob. *Songs of Praise Discussed; A Handbook to the Best-known Hymns and to Others Recently Introduced.* London, [1933] 1952.
Treats texts and music.

Polack, W. G. *Handbook to the Lutheran Hymnal,* 2d rev. ed. St. Louis, Mo., 1942.
Emphasis on texts, but melodies are not overlooked.

Notes

Introduction

1. Unless otherwise indicated, quotations from Luther are taken from Walter E. Buszin, *Luther on Music*, reprinted 1958 by the Lutheran Society for Worship, Music, and the Arts by permission of G. Schirmer Inc., New York, N. Y.

2. The term "hymn mass" (Ger.: *Liedmesse*) refers to the practice of substituting for the prose texts of the five great songs of the liturgy the following Lutheran chorales that emerged in the early years of the Reformation and which were used for just that purpose: "Kyrie, God Father in Heaven Above" (the Kyrie hymn); "All Glory Be to God on High" (the Gloria hymn); "We All Believe in One True God" (the Credo hymn); "Isaiah, Mighty Seer in Days of Old" (the Sanctus hymn); and "O Christ, Thou Lamb of God" (the Agnus hymn).

3. Drawn from E. M. Plass, *What Luther Says* (St. Louis, 1959), p. 982.

Chapter I

1. Anamnesis is usually rendered "remembrance" in English. It connotes far more than mere mental recall, however. It refers to the reality of a past event as it comes alive in the words and actions of worship.

2. *Contemporary Worship 6: The Church Year—Calendar and Lectionary* (1973). On this section see also A. A. McArthur, *The Christian Year and Lectionary Reform* (London, 1958); and N. M. Denis-Boulet, *The Christian Calendar* (London, 1960).

3. This complex history of the evolution of the Western traditions is most recently detailed in *The Church at Prayer: The Eucharist*, ed. A. G. Martimort (Shannon, 1973), pp. 28—53. Compare G. Dix, *The Shape of the Liturgy* (Westminster, 1945); R. Staehlin, "Die Geschichte des christlichen Gottesdienstes von der Urkirche bis zur Gegenwart," *Leiturgia*, I, ed. Mueller & Blankenburg (Kassel, 1954); and Luther D. Reed, *The Lutheran Liturgy*, rev. ed. (Philadelphia, 1959).

4. This concept is developed by such theologians as Regin Prenter, *The Word and the Spirit* (Minneapolis, 1965) and Peter Brunner, *Worship in the Name of Jesus*, tr. M. H. Bertram (St. Louis, 1968).

5. For more detailed historical material on the liturgy of the hours see C. W. Dugmore, "Canonical Hours," *A Dictionary of Liturgy and Worship* ed. J. G. Davies (New York, 1972), pp. 113—120. See also H. Goltzen, "Der Taegliche Gottesdienst," *Leiturgia*, III (Kassel, 1956), pp. 100—294; and Reed, op. cit., pp. 388—449.

6. Quoted in Eberhard Weismann, "Der Predigtgottesdienst und die verwandten Formen," *Leiturgia*, III, pp. 23—24.

7. English translations of Luther's liturgical writings are in *Luther's Works*, 53, American Edition (Philadelphia, 1965).

8. For this section see Weismann, op. cit., and Friedrich Kalb, *Grundriss der Liturgik* (Munich, 1965).

9. B. M. Schmucker, "The First Pennsylvania Liturgy," *The Lutheran Church Review*, I (1882), pp. 16—27; 161—172.

10. Quoted from Luther D. Reed, "The Common Service in the Life of the Church," *The Lutheran Church Quarterly*, 12 (1939), pp. 9—10.

11. Henry Eyster Jacobs, *A History of the Evangelical Lutheran Church in the United States* (New York, 1893), p. 506.

12. "The Lutheran Sources of the Common Service," *The Lutheran Quarterly*, 21 (1891), p. 239.

13. On the entire section see Luther D. Reed, *The Lutheran Liturgy*, pp. 161—227.

14. Ibid., pp. 453—462.

15. See the discussion in Arthur Carl Piepkorn, "The Protestant Worship Revival and the Lutheran Liturgical Movement," *The Liturgical Renewal of the Church*, ed. Massey Shepherd (New York, 1960), p. 87.

16. See his *A Manual in Worship* (Philadelphia, 1946).

Chapter II

1. For a discussion of Lutheran worship and church music practices on the Continent the following writings are helpful: *Luther's Works*, Vol. 53, "Liturgy and Hymns," ed. Ulrich Leupold (Philadelphia, 1965); Emil Sehling, *Die evangelischen Kirchenordnungen des XVI. Jahrhunderts* (Leipzig, 1902—13); Leonard Fendt, *Der Lutherische Gottesdienst des 16. Jahrhunderts* (Munich, 1923); Vilmos Vajta, *Luther on Worship* (Philadelphia, 1958); Jaroslav Pelikan, *Luther and the Liturgy*, in *More About Luther*, Martin Luther Lectures, Vol. 2 (Decorah, Iowa, 1958); for the 17th century see especially Friedrich Kalb, *Theology of Worship in 17th-Century Lutheranism* (St. Louis, 1965); for the most detailed treatment of the development of Lutheran church music see Friedrich Blume, *Protestant Church Music* (New York, 1974); for various views of worship at Bach's time see Guenther Stiller, *Johann Sebastian Bach und das Leipziger gottesdienstliche Leben seiner Zeit* (Kassel and Basel, 1970) and Bernard Knick, *St. Thomas zu Leipzig: Schule and Chor* (Wiesbaden, 1963).

For American Lutheran worship and church music practices two basic histories may be helpful: Lars Qualben, *The Lutheran Church in Colonial America* (New York, 1940), and Abdel Ross Wentz, *A Basic History of Lutherans in America*, rev. ed. (Philadelphia, 1964). More particular information may be found in such works as *Church Music and Musical Life in Pennsylvania* (Philadelphia, 1927); *Documentary History of the Evangelical Lutheran Ministerium of Pennsylvania and Adjacent States* (Philadelphia, 1898); and Harry Kreider, *The Beginnings of*

Lutheranism in New York (New York, 1949). A view of the Bavarian Lutheran communities in Michigan may be found in Theodore Graebner, *Church Bells in the Forest* (St. Louis, 1944); information on the music of the Saxon immigrants may be found in *Moving Frontiers: Readings in the History of The Lutheran Church—Missouri Synod*, ed. Carl S. Meyer (St. Louis, 1964), and in Carl Schalk, *The Roots of Hymnody in The Lutheran Church—Missouri Synod* (St. Louis, 1965). Materials relating to the Norwegian immigrants include J. Magnus Rohne, *Norwegian American Lutheranism up to 1872* (New York, 1926); Theodore Blegen, *Norwegian Migration to America. The American Transition* (Northfield, Minn., 1940); E. Clifford Nelson, *The Lutheran Church Among Norwegian Americans: A History of the Evangelical Lutheran Church* (Minneapolis, 1960); and *Norsemen Found a Church*, ed. J. C. K. Preus (Minneapolis, 1953). The development of the *Common Service* and its antecedents in America are treated at great length in Luther D. Reed, *The Lutheran Liturgy*, rev. ed. (Philadelphia, 1959).

Among the congregational histories that have been helpful in this chapter are *The Old Trappe Church*, ed. Ernest T. Kretschmann (Philadelphia, 1893); Herman F. Zehnder, *Teach My People Thy Truth: The Story of Frankenmuth, Michigan* (printed privately, 1970); N. N. Ronning, *The Saga of Old Muskego* (Waterford, Wis., 1943); and *The History of First English Evangelical Lutheran Church in Pittsburgh, 1837—1909* (Philadelphia, 1909).

Four dissertations available in microfilm are worthy of mention in connection with the music, worship, and hymnody of American Lutheranism: Gerhard M. Cartford. *Music in the Norwegian Lutheran Church: A Study of Its Development in Norway and Its Transfer to America, 1825—1917* (University of Minnesota, 1961); Arnold Lehmann, *The Music of the Lutheran Church, Synodical Conference, Chiefly the Areas of Missouri, Illinois, Wisconsin, and Neighboring States, 1839—1941* (Western Reserve University, 1967); Carlton Y. Smith, *Early Lutheran Hymnody in America from the Colonial Period to the Year 1850* (University of Southern California, 1956); and Edward Wolf, *Lutheran Church Music in America during the Eighteenth and Early Nineteenth Centuries* (University of Illinois, 1960).

2. *Luther's Works*, American ed., 53 (Philadelphia, 1965), 61.

3. The development in the course of the century of a series of de tempore hymns replacing the Gradual and reflecting the theme of the day from the Gospel became an important part of Lutheran worship. While these hymns varied occasionally from place to place, there was a basic general agreement as to the choice of the de tempore hymn for a particular Sunday of the church year.

4. Sidney Moore, *Sursum Corda*, quoted in Wm. Reynolds, *A Survey of Christian Hymnody* (New York, 1963).

5. This admittedly fictionalized account, found in Moser's *Die evangelische Kirchenmusik in volkstuemlichem Ueberblick* (Stuttgart, 1926) is, however, based on a thoroughly realistic understanding of the customs and practices of the time. The English translation is from Theodore Graebner, *The Borderland of Right and Wrong* (St. Louis, 1945).

6. This Lutheran congregation was founded in 1649 by Dutch Lutherans and subsequently named Trinity in 1729. In 1749 a schism of German members formed Christ Church, the two groups reuniting in 1784 and meeting at Christ Church. In 1822 St. Matthew was organized, without schism, for the English-speaking members, Christ

Church remaining for the German-speaking members. In 1831 Christ Church building was sold, both congregations using St. Matthew's building. Thus St. Matthew, which still exists, is the sole survivor of the old New York congregation.

7. T. Graebner, *Church Bells in the Forest* (St. Louis, 1944), p. 68.

8. *Ibid.*, p. 47.

9. Translation in *Moving Frontiers*, ed. C. S. Meyer (St. Louis, 1964), p. 182.

10. C. Eissfeldt, translated by T. Laetsch in *Concordia Historical Institute Quarterly*, IV (1931), 67.

11. T. Buenger in *Concordia Historical Institute Quarterly*, IX (1936), p. 70.

Chapter III

1. Dietrich Bonhoeffer, *Life Together* (New York and Evanston, 1954), p. 58.

2. *The Book of Concord*, tr. and ed. Theodore Tappert (Philadelphia, 1959), p. 32.

3. See chapter V in this *Handbook* for a more detailed study of this music.

4. I wish to acknowledge the assistance of Erik Routley (via his book *The Music of Christian Hymnody*) for much of the shape and substance of this portion of this chapter.

5. Erik Routley, *The Music of Christian Hymnody* (London, 1957), p. 5.

6. For a more detailed analysis of the poetic structure of hymn texts see Austin Lovelace, *The Anatomy of Hymnody* (New York and Nashville, 1965).

7. Technically, a single line is a verse; a series of lines or verses makes a stanza.

8. Bernard Manning, *The Hymns of Wesley and Watts* (London, 1942).

9. Routley, op. cit., pp. 91—92.

10. See, for example, Graham George's tune "The King's Majesty" both for its rhythmic elasticity and for its occasional thickening of harmonic texture. *EpH*, 64, 1st tune.

11. St. Louis, 1969. It was supplementary to *The Lutheran Hymnal* (1941).

12. Published in 1969 and 1972, respectively, by Concordia, Fortress, and Augsburg.

13. A possible exception would be the festival services in which clergy and choir recess out of the church at the close of the service.

14. If the service bulletin is to achieve maximum effectiveness, it must list all, not merely some, parts of the service *in the order in which* they follow.

15. See especially chapters IV and V in this *Handbook* for more detailed suggestions regarding the singing of hymns in alternation.

Chapter IV

1. The liturgical function of the choir has also been articulated by Carl Halter, *The Practice of Sacred Music* (St. Louis, 1955), and Carl F. Schalk, "Choral Music in Today's Church," unpublished course outline, '74 Inter-Lutheran Church Music Institutes, sponsored by the Lutheran Church in America, American Lutheran Church, and The Lutheran Church—Missouri Synod.

2. A key role is assigned to the choir in the method for introducing new hymns (and thus also other liturgical music) to the congregation outlined in Ralph D. Gehrke, *Planning the Service; a Workbook for Pastors, Organists, and Choirmasters* (St. Louis, 1961), pp. 7—8.

3. The anthem was often specified after the third collect at the end of the service and thus, though identified in the rubrics, was placed outside the service. Elwyn A. Wienandt and Robert H. Young, *The Anthem in England and America* (New York, 1970), p. 8.

4. See the author's "Polychoral Music, Michael Praetorius, and the Fifty Days of Easter," *Church Music* 73·1, 17—27.

5. The term "liturgical" as employed in the ensuing discussion refers to all texts of the liturgy potentially available for choral performance, those specifically assigned in the present day to the choir as well as those at one time designated for choral performance but now given to the congregation or the pastor. Thus, for example, it not only includes the gradual or psalm of the day but also the congregational Kyrie.

6. The Common Service or Holy Communion of *The Lutheran Hymnal*, authorized by the synods constituting the Evangelical Lutheran Synodical Conference of North America (St. Louis, 1941); the *Service Book and Hymnal*, authorized by the Lutheran churches cooperating in the Commisson on the Liturgy and Hymnal (Minneapolis, 1958); the *Worship Supplement*, authorized by the Commission on Worship, The Lutheran Church—Missouri Synod and the Synod of Evangelical Lutheran Churches (St. Louis, 1969), are followed. Adaptation to subsequent liturgical formulations can readily be made.

7. *The Church Year Calendar and Lectionary*, prepared by the ILCW as *CW6* (Minneapolis: Augsburg Publishing House; Philadelphia: Board of Publication, Lutheran Church in America; and St. Louis: Concordia Publishing House, 1973), appoints a psalm for each Sunday or festival of the church year. See "Psalms and Canticles," below, for specific examples of settings of complete psalms.

8. *The English Hymnal*, new ed. (London, 1933).

9. *The Hymnal of the Protestant Episcopal Church of the United States of America 1940* (New York, 1940).

10. See "Psalms and Canticles," below.

11. The history of the Hymn-of-the-Week tradition, with emphasis on its theological and practical signficance, is outlined in Ralph D. Gehrke, "The Hymn-of-the-Week Plan," *Concordia Theological Monthly* XXXII, 11 (Nov. 1961), 697—704.

12. In recent years Augsburg Publishing House, Concordia Publishing House, The Lutheran Society for Worship, Music, and the Arts, and others have distributed Hymn-of-the-Day lists drawing upon hymns in *SBH*, *TLH*, and *WS*, and traditional and ILCW pericopes. That of Ralph Gehrke, *Planning the Service*, though Germanic in emphasis, is the most solid historically, and it provides church musicians with the most valuable hymnic resources. The Gehrke list has been revised to relate to the ILCW's *CW 6* and to include hymns of *WS*; see Edward W. Klammer, "A New Approach to the Hymn of the Week," *Church Music* 75·1, 23—25.

13. Additional comments on the Hymn of the Day and a list of choral collections are to be found under "Hymns and Chorales" below.

14. Paul F. Bosch, "A Form for Praise," *The Circle. Worship Supplement* (October 1974).

15. *The Plainsong Setting of the Service from the Service Book and Hymnal of the Lutheran Church in America*, authorized by the Churches Co-operating in the Commission on Liturgy (Minneapolis, 1958), 13—19.

16. Paul G. Bunjes, "A Hymn to the Holy Trinity" (St. Louis, 1958).

17. Cycles of Gospel motets for the church year have been written by such early composers as Melchior Vulpius, Melchior Franck, Christoph Demantius, and such contemporary composers as Jan Bender, Gerhard Krapf, and Richard Hillert.

18. Collections containing music in these styles are listed under "Psalms and Canticles" below.

19. See *Church Music* 69:1, entire issue, subtitled "Singing the Psalms and the Propers."

20. Paul G. Bunjes, *The Formulary Tones Annotated* (St. Louis, 1965). The formulary tones have been applied to two canticles for choir, to be performed in alternation with congregational singing of related chorale stanzas: Paul G. Bunjes, "Chant-Chorale for Advent, on the Benedictus and 'Let the Earth Now Praise the Lord'" (St. Louis, 1961); also "Chant-Chorale for Christmas, on the Magnificat and 'All Hail to Jesus' Hallowed Name'" (St. Louis, 1961).

21. *Psalms for the Church Year; for Congregation and Choir*, ed. Paul Bunjes, F. Samuel Janzow, and Carl Schalk (Minneapolis, 1975). Another type of chant for choir and congregation is proposed by Charles Anders, "Psalm 46: God Is for Us a Refuge and Strength" (Minneapolis, 1969), and "Psalm 119: They Are Happy Whose Life Is Blameless" (Minneapolis, 1970). In these the choir sings the psalm set to an unaccompanied chant, and the congregation sings a refrain.

22. The ILCW *Calendar and Lectionary* assigns the St. Matthew, St. Mark, and St. Luke accounts in successive years to the Sunday of the Passion (Palm Sunday).

23. A brief historical survey of musical Passions is given in Basil Smallman, *The Background of Passion Music* (Naperville, Ill., 1957). See also Victor E. Gebauer, "Passion Settings for the Parish," *Church Music* 73·1, 8—16.

Chapter V

1. For a concise presentation of the development of these ideas see Reuben Pirner, "Instruments in Christian Worship: A Historical-Theological Perspective," *Church Music* 70·1, 1—7.

2. Peter Brunner, *Worship in the Name of Jesus* (St. Louis, 1968), p. 276.

3. For another treatment of this subject see Paul Bunjes, "A Classification of Basic Organ Voices," *Church Music* 67·1, pp. 34—37.

Tables: The Church Year, the Mass, and Various Lutheran Orders

TABLE A The Church Year

SBH/TLH	CW-6
The Season of Advent	Advent Season
The First Sunday in Advent	First Sunday in Advent
The Fourth Sunday in Advent	The Fourth Sunday in Advent
. . .	. . .
The Christmas Season	Christmas Season
Christmas Day, the Nativity of Our Lord	The Nativity of Our Lord, *Christmas Day*
The First Sunday after Christmas	First Sunday after Christmas
The Second Sunday after Christmas	Second Sunday after Christmas
The Circumcision of Our Lord (Jan. 1) The Holy Name of Jesus*	
The Season of Epiphany	Epiphany Season
The Epiphany of Our Lord (Jan. 6)	The Epiphany of Our Lord (Jan. 6)
The First Sunday after The Epiphany	The Baptism of Our Lord, *First Sunday after the Epiphany*
	Second Sunday after the Epiphany
. . .	. . .
The Sixth Sunday after The Epiphany The Transfiguration of Our Lord*	Eighth Sunday after the Epiphany The Transfiguration of Our Lord, *Last Sunday after the Epiphany*
Septuagesima	
Sexagesima	
Quinquagesima	
The Season of Lent	Lenten Season
Ash Wednesday	Ash Wednesday
Invocabit (Invocavit*)	First Sunday in Lent
Reminiscere	
Oculi	
Laetare	. . .
Judica, Passion Sunday	Fifth Sunday in Lent

Palmarum
Holy Week
  Monday
  Tuesday
  Wednesday
  Maundy Thursday
  Good Friday
  Saturday, Easter Eve.

The Easter Season
  Easter Day. The Resurrection of
    Our Lord.
  Easter Monday
  Easter Tuesday
Quasi Modo Geniti
Misericordia
Jubilate
Cantate
Rogate
The Ascension of Our Lord
Exaudi, The Sunday after the Ascension

The Day of Pentecost, Whitsunday
The Season After Trinity
  Trinity Sunday

  The First Sunday after Trinity
    (The Second Sunday after Pentecost**)
  . . .
  The Twenty-sixth Sunday after Trinity
    (The Twenty-seventh Sunday after
    Pentecost**)
  The Last Sunday after Trinity

St. Andrew—Nov. 30
St. Thomas—Dec. 21
St. Stephen—Dec. 26
St. John—Dec. 27
The Holy Innocents—Dec. 28

The Conversion of St. Paul—Jan. 25
The Presentation of Our Lord—Feb. 2
  and the Purification of Mary*
St. Matthias—Feb. 24

Holy Week
  Sunday of the Passion, *Palm Sunday*
  Monday in Holy Week
  Tuesday in Holy Week
  Wednesday in Holy Week
  Maundy Thursday
  Good Friday
  Saturday in Holy Week

Easter Season
  The Resurrection of Our Lord,
    Easter Day
    Easter Evening or Easter Monday

  Second Sunday of Easter

  . . .

  Sixth Sunday of Easter
  The Ascension of Our Lord
  Seventh Sunday of Easter
  The Day of Pentecost

The Season after Pentecost

  The Holy Trinity, *First Sunday
    after Pentecost*
  Second Sunday after Pentecost

  . . .

  Twenty-seventh Sunday after Pentecost

  Last Sunday after Pentecost,
    Christ the King

St. Andrew—Nov. 30
St. Thomas—Dec. 21
St. Stephen—Dec. 26
St. John—Dec. 27
The Holy Innocents—Dec. 28
The Name of Jesus—Jan. 1
The Confession of St. Peter—Jan. 18
The Conversion of St. Paul—Jan. 25
The Presentation of Our Lord—Feb. 2

  St. Matthias—Feb. 24

The Annunciation—March 25
St. Mark—April 25
St. Philip and St. James—May 1

The Nativity of St. John, the
    Baptist—June 24
St. Peter and St. Paul—June 29
The Visitation—July 2
St. Mary Magdalene—July 22*
St. James the Elder—July 25
The Transfiguration of Our Lord—Aug. 6**

St. Bartholomew—Aug. 24

St. Matthew—Sept. 21
St. Michael and All Angels—Sept. 29
St. Luke—Oct. 18
St. Simon and St. Jude—Oct. 28
Reformation Day—Oct. 31
All Saints' Day—Nov. 1

 *TLH only
**SBH only

The Annunciation of Our Lord—March 25
St. Mark—April 25
St. Philip and St. James—May 1
The Visitation—May 31
The Nativity of St. John, the
    Baptizer—June 24
St. Peter and St. Paul—June 29

St. Mary Magdalene—July 22
St. James the Elder—July 25

Mary, Mother of Our Lord—Aug. 15
St. Bartholomew—Aug. 24
Holy Cross Day—Sept. 14
St. Matthew—Sept. 21
St. Michael and All Angels—Sept. 29
St. Luke—Oct. 18
St. Simon and St. Jude—Oct. 28
Reformation Day—Oct. 31
All Saints' Day—Nov. 1

TABLE B The Mass

Missale Romanum 1570	*Missale Romanum 1970*
Confiteor (Celebrant & Ministers)	
Introit	Introit
	In nomine . . .
	Gratia Domini . . .
	Corporate Confession
Kyrie (ninefold)	Kyrie (sixfold)
Gloria in excelsis	Gloria in excelsis
Salutation and Collect	Salutation and Collect
	First Reading
	Responsorial Psalm

Missale Romanum 1570, cont.	*Missale Romanum 1970, cont.*
Epistle	Second Reading
Gradual/Alleluia or Tract	Alleluia
Gospel with Acclamations	Salutation/Response Gospel with Acclamations
(Sermon)	Homily
Nicene Creed	Nicene Creed
Offertory:	Offertory:
Offertory Antiphon	Offertory Antiphon
Salutation and Collect	Presentation of Bread & Wine
	Benedictus es . . . panem . . .
Suscipe, sancte Pater . . .	Elevation of Bread
	Benedictus Deus . . . per huius
Deus, qui humanae substantiae . . .	aquae et vini mysterium . . .
Mixing of Water with Wine	Mixing of Water with Wine
	Benedictus es . . . vinum . . .
Offerimus tibi . . .	Elevation of Wine
In spiritu humilitatis . . .	In spiritu humilitatis . . .
Veni, sanctificator . . .	
(Offering of incense)	(Offering of incense)
Lavabo inter innocentes	Lava me, Domine . . .
Suscipe, sancta Trinitas . . .	
Orate, fratres . . .	Orate, fratres
Prayer over the Gifts	Prayer over the Gifts
Canon:	Canon:
Preface	Preface:
Salutation/Response	Salutation/Response
Sursum corda	Sursum corda
Vere dignum	Vere dignum
Proper Preface	Proper Preface
Sanctus/Benedictus	Sanctus/Benedictus
	[Eucharistic Prayer 1]*
Te igitur . . .	Te igitur . . .
In primis . . .	in primis . . .
Memento, Domine, famulorum . . .	Memento, Domine, famulorum . . .
Communicantes . . .	Communicantes . . . [altered]
Hanc igitur . . .	Hanc igitur . . .
Quam oblationem . . .	Quam oblationem . . .
Verba (Qui pridie . . .)	Verba (Qui pridie . . .) [altered]
	Acclamation: Mysterium fidei . . .
Unde et memores . . .	Unde et memores . . .
Supra quae propitio . . .	Supra quae propitio . . .

Missale Romanum 1570, cont.	*Missale Romanum 1970, cont.*
Supplices te rogamus . . .	Supplices te rogamus . . .
Memento etiam, Domine . . .	Memento etiam, Domine . . .
Nobis quoque . . .	Nobis quoque . . . [altered]
Per quem . . .	Per Christum . . . per quem . . .
Doxology: Per ipsum . . .	Doxology: Per ipsum . . .
Communion:	Communion:
Our Father with Embolism	Our Father with Embolism [altered]
	and Doxology
Pax Domini . . .	Domine Jesu Christe, Fili . . . [abbr.]
Fraction and Commixture	Pax Domini . . .
Agnus Dei	Kiss of Peace
Domine, Jesu Christi, qui . . .	Fraction and Commixture
(Kiss of peace)	Agnus Dei
Domine Jesu Christe, Fili . . .	Domine Jesu Christi, qui . . . [abbr.]
Perceptio corporis tui . . .	or, Perceptio corporis . . . [altered]
Domine, non sum dignus . . .	Domine, non sum dignus . . .
Communion (of Celebrant and	Communion (of Celebrant and
People separated)	People integrated)
	Communion Antiphon
Ablutions	Ablutions
	Silence
Communion Antiphon	Post-Communion Collect
Post-Communion:	Post-Communion:
Salutation and Post-Communion Collect	Salutation/Response
Salutation and Ite, missa est	
or Benedicamus	Benediction
Placeat tibi . . .	Ite missa est . . .
Benediction	
Last Gospel	*Three additional Eucharistic
	Prayers are provided

TABLE C The Formula missae (1523)*

(Sermon)

Introit   according to traditional usage, but "we prefer the Psalms from which they were taken"

Kyrie	ninefold, with the various melodies for the different seasons
Gloria in excelsis	
Collect	only one
Epistle	
Gradual with Alleluia	sequences and proses not to be used except for the short one for the Nativity *Grates nunc omnes*
Gospel	
Nicene Creed	sung
(Sermon)	either here or possibly before the Introit
Preparation of the bread and wine	in the customary manner
Preface	
Words of Institution	
Sanctus	sung by the choir with the Elevation at the singing of the Benedictus as is customary
Lord's Prayer	
Pax Domini	

The Communion
  Agnus Dei
  Proper Communion	

The Post-Communion
  Collect
  Benedicamus Domino
  Aaronic Benediction
	either the customary one or that from Numbers 6 or from Psalm 67

*See *Luther's Works* Vol. 53, American Edition (Philadelphia, 1965)

TABLE D The *Deutsche Messe* (1526)*

The Hymn or German Psalm (Introit)

The Kyrie	threefold, chanted to the first Gregorian Psalm tone
The Collect	one, monotoned by the priest
The Epistle	chanted to the eighth Gregorian Psalm tone
The German Hymn	"We Now Implore God the Holy Ghost" or some other hymn sung "with the whole choir"
The Gospel	chanted to the fifth Gregorian Psalm tone
The Creed	sung to the German versification "We All Believe in One True God"
The Sermon	preached on the Gospel for the day

Paraphrase of the Lord's Prayer

Admonition to the Communicants	either read from the pulpit after the sermon or at the altar

The Words of Institution

The Distribution of the Elements	Luther suggests the following procedure: consecration of the bread and its distribution during which the German Sanctus "Isaiah, Mighty Seer in Days of Old" is sung; consecration of the wine and its distribution, during which such other hymns as "O Lord, We Praise Thee," "Jesus Christ, Our Blessed Savior," and the German Agnus Dei "O Christ, Thou Lamb of God" may be sung. Men and women were not to commune together, but the women after the men. The elevation of the elements was retained.

The Collect

The Aaronic Benediction

*See *Luther's Works* Vol. 53, American Edition (Philadelphia, 1965)

TABLE E The *Psalmodia sacra* (1553)*

The Mass
Introit

Kyrie   according to season and rank of the service

Gloria in excelsis   or "Allein Gott in der Hoeh' sei Ehr'" could
                                     "sometimes" also be sung

Epistle

Alleluia   with Sequence for feast days; on other days
                                     a German psalm hymn could be sung

Sermon with Litany   hymn verses before and after the sermon
                                     were most likely sung

Latin Creed   or "Wir glauben all an einen Gott"

Exhortation and Preface

Preface

Sanctus   or "Jesaia, dem Propheten, das geschah"

Altar prayers

Words of Institution

Distribution   during which such hymns as "Jesus Christus,
                                     unser Heiland", "Gott sei gelobet," and others
                                     were sung

Agnus Dei   or "O Lamm Gottes, unschuldig"

Prayer of Thanksgiving

Prayer for the Church

Benediction

Concluding hymn ("Erhalt uns, Herr")

Matins
Invitatory   usually only on the highest feasts

Martins, cont.

Antiphon	chanted by the pastor or sung as a motet by the choir
Psalms (3)	*Beatus vir, Quare fremuerunt, Domine quid,* or others
Antiphon	chanted by the pastor or sung as a motet by the choir
Gospel	*latine in choro,* then repeated by a boy in German, *ante chorum;* on highest feasts sung in Latin by the cantor
Responsory	
(Sermon)	most likely, but not specifically mentioned by Lossius
Te Deum	in Latin
Benedicamus Domino	sung by the pastor or choir

Vespers

Antiphon	sung by boys "specially chosen and trained to do it"
Psalm	
Antiphon	
Gospel	sung by a boy, with Responsory added
Hymn (1 or more)	Latin or German
Antiphon to the Magnificat	
Magnificat	
Antiphon to the Magnificat	could also be played on the organ
Benedicamus Domino	sung by selected boys

*See Hans Joachim Moser, *Die evangelische Kirchenmusik in Deutschland* (Berlin-Darmstadt, 1954), pp. 324—325; and Friedrich Blume, *Geschichte der evangelischen Kirchenmusik.* 2d, rev. ed. (Kassel, 1965), pp. 37—38.

TABLE F Relationship Between 16th-Century Orders*

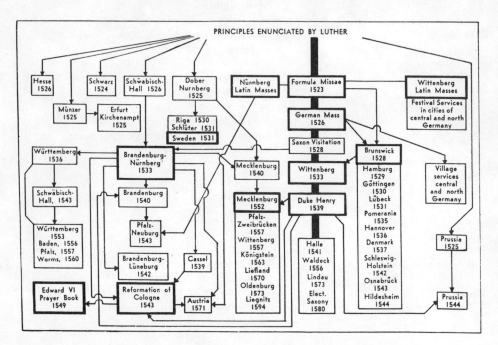

*From Luther D. Reed, *The Lutheran Liturgy*, rev. ed. (Philadelphia, 1959), p. 91.

TABLE G Leipzig Church Orders at the Time of J. S. Bach*

Organ Prelude (?)

The Introit	usually sung as a polyphonic motet in Latin
The Kyrie	usually alternated Sunday for Sunday between the Latin *Kyrie fons bonitatis* sung by the choir and the German "Kyrie, Gott Vater in Ewigkeit" sung by the congregation
The Gloria in excelsis	intoned by the pastor, followed either by the "Et in terra pax . . ." sung by the choir, or by "Allein Gott in der Hoeh' sei Ehr'" sung by the congregation

The Salutation and Response	chanted in Latin between pastor and choir
The Collect	chanted in Latin
The Epistle	chanted
The Hymn	the hymn suited to the Gospel was sung alternately by the congregation, choir, and organ; occasionally a Litany was chanted at this point
The Gospel	chanted
The Creed (Latin)	intoned by the pastor, the choir continuing
The Cantata (*Stueck* or Concerto)	
The Creed (German)	in Luther's version, "Wir glauben all an einen Gott"
The Sermon	usually preceded by the hymn "Herr Jesu Christ, dich zu uns wend"; the sermon concluded with various prayers, intercessions, announcements, and several stanzas of an appropriate hymn
(The Cantata)	the second part on those occasions when the cantata was divided
The Preface	chanted alternately in Latin between the deacon and the choir
The Sanctus	sung in parts by the choir
The Lord's Prayer	
The Words of Institution	
The Distribution of the Elements	during this time the singing of German hymns by the congregation occurred, as well as the singing of Latin motets by the choir
The Collect	chanted
The Benediction	chanted

*See Guenther Stiller, *Johann Sebastian Bach und das Leipziger gottesdienstliche Leben seiner Zeit* (Kassel, 1970).

TABLE H The *Kirchen-Agende* (1748) and its Revision (1786)*

Kirchen-Agende, 1748

The Hymn	"Nun bitten wir den heiligen Geist" or a verse of "Komm, heiliger Geist, Herre Gott"

The Confession of Sins:
  Exhortation**
  Confession
  Kyrie paraphrase
	spoken, the pastor at the altar

The Gloria in excelsis	sung in the metrical version "Allein Gott in der Hoeh' sei Ehr'"
The Salutation	
The Collect for the Day	taken from the Marburg hymn book
The Epistle	
The Hymn	"the principal hymn selected by the pastor, from the hymns in the Marburg Hymn-book"
The Gospel	
The Creed	"the pastor repeats devoutly the Creed, in verse, 'Wir glauben all'"
The Hymn	either "Liebster Jesu, wir sind hier" or "Herr Jesu Christ, dich zu uns wend"

The Sermon
  Prayer or Exordium
  Lord's Prayer
  Text/Gospel (read again)
  Sermon
	limited, according to the Agenda, to three quarters of an hour or at most one hour

The General Prayer or Litany
  (or Communion service;
  see below)	

The Lord's Prayer	ordinarily from the pulpit at the close of the sermon
Announcements	
The Votum	
The Hymn (Offering?)	

The Salutation and Response

The Collect

The Benediction

When Holy Communion was celebrated, the service after the sermon was as follows:

Preparation of Bread and Wine

Versicles	spoken between pastor and congregation, with
Salutation/Response	an abbreviated spoken Sanctus
Sursum corda	
Sanctus (no Benedictus)	
Exhortation to the Communicants	from the *Deutsche Messe* of 1526
and paraphrased Lord's Prayer	
The Lord's Prayer	
The Words of Institution	pastor directed to "pray"
	these words
The Invitation	

The Distribution of the Elements

The Thanksgiving Versicle (Benedicamus)

The Post-Communion Collect (Luther)

The Aaronic Benediction and The Trinitarian Blessing

Revised *Agende*, 1786

Hymn (free choice)

Confession
  Exhortation***
  Confession
  Kyrie paraphrase

Prayer *ad libitum*

Epistle

Hymn (free choice)

Sermon:
   Prayer
   Lord's Prayer
   Gospel or free text
   Sermon

General Prayer (longer form)

Votum

Hymn (Offering?)

Preparation of Bread and Wine

Versicles
   Salutation/Response
   Sursum corda
   Sanctus

Exhortation and paraphrased Lord's Prayer

Lord's Prayer

Words of Institution

Invitation

Distribution (revised formula)

Thanksgiving Versicle (Benedicamus)

Post-Communion Collect (Luther)

Aaronic Benediction

Trinitarian Blessing

*For a reconstruction of the original text, see *Hallesche Nachrichten*, ed. W. J. Mann and B. M. Schmucker (Allentown, 1886), pp. 211 ff. For English translations compare C. W. Schaeffer in Henry Eyster Jacobs, *A History of the Evangelical Lutheran Church in the United States* (New York, 1893), p. 269; B. M. Schmucker, "The First Pennsylvania Liturgy," *The Lutheran Church Review,* I (1882), pp. 16—27, 161—172, and the account in the *Documentary History of the Evangelical Lutheran Ministerium of Pennsylvania and Adjacent States* (Philadelphia, 1898), pp. 13 ff. For text of the Revision see *Kirchen-Agende der Evangelisch-Lutherischen Vereinigten Gemeinden in Nord America* (Philadelphia, 1786).

**Rubrics for orientation at the altar are included throughout.

***Rubrics on orientation are omitted.

TABLE I Loehe's *Agende* (1844)*

The Hymn	Loehe suggests "Komm, heiliger Geist, erfuell," "Komm heiliger Geit, Herre Gott," or a similar hymn
The Versicle and Response	
The Confession and Absolution	
The Introit and Gloria Patri	To be sung by the choir where one is at hand or, where no choir is available, may be read by the pastor, or a psalm may be sung by the congregation.
The Kyrie	To be sung in alternation by pastor and congregation, or by choir and congregation
The Gloria in excelsis	Intoned by the pastor, continued by the congregation, or the people may sing "Allein Gott in der Hoeh' sei Ehr'" in response to the intonation
The Salutation	
The Collect	Chanted by the pastor, the people responding "Amen."
The Epistle	Chanted
The Hallelujah	By the congregation. On festivals the Gradual, Sequence, or Prose may be sung before the Hallelujah.
The Hymn	Based on the Gospel and appropriate to the celebration. The offerings are collected during the singing of the hymn.
The Salutation	
The Gospel	Chanted
The Nicene Creed	May be spoken, sung, or chanted to Luther's metrical version
The Sermon	Should be based on the Gospel and not exceed three quarters of an hour. The sermon concludes with special intercessions and prayers.
The Offertory	Sung by the congregation to "Schaffe in mir Gott ein reines Herze"

The Prayer	
The Preface and Proper Preface	
The Sanctus	To be sung by the congregation kneeling, followed by a "short but deep silence"
The Words of Institution	To be chanted
The Agnus Dei	Sung by the congregation as "Christe, du Lamm Gottes"
The Lord's Prayer	
The Pax	
The Distribution of the Elements	The men communed first, then the women. During the distribution Loehe suggests the following hymns be sung: "Jesaiah, dem Propheten, das geschah"; "Jesus Christus, unser Heiland"; "Gott sei gelobet und gebenedeiet"; and "Ich danke dem Herrn"
The Nunc dimittis	Or the hymn "Mit Fried und Freud ich fahr dahin" may be sung
The Post-Communion Versicle & Collect	
The Salutation	
The Benedicamus	
The Benediction	Announcements were to be made at the conclusion of the service

*See *Agende fuer christliche Gemeinden des lutherischen Bekenntnisses.* Herausgegeben von Wilhelm Loehe (Noerdlingen, 1844).

TABLE J The Saxon *Kirchen-Agende* (1856)*

The Kyrie	To be sung as the hymn version "Kyrie, Gott Vater in Ewigkeit"
Gloria	Following the intonation of the pastor, the congregation sang all verses of "Allein Gott in der Hoeh' sei Ehr'"
The Salutation and Response	

The Antiphon	Chanted by the pastor and congregation, normally one antiphon; on festivals, however, two were prescribed
The Collect for the Day	
The Epistle	The congregation stands
The Chief Hymn of the Day	
The Gospel	The congregation stands
The Creed	Sung by the congregation in Luther's version "Wir glauben all an einen Gott, Schoepfer"
The Sermon	After the sermon had been introduced, a hymn verse was often sung. After the sermon the pastor led the congregation in prayer of confession, pronounced the absolution, led in the general prayer, special supplications, announcements, and concluded with the Lord's Prayer, all from the pulpit
The Offertory (or order without Communion; see below)	"Schaffe in mir, Gott, ein reines Herze" sung by the congregation during the singing of which the pastor prepares the elements
The Preface and Propers Preface	Chanted by the pastor
The Sanctus	Sung by the congregation
The Lord's Prayer	Chanted by the pastor, the congregational singing "For Thine is the Kingdom . . ."
The Words of Institution	
The Agnus Dei	Sung by the congregation to the hymn "Christe, du Lamm Gottes"
The Distribution of the Elements	
The Post-Communion Versicle & Collect	
The Benediction	
The Hymn	The congregation sang "Gott sei gelobet und gebenedeiet" or another appropriate verse

If Communion was not celebrated, the service after the sermon was as follows:

A Hymn

The Antiphon and Collect   Chanted by the pastor

The Benediction

A Closing Hymn Verse   After a stanza of "Gott sei gelobet und
                gebenedeiet" or a similar stanza, the congre-
                gation prayed silently the Lord's Prayer

*See *Kirchen-Agende fuer Evang.-Luth. Gemeinden ungeaenderter Augburgischer Confession. Zusammengestellt aus den altern rechtglaeubigen Saechsischen Kirchen-Agenden* (St. Louis, 1856).

TABLE K The *Church Book* (1868)*

The Invocation

The Confession of Sins and Absolution
 Beloved in the Lord . . .
 Versicles/Responses
 Almighty God, our Maker . . .
 O Most Merciful God . . .
 Almighty God, our heavenly Father . . .

The Introit with Gloria Patri   Or a general Introit may be used rather
                than the appointed one for the church
                year

The Kyrie   Sixfold

The Gloria in excelsis   Or the Te Deum or another hymn of praise

The Salutation and Response

The Collect

(Old Testament)

The Epistle for the Day

The Hallelujah   Or a sentence for the season, or a
                psalm or hymnody may be used after the
                Hallelujah

The Gospel for the Day   With Acclamations

The Creed   If there is Communion, the Nicene
                Creed shall always be used

The Hymn	
The Sermon	
The Offertory	Or the 2d and 3d stanzas of Watts' hymn "O Thou That Hear'st When Sinners Call" (*CB*, 356) may be used
The General Prayer	
The Lord's Prayer (or order with Communion; see below)	After the Lord's Prayer the minister may make any announcements, the offerings may be gathered, and a hymn may be sung
The Benediction	

If Communion is celebrated, there shall follow after the General Prayer:

The Hymn (Offering?)	During the singing of this hymn the minister shall prepare the vessels
The Preface Salutation/Response Sursum corda Vere dignum Proper Preface	
The Sanctus	
The Exhortation	
The Lord's Prayer	With hands extended over the bread and wine
The Words of Institution	
The Agnus Dei	
The Distribution of the Elements**	
The Pax Domini	
The Nunc Dimittis	
The Thanksgiving	
The Aaronic Benediction	

*"Order of Morning Service" from the *Church Book* can be found in *Lutheran Confessional Theology in America 1840—1880*, ed. Theodore G. Tappert (New York, 1972) pp. 340—351.

**In the German version of 1877 the Pax precedes the Distribution.

TABLE L The *Common Service* (1888)*

The Order of Morning Service, or the Communion

The Invocation

The Confession of Sins and Absolution
   Beloved in the Lord . . .
   Versicles/Responses
   Almighty God, our Maker . . .
   O most merciful God . . .
   Almighty God, our heavenly Father . . .

The Introit	Or a psalm or a hymn may be used
The Kyrie	Threefold
The Gloria in excelsis	Or another canticle or hymn of praise, but the Gloria should always be used on festivals and when there is Communion
The Salutation and Response	
The Collect	A full set is provided
(Other Scripture)**	
The Epistle for the Day	
The Hallelujah***	Or a sentence for the season may be sung with The Hallelujah, or a psalm or hymn after the Hallelujah
The Gospel for the Day	With Acclamations
The Creed	If there is Communion, the Nicene Creed shall always be used
The Hymn	
The Sermon and Votum	
The Offertory	After the Offertory the offerings of the congregation are gathered, and the minister shall announce any special petitions requested
The General Prayer (or order with Communion; see below)	

The Lord's Prayer

The Hymn   Or a doxology if there is no Communion

The Benediction

If Communion is celebrated, after the General Prayer shall follow:

The Hymn

The Preparation of Bread and Wine

The Preface
   Salutation/Response
   Sursum corda
   Vere dignum
   Proper Preface

The Sanctus

The Exhortation

Lord's Prayer

Words of Institution

The Pax Domini

The Agnus Dei

The Distribution

The Nunc dimittis

The Thanksgiving
   O give thanks . . .
   Collect (Luther)

The Benedicamus

The Benediction

The Common Service for the use of Evangelical Lutheran Congregations (Charleston, 1888). In November 1888 the Joint Committee declared this publication to be "the correct exhibition of the standard text" (Reed, p. 190).
**Not in *CSB* (1918)
***Full set of Graduals in *CSB*. Hallelujah or Lenten Tract as alternates.

TABLE M Danish-Norwegian Liturgies*

The Ritualet of 1685—1688	The Rescript of 1802	American Haugeanism c. 1900
The Opening Prayer (congregation kneeling)	The Opening Prayer	The Opening Hymn
The Kyrie	The Hymn	Free Prayer (by a layman)
The Gloria in excelsis (later a hymn)	The Collect	The Hymn (pastor at the altar)
The Salutation	The Epistle	Salutation (congregational response omitted)
The Collect	The Hymn	The Collect
The Epistle	The Sermon	The Epistle
The Hymn (in place of the Hallelujah)	The General Prayer	The Gospel
The Gospel (with "Praise be to Thee, O Christ," by the congregation)	The Blessing (Benediction)	The Hymn
The Creed (or hymn)	The Hymn	The Sermon
The Sermon	The Collect	Free Prayer or General Prayer
Exordium	The Hymn	The Hymn
Unison Lord's Prayer	The Closing Prayer	The Collect
Text	The service of Holy Communion was unchanged	The Benediction
Sermon		The Hymn
The General Prayer		Free Closing Prayer

298

The Lord's Prayer

The Benediction

The Hymn (baptism followed)

The Exhortation

The Lord's Prayer

The Words of Institution

The Distribution (the Agnus Dei sung
three times during the distribution)

The Hymn of Thanksgiving

The Benediction (sign of the cross)

The Hymn

The Closing Prayer

The Service of Holy Communion was simplified and, as with the rest of the service, was not chanted.

*From E. Clifford Nelson, *The Lutheran Church Among Norwegian-Americans*, II (Minneapolis, 1960), 342—343.

TABLE N Matins and Vespers

(The Lutheran Hymnal, 1941, and Service Book and Hymnal, 1958)

Matins	*Vespers*
Opening Versicles	Opening Versicles
Invitatory and Venite	Psalm(s) and Gloria Patri
Office Hymn	Lesson(s)
Psalm(s) and Gloria Patri	Responsory
Lesson(s)	(Offering)
Responsory	Office Hymn
Sermon	Versicle
(Offering)	Magnificat or Nunc dimittis
Te Deum or Benedictus	Kyrie
Kyrie	Our Father
Our Father	Salutation and Collect for the Day
Salutation and Collect for the Day	Salutation and Collect for Peace* Versicle and Collect for Peace**
Salutation and Collect for Grace* Versicle and Collect for Grace**	Benedicamus
Benedicamus	Benediction
Benediction	

*TLH
**SBH

TABLE O *The Lutheran Hymnal* (1941), the *Service Book and Hymnal* (1958), and *Lutheran Book of Worship* (1978)

The Lutheran Hymnal (1941)— *Service Book and Hymnal* (1958)	*Lutheran Book of Worship* (1978)
In the Name . . .	Brief Order of Confession and Forgiveness (separate from The Holy Communion)
Confession of Sin	

The Lutheran Hymnal (1941)— Service Book and Hymnal (1958), cont.	Lutheran Book of Worship (1978), cont.
Introit/Gloria Patri	The Entrance Hymn (or Psalm)
	Apostolic Greeting
Kyrie (Deacon's Litany*)	Kyrie (Deacon's Litany)
Gloria in excelsis	Gloria in excelsis (or "Worthy is Christ . . .")
Salutation and Collect	Salutation and Prayer of the Day
Old Testament Lesson*	First Lesson
(Psalm)*	Psalm
Epistle	Second Lesson
Gradual/Tract	Verse (Alleluia or Tract)
Gospel with Acclamations	Gospel with Acclamations
Nicene Creed	Sermon
Hymn	Hymn of the Day
Sermon	Nicene or Apostles Creed
Offering	The Prayers
Offertory Preparation of Bread and Wine	The Pax Domini
	The Offering
Prayer of the Church	The Offertory and Offertory Prayer Preparation of Bread and Wine
Hymn	

Preface
  Salutation/Response
  Sursum corda
  Vere dignum
  Proper Preface
	The Great Thanksgiving
	  Salutation/Response
	  Sursum corda
	  Vere dignum
	  Preface

Sanctus/Benedictus	Sanctus/Benedictus

The Lutheran Hymnal (1941)— Service Book and Hymnal (1958), cont.	Lutheran Book of Worship (1978), cont.

Prayer of Thanksgiving:*
  Praise
	Prayer of Thanksgiving:*
	  Praise
	  Salvation history

Words of Institution
  Anamnesis
  Epiclesis
	Words of Institution
	  Anamnesis/Maranatha
	  Epiclesis
	  Memorial

Doxology	Doxology
Lord's Prayer**	Lord's Prayer
Pax Domini	(Fraction)
Agnus Dei	

Communion
  Blessing
	Communion
	  Agnus Dei or other hymns
	  Blessing

Post-Communion:
  Nunc dimittis
  O give thanks . . .
  Collect
  Salutation and Benedicamus
	Post-Communion:
	  "Thank the Lord . . ." or "Lord,
	  now you let . . ."
	  Prayer

Aaronic Benediction with Trinitarian Blessing***	Blessing (Trinitarian or Aaronic)
	Dismissal
	*(If there is no Communion)
	The Offering
	The Offertory
	The Prayers
	Lord's Prayer
	The Blessing

*Not in *TLH*
**In *TLH* the Lord's Prayer is followed
by the Words of Institution

****TLH* omits the Trinitarian Blessing

*Or Words of Institution which may be
preceded by a brief prayer of thanks.

Notes on the Contributors

Eugene Brand is director of the office of studies and international scholarship and exchange of Lutheran World Ministries, project director for the Inter-Lutheran Commission on Worship, and a member of the editorial board of *Church Music.*

Herbert Gotsch teaches at Concordia Teachers College, River Forest, Ill., and is a member of the editorial staff of *Church Music.*

Richard Hillert teaches at Concordia Teachers College, River Forest, Ill., is widely recognized as a composer, and is a member of the Liturgical Music Committee of the Inter-Lutheran Commission on Worship and assistant editor of *Church Music.*

Edward W. Klammer is the editor of many church music publications, has long been associated with the music department of Concordia Publishing House, is a member of the Hymn Music Committee of the Inter-Lutheran Commission on Worship, and is a member of the editorial staff of *Church Music.*

Adalbert Raphael Kretzmann, pastor of St. Luke Lutheran Church, Chicago, Ill., is a widely respected authority on church art and architecture and a member of the editorial board of *Church Music.*

Carlos R. Messerli teaches at Concordia Teachers College, Seward, Nebr., and is a member of the Liturgical Music Committee of the Inter-Lutheran Commission on Worship.

Louis G. Nuechterlein is pastor of Cheshire Lutheran Church, Cheshire, Conn.

Carl Schalk teaches at Concordia Teachers College, River Forest, Ill., has edited many church music publications, and is a member of the Hymn Music Committee of the Inter-Lutheran Commission of Worship and the editor of *Church Music.*